Supermarine
Seafire

Other Titles in the Crowood Aviation Series

Supermarine
Seafire

Kev Darling

The Crowood Press

First published in 2008 by
The Crowood Press Ltd
Ramsbury, Marlborough
Wiltshire SN8 2HR

www.crowood.com

British Library Cataloguing-in-Publication Data
A catalogue record for this book is available from the British Library.

ISBN 978 1 86126 990 4

Typeset by Florence Production Ltd, Stoodleigh, Devon
Printed and bound in Great Britain by The Cromwell Press Ltd

Contents

Introduction

The issue of air power at sea has always been a controversial one. Land-based air forces have always considered themselves more than capable of defending the fleet, yet sea-based air power has often proved better placed to do so.

It is, therefore, hardly surprising that the emergence of the Fleet Air Arm as a viable fighting force was not a straight-forward process. The merger of the Royal Naval Air Service with the Royal Flying Corps, which produced the Royal Air Force in 1918, meant that the newly-created air arm possessed aircraft designed to support naval operations together with the necessary expertise. While the Admiralty was allowed to build aircraft carriers, the control of the aircraft that operated from them remained with the Air Ministry. The navy did the best it could, but a basic lack of under-standing of naval air needs meant that the aircraft provided were less than ideal. Eventually, however, the Admiralty gained control over its air assets and set about bringing them up to an improved standard.

Having rid itself of various out-dated biplanes – although not the indispensable Swordfish – the Fleet Air Arm progressed via a series of monoplane fighters to the Seafire. Often photographed in an undig-nified pose following one of the flight deck accidents commonly suffered by the type, the Seafire might not have been the greatest naval fighter. It was, however, one with an impeccable pedigree. Hurriedly developed from the Spitfire, the Sea Spitfire, as it was initially known, revealed design defects that had not become apparent in the land-based versions.

Short of a complete redesign of the rear fuselage and tail assembly, however, the manufacturer's best suggestion was to allow the various separations and wrinkles to continue until they reached a set limit, at which point extensive repairs would be required. Yet even with this limitation, Seafire pilots carried out their tasks with distinction and even managed to shoot down some enemy aircraft in the process. Although the emergence of more capable American naval fighters seemed to mark the end of the Seafire as a front-line fighter, the choice facing Britain at the end of the war to purchase or return them meant that the Seafire was reinstated. It served during the early stages of the Korean War but was replaced by the Hawker Sea Fury.

Surprisingly little has been published about the Seafire and some of that is contradictory. However, with help from the Fleet Air Arm Museum at Yeovilton, Air Britain, Ray Sturtivant, Laurence M. Bean, Will Blunt, Stephen Fox, Rick Harding, Chris Michel/Airframe Assem-blies (Isle of Wight) Ltd, Mark Russell and Peter Russell Smith, I have managed to piece together what I hope is a reasonable history of the Seafire and its exploits. As it was a stalwart of the British Pacific Fleet, the forgotten navy, I would like to dedicate this book to all who were involved with the Seafire throughout its service life.

Kev Darling
Wales, 2007

CHAPTER ONE

Hearts of Oak

John 'Jackie' Fisher, more formally Admiral of the Fleet Lord Fisher of Kilverstone, is recognized as one of the Royal Navy's most outstanding leaders. He was also one of the most innovative.

The man behind the *Dreadnought*, the all big-gun battleship, and the battlecruiser also replaced steam power with oil fuel and introduced submarines to the Royal Navy during his first period as First Sea Lord. Fisher also ordered a large number of aircraft, including the small airships, often called 'blimps', which proved to be of great value for reconnaissance during the early part of World War I.

In 1910 four Royal Navy officers were selected for pilot training. One of them, Lt C.R. Samson RN, became the first British airman to fly an aeroplane from a ship. In January 1912, Samson flew a Short pusher biplane equipped with buoyancy floats from a steeply-sloped launching ramp mounted on the bow of HMS *Africa* moored in the estuary of the River Medway. Actually, Samson was not the first however, the honour going to an American, Eugene P. Ely. In November 1910 Ely flew a Curtiss pusher biplane from a specially-constructed platform mounted on the forecastle of the cruiser the USS *Birmingham*.

The following May Samson flew a similar aircraft from the pre-Dreadnought battleship HMS *Hibernia*. The launch ramp was set at a less steep angle compared with that on the *Africa*. And this time the ship was under way, steaming at 10.5kt (18.9km/h). A third series of trials during the summer involved the cruiser *London*. Although use of such ramps was found to be a dead end – the forward guns were rendered unusable – it did pave the way for further experiments in naval aviation.

The RNAS is Established

While these trials were in progress the army had established the Royal Flying Corps (RFC), which comprised military and naval wings and a central flying school. This was not an arrangement that found favour with the Admiralty, however, and on 1 July 1914 the Naval Wing ceded from the RFC to become the Royal Naval Air Service (RNAS). To complement this change, the Admiralty established an Air Department commanded by Capt Murray Seuter RN. Later that month the RNAS fielded three airships and seventeen aeroplanes to represent it at the naval review held at Spithead.

Having established that naval aviation was a viable proposition, the Admiralty set up operating bases: the Isle of Grain in 1912, Calshot, Cromarty, Felixstowe and Great Yarmouth in 1913. Training and development continued with the result that over 100 pilots were available at the beginning of 1914. Work, which would lead to the development of aircraft carriers, was also in progress. HMS *Hermes*, originally a cruiser, and *Ark Royal*, which started life as a merchant ship, were among the vessels converted to act as seaplane carriers. More adventurous was the Cunard liner *Campania*, which had a 200ft (60m) wooden deck built over her forecastle. The Fairey company's new seaplane, also called Campania, was able to take off from it using a wheeled trolley placed under the floats.

Enter the Aircraft Carrier

Many solutions were tried before the first aircraft carrier appeared. One of these was to launch aircraft from lighters towed at speed by destroyers. This at least got landplane fighters into the air but the aircraft had to be ditched at the completion of its sortie. The first move that was to lead to a practical aircraft carrier was the conversion of HMS *Furious*. Originally laid down as one of a class of three battlecruisers, *Furious* was modified during construction with a sloping launch platform mounted in the space intended for the forward 18in gun turret. Beneath it was an enclosed hangar with space for eight seaplanes, workshops and stowage for 1,200gal (5,455ltr) of petrol. Deck landing trials using wheeled aircraft – a Sopwith Pup – were undertaken during mid-1917. The pilot, Sqn Cdr Dunning, managed two successful attempts but was killed during his third touchdown. As a result, it was recommended that the ship be rebuilt to accommodate a landing-on deck and a hangar.

Thus modified *Furious* was released for service in mid-1918, but the ship was again rebuilt in 1921 with a full-length deck. A separate lower-level flying-off deck was deleted in 1932. Two innovations introduced during the conversion included the rounding down of the deck's trailing edge and the first examples of arrestor wires. *Furious'* two sister ships were also converted into aircraft carriers. *Courageous* and *Glorious* were commissioned in 1928 and 1930 respectively. They were preceded into service by the first purpose-designed aircraft carrier, which had been ordered in 1917 and commissioned in 1923. Like the earlier seaplane carrier, this ship was also called *Hermes*.

Then came *Eagle* – converted from a Chilean battleship – which was commissioned in 1924. But another *Ark Royal*, launched in 1937 and commissioned the following year, was the first large British carrier designed from scratch, predicated on the basis of experience gained from the converted vessels and incorporating experience gained from carrier operations in the 1920s and 1930s. The *Ark* featured a flight deck, which provided much of the ship's strength. She was followed by the Illustrious class, which, with their armoured flight decks, were to prove their worth in the coming conflict. The name ship was commissioned in 1940 and the last of the class, *Victorious*, remained in service until 1969.

The Royal Navy had its aircraft carriers but it had lost control over the aircraft that operated from them. On 1 April 1918 the RFC and RNAS merged to form the Royal Air Force. The RNAS' contribution to the marriage was a substantial one. By the end of the war its strength stood at 2,949 aircraft and 103 airships operated at

A Sopwith Camel leaves a ship with a very famous name: HMS *Ark Royal*. It was also one of the few aircraft carriers to utilize a mizzen mast for longitudinal stability. In 1935 the vessel was re-named *Pegasus* to enable the original name to be transferred to the new fleet carrier, HMS *Ark Royal*. FAAM Yeovilton

Confirmation that carrier-borne aviation was feasible was provided by Sqn Cdr E.H. Dunning when he landed a Sopwith Pup aboard the partly-converted HMS *Furious* in August 1917. Unfortunately, Edwin Harris Dunning was killed on 7 August while attempting another landing on *Furious* in Scapa Flow. FAAM Yeovilton

126 bases by 67,000 officers and ratings. This had grown in just four years from an establishment of forty landplanes, thirty-one seaplanes and seven airships manned by 130 officers and 700 petty officers and ratings.

During this period the RNAS had undertaken some brave but perilous missions. On 22 September 1914 the Eastchurch, Isle of Sheppey-based squadron supplied four aircraft for the first ever air raid on German territory. On Christmas Day, seven aircraft left the seaplane carriers *Engadine*, *Riviera* and *Empress* to bomb German hangars at Nordholx near Cuxhaven. While many operations were undertaken by waterborne aircraft the service was to acquire land-planes: Sopwith Camels, Pups and One-and-a-Half Strutters. In fact, the navy's fighter strength was now on a par with that of the RFC.

Fleet Air Arm is Formed

After reaching a peak in 1918, naval air strength of the newly-formed RAF was quickly reduced to a single spotter reconnaissance squadron, a fighter flight and half of a torpedo squadron. There was also a seaplane flight and a flying boat flight. These changes followed a massive reduction in funding as social programmes were now given priority over military spending. It took the next twenty years for the Admiralty to place both the aircraft and their carriers under unified control. The process was completed in May 1939, just in time for another war. In 1921 the Admiralty managed to secure agreement that observers would be drawn from the navy, while in 1923 a Committee of Inquiry recommended that at least 70 per cent of pilots should also be of naval origin, holding dual naval and RAF ranks. In April 1924 the title Fleet Air Arm was adopted even though it was still officially part of the RAF. The final stage came in 1937 with an announcement in the House of Commons that complete control of the Fleet Air Arm was to be transferred to the Admiralty. This was followed by the establishment of new land bases at Donibristle, Eastleigh, Evanton, Ford, Hatston, Lee-on-Solent, St Merryn and Worthy Down.

During this period naval aircraft strength grew slowly. By January 1924 the inventory was seventy-eight aircraft in thirteen flights; by October this had become 128 aircraft in eighteen flights. Six years later this had

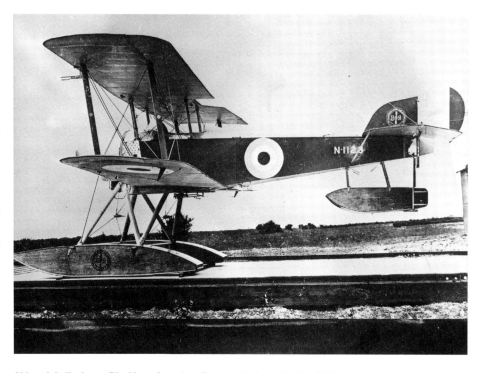

Although it displays a Blackburn Aeroplane Company badge on the fin, this is actually a Sopwith Baby built under contract. This picture illustrates an alternative way of carrying fighter aircraft aboard capital ships. Instead of launching them from flight decks, the resident aircraft could either take-off from a turret ramp or be craned-off to the sea to take-off under its own power. While the former was workable it did mean that the gun turret was unusable for its original purpose. Whichever method was adopted, the pilot had to alight alongside his ship to be recovered while the vessel was still underway. BBA Collection

Although the Parnell Peto never entered service with the Royal Navy it did represent the dual policy pursued between the wars of operating wheeled aircraft from carriers and float-equipped aircraft, as seen here, from capital ships and cruisers. While the Peto performed well enough, the fleet fighter contract went to the Fairey Flycatcher. BBA Collection

grown to 144 aircraft in twenty-four flights. When flights were replaced by squadrons in 1932, 156 aircraft were in service with twenty-six flights. Squadrons now comprised between nine and twelve aircraft concentrated on aircraft carriers or land bases. A handful of ship's flights was retained for aircraft operating from capital ships and cruisers. When hostilities resumed in September 1939 the Fleet Air Arm had twenty squadrons with 340 aircraft, of which 225 were under squadron control, the remainder being dispersed among ship's flights.

Naval Aircraft Development

The aircraft delivered to the Admiralty during the inter-war period were a mixed bag. The Fairey Flycatcher biplane entered service in 1923. Designed as a fleet fighter, it was a ruggedly-built machine, which was easy to fly, suitable for aerobatics and, most importantly, easy to land aboard an aircraft carrier. It introduced many new features, including flaps running along the entire trailing edges of both wings with their outer sections also acting as ailerons. Thus equipped the Flycatcher was able to achieve exceptionally short landing and take-off runs. Another innovation was the hydraulic wheel brake system used in conjunction with the fore and aft arrester wires that were favoured by carriers of the time. The Flycatcher served until 1934 when it was replaced by the Hawker Nimrod, which closely resembled its land-based counterpart, the Fury. But there some were significant changes: wingspan was bigger and flotation boxes were built into the wings and fuselage. This made it slower than the Fury but the Nimrod still represented a worthwhile advance on the Flycatcher. The first production machines lacked arrester gear fitted, this omission being rectified in the Mk II, which featured a hook under a strengthened fuselage.

The Gloster Sea Gladiator was to be the naval fighter squadrons' last biplane fighter. This was another land-based design adapted for ship-board operations with a strengthened structure to absorb the punishment of deck landings. Catapult launching hooks were also featured and a collapsible dinghy was carried between the undercarriage legs. The Sea Gladiator entered service in December 1938 and the type remained in front-line service until 1941. The Sea Gladiator's finest hour

Most illustrations show the Fairey Flycatcher with floats, but as revealed here by S1286, a wheeled option was also available. The type remained in service until the early 1930s. BBA Collection

Although the Admiralty was less than happy to have the Air Ministry controlling its air assets, their Lordships were content to accept the Hawker Nimrod for service aboard their aircraft carriers. In essence it was a naval version of the land-based Hawker Fury fighter, which retained the good looks of the entire family. BBA Collection

probably came in 1940 during the defence of Malta when a handful of fighters (in RAF hands) offered a heroic resistance to superior Axis forces.

The Fairey Fulmar was a monoplane mounting eight machine guns and powered by a Rolls Royce Merlin. But carrying an observer as well as a pilot, the thick-winged Fulmar was underpowered. In comparison with land-based opponents it lacked agility and was a slow climber. The Blackburn

Skua had been conceived to combine the roles of fighter and dive-bomber. With its 900hp Bristol Perseus radial engine, it was also a two-seater and had a top speed of just 225mph (360km/h). Even so, the type scored the Fleet Air Arm's first aerial victory of World War II and sank the cruiser *Konigsberg* during the Norwegian campaign. The Roc was based on the Skua and had a four-gun power-operated turret behind the pilot, like the Boulton Paul Defiant but

Prior to the appearance of monoplanes, the fleet's main aerial workhorse was the Fairey IIIF. Here an unidentified float-equipped example is launched by a capital ship's catapult. FAAM Yeovilton

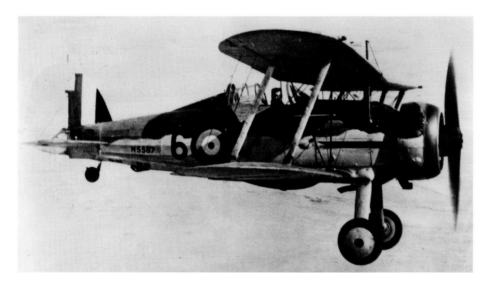

Once the Hawker Nimrod was established in service it was common practice to keep the emerging Fleet Air Arm equipped with naval versions of land-based equivalents. Pictured here, Gloster Sea Gladiator N5567 displays the camouflage scheme adopted after war was declared in September 1939. According to legend, three Sea Gladiators, named Faith, Hope and Charity, played a vital role in the defence of Malta. Will Blunt Collection

With the arrival of the Hawker Sea Hurricane, the Fleet Air Arm gained its first single seat monoplane fighter able to meet land-based counterparts on equal terms. The conversion involved the standard Hurricane design being reworked to enable it to cope with the rigours of ship-board operations. Although it featured an arrester hook, the Sea Hurricane was one of the few shipboard fighters never to be fitted with folding wings, although such a conversion had been considered. While it was intended to deploy as many Sea Hurricanes as possible on board carriers, the lack of available flight decks meant that another temporary measure had to be employed. This was the so-called 'Catafighter', a Hurricane launched from ramps mounted on merchant ships (catapult armed merchantmen or CAM ships) or warships to defend convoys from marauding Focke-Wulf Fw 200 Condors.

Once launched, however, the aircraft could not return to the ship and had to ditch in the sea. While the Catafighter represented a useful temporary expediency, the loss of an aircraft – and the potential loss of an experienced pilot – was less welcome. Fortunately for the Sea Hurricane pilots, their aircraft were soon fitted with a pair of 45gal (205ltr) overload tanks which offered the option of returning to friendly territory if within range. The arrival of escort carriers from the USA meant that a measure of anti-submarine protection could be given to each convoy while the Sea Hurricane pilots now had decks to return to, albeit small ones.

Sea Hurricanes were deployed on the Russian convoys where they provided much-needed air support. In a warmer climate they provided support to the convoys battling their way through to Malta. Although the Sea Hurricane lacked the racy looks of the Spitfire/Seafire, the skill, determination and courage of its pilots ensured that the convoys reached their destinations with losses reduced. The Sea Hurricane remained in front line service with the FAA until mid-1944, having been superseded by the Supermarine Seafire.

Lacking sufficient suitable modern fighters, the Royal Navy had to turn to the USA. The first of the American fighters to join the FAA was the Grumman Wildcat, known initially in British service as the Martlet. Featuring the short dumpy fuselage and retractable undercarriage that had characterized Grumman's previous biplane fighters, the Martlet was a monoplane with four wing-mounted 0.50in machine-guns.

considerably slower. The Roc saw limited service and the Skua's employment in the fighter role was also limited. But the Fulmar was able to remain airborne on patrol for long periods and saw extensive service. Despite its deficiencies the Fulmar rendered valuable service and the type was credited with the destruction of 112 enemy aircraft between September 1940 and August 1942. This represented nearly a third of the Fleet Air Arm's total of air-to-air victories throughout the war.

The Blackburn Roc represented an attempt by the Admiralty to introduce a turret fighter to the Fleet Air Arm. The underlying premise was that the concentration of firepower from one closely-grouped source would be enough to disable any enemy aircraft. Unfortunately for all concerned, the Roc was too slow and the turret fighter concept was flawed, as the land-based Boulton Paul Defiant later proved. BBA Collection

The Blackburn Skua was designed to combine the roles of fighter and dive-bomber. A Skua did, however, claim the honour of scoring the Fleet Air Arm's first victory in World War II by shooting down a Dornier flying boat. Will Blunt Collection

Powered by an early version of the Rolls-Royce Merlin, the same engine used by the Spitfire and Seafire, the Fairey Fulmar is probably best described as workmanlike. Based on the earlier Battle bomber, this two-seat fighter had exceptionally good range and heavy firepower with eight wing-mounted Browning machine-guns. It was let down by a top speed inferior to that of land-based opponents. Will Blunt Collection

A Sea Hurricane IB of No. 800 Squadron prepares to leave the carrier HMS *Indomitable*. The type's major failing, and one it shared with the first Seafires, was the lack of wing-folding, although a conversion was considered. Will Blunt Collection

The type's folding wings were much appreciated aboard the smaller British carriers and replaced the Sea Gladiator from September 1940. The Martlet shot down its first German aircraft on Christmas Day.

The next batch of aircraft supplied to the Royal Navy were designated Mks IV and V and differed from the earlier machines in that they were supplied under the Lend-Lease arrangement, the earlier fighters having been purchased outright. These aircraft began entering service in July 1942. The Grumman Martlet/Wildcats remained in front-line service until the end of the war, when, like the later Grumman Hellcats and Chance-Vought Corsairs, they had to

be purchased or returned to the USA. The FAA was once again reliant on British-built fighters. Against this background it is hardly surprising that the Admiralty should press for the development of a naval version of the highly successful Supermarine Spitfire.

Supermarine Aviation Works

Supermarine Aircraft, builder of the Spitfire and Seafire, owed its existence to Noel Pemberton Billing. The son of a Birmingham iron founder, he was a larger than life character who ran away to sea at the age

of fourteen. In South Africa he did a number of different jobs: bricklayer, tram conductor and mounted policeman. He was wounded during the Boer War. Returning home, he opened a garage in Surrey and later developed an interest in aviation. By 1904 he had built a glider. He was awarded a Royal Aero Club Aviator's Certificate in 1912. In October 1913, after a brief spell of buying and selling steam yachts, Pemberton Billing decided to enter the world of aircraft manufacture, acquiring premises at Woolston alongside the River Itchen near Southampton to build flying boats under the name of Supermarine, his telegraphic address.

On a wet flight deck the ground crew await the pilot's signal that he is about to start his Sea Hurricane's engine. Although it is not possible to read the aircraft's codes, it is highly likely that these are No. 800 Squadron machines preparing for a patrol aboard HMS *Indomitable*. BBA Collection

While the Sea Hurricane represented an acceptable stop-gap, the sheer lack of aircraft forced the Admiralty to look to the United States for additional fighters like the tubby Grumman Martlet, later renamed Wildcat in line with US Navy convention. Wildcat AJ148 was on the strength of No. 888 Squadron, which flew from HMS *Formidable* during operations in the Indian Ocean. United States Navy

Pemberton Billing's first design was the innovative PB.1, which was exhibited at the Olympia Aero Show in March 1914. During the war, he produced the Nighthawk quadraplane, a cannon-armed, searchlight-equipped 'Zeppelin killer' for the Admiralty. But in 1916 Pemberton Billing became interested in politics and sold his interest in the company to works manager Hubert Scott-Paine, who became managing director of the re-registered Supermarine Aviation Works. The year was significant for the company for another reason: Reginald J. Mitchell joined its staff.

The Supermarine N.1B Baby represented the kind of aircraft Pemberton Billing had envisaged although none had entered service before hostilities ended in 1918. As with other aircraft manufacturers, Supermarine was affected by the post-war slump in the aviation market and was forced to diversify into activities ranging from building bodies for Model T Fords to the production of lavatory seats. Yet Supermarine continued to design flying boats in anticipation of a burgeoning civil market.

The first fruit of these labours was the Channel Type, which emerged in 1919. Both crew and passengers were exposed to the elements, yet the aircraft saw service in South America, Bermuda, Chile, Japan and Norway. It was also operated by the fledgling airlines based in the south of England and engaged on the cross-channel passenger run. During the 1920s, Scott-Paine was bought out and Supermarine became a limited company with James Bird as managing director and Mitchell as chief designer. Further premises were acquired at Hythe to facilitate the production of flying boats.

the Schneider Trophy races held between 1925 and 1931. Such competitions helped accelerate the pace of aircraft design. For Supermarine this effort reached its climax with the S.6B, which not only enabled Britain to hold the Schneider Trophy in perpetuity but also to set a new world speed record. The first Supermarine design to achieve victory in the series was the Sea Lion II. In 1922 this aircraft wrested an outright win from an Italian government-sponsored team which had already won two races and only needed a third to retain the trophy.

The American team won the following year and it was not until 1925 that Supermarine unveiled its next contender, the S.4. Although it achieved a remarkable 226.75mph (362.8km/h), it crashed on the eve of the race. Undaunted, Supermarine set about designing a successor, helped by government cash.

The result of this extra finance was a team of three S.5s, one of which won at an average speed of 281.65mph (450.64km/h). Another S.5 was second. In 1929 Supermarine joined forces with Rolls-Royce to produce the S.6 powered by the 1,900hp 'R' engine. The sleek seaplane averaged 328.63mph (525.81km/h) to win a clear victory over its Italian rival. On 12 September 1929 an S.6 reached 357.7mph (572.32kmh), although this was not ratified as a world speed record. After two victories Supermarine was confident of winning the final contest in 1931, but with six months to go the British Government withdrew its financial support. All looked lost until Lady Huston offered the company £100,000 to cover the cost of equipping the team. The

result of their hurried efforts was the Supermarine S.6B powered by an uprated engine, which offered a guaranteed a short sprint output of 2,300hp. Finding enough area for cooling purposes on such a stream-lined design was a major problem, however. The answer was the installation of double skin radiators on the upper wing surfaces and floats.

Yet this effort seemed to be wasted as the Italian opposition was unable to field a candidate. As a result, the Supermarine S.6B merely had to complete the course to win, which it did, reaching a speed of 340.08mph (544.13km/h). Supermarine then fitted the aircraft with a special sprint engine to enable it to set a new world speed record of 407.5mph (652km/h) on 29 September 1931. These winning Supermarine seaplanes pioneered all-metal construction. Their design also involved use of the National Physical Laboratory's wind tunnel at Teddington as well as the duplex water tank for float development at Vickers' St Albans works.

Supermarine had become a division of Vickers Armstrong in 1928. It was now part of a large conglomerate whose interests included ship-building, locomotive and armament manufacture. Yet Supermarine was able to maintain its independence. While Vickers concentrated on bombers at its Weybridge factory, Supermarine continued to turn out flying boats. But this was to change. The lessons learned during the quest for the Schneider Trophy were about to be put to a different use by Mitchell and his team. The immortal Spitfire and its various offshoots, which included the Seafire fleet fighter, were on their way.

Schneider Trophy Success

As the company's experience in designing and manufacturing flying boats expanded, so the orders increased. To cater for varied customer requirements Supermarine evolved several separate ranges of aircraft. The first covered general-purpose single-engined amphibians, while the second and more profitable one included twin-engined flying boats, mainly aimed at fulfilling RAF contracts. All these designs resulted in graceful aircraft. The line began with the Southampton of 1925 and ended in 1936 with the Stranraer.

A complete contrast was provided by the company's production of aircraft to contest

Seen on the Calshot slipway, Supermarine S.6B S1596 awaits its next flight. In the final Schneider Trophy race the British team secured the Trophy for all time. BBA Collection

N220 was the Supermarine S.5 racer built to contest the Schneider Trophy race. Although not successful, it did pave the way for the Supermarine S.6B racer. BBA Collection

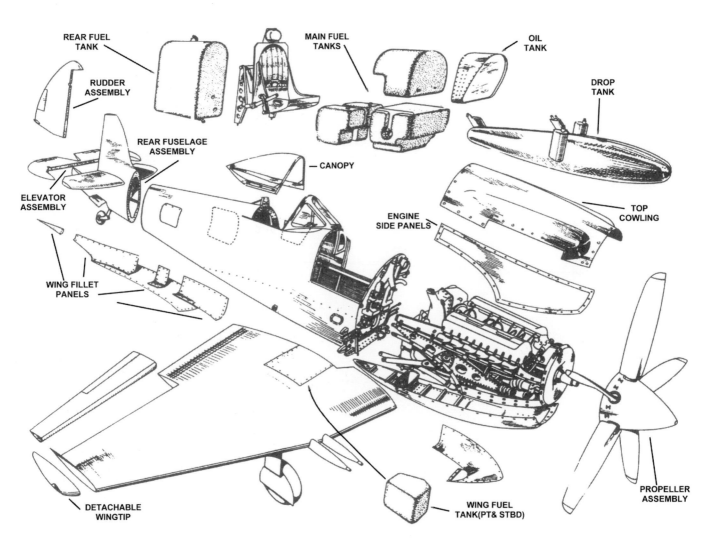

REAR FUEL TANK
RUDDER ASSEMBLY
REAR FUSELAGE ASSEMBLY
ELEVATOR ASSEMBLY
WING FILLET PANELS
DETACHABLE WINGTIP
MAIN FUEL TANKS
CANOPY
ENGINE SIDE PANELS
WING FUEL TANK(PT& STBD)
OIL TANK
DROP TANK
TOP COWLING
PROPELLER ASSEMBLY

The Spiteful/Seafang series of piston-engined fighters represented the final expression of the Spitfire–Seafire line. This diagram illustrates the Spiteful, the Seafang being similar except for an arrester hook and folding wings. Eric Morgan collection

CHAPTER TWO

Seafire Heritage

In 1931 Supermarine responded to Air Ministry Specification F7/30, which called for the development of a single-seat fighter for the Royal Air Force. Also known as Operational Requirement OR.1, the specification had been put out to tender in October 1930. It had been prompted by the belated realization that Britain was falling behind in the development of modern combat aircraft and also that Europe was drifting towards war. The basic requirements of F7/30 included a high rate of climb, the best speed possible above 15,000ft (4,600m), good all-round vision for the pilot, excellent manoeuvrability, ease of maintenance and, importantly, ease of construction for high-volume manufacture. It was intended that prototypes should be ready for flight in 1934.

In many ways Supermarine could be seen as an outsider. Although well-known for its elegant flying boats, it was the Schneider Trophy racers, plus the designing skill of R.J. Mitchell, that prompted the company to tender. This was an important contract and Supermarine was not alone in making a submission. Blackburn, Parnell and Westland submitted biplane designs, while monoplane entrants included one from Boulton Paul. After the usual elimination process, the Air Ministry invited Supermarine to develop its submission into the Type 224. The contract was completed in late 1932. Although the company had delivered a fairly comprehensive outline draft to the Air Ministry, it was only at this stage that the client began to add fine details to its initial requirement. As a result, the Type 224 was to feature wing-mounted machine-guns and be able to carry four 20lb bombs for ground attack.

The Type 224

The Type 224 that emerged in 1934 was radical in many respects, yet overall it represented a dead-end. The most obvious departure from previous monoplane fighter concepts was the cranked wing. This had been selected to eliminate the external bracing featured by earlier designs. The wing itself was conservatively built. It was much thicker than was really necessary, reflecting fears about the flutter problems that had been evident with the seaplane racers. The wing was deep enough to house the radiators and condensers, which were mounted at the leading edges to cool the 600hp Rolls-Royce Goshawk engine. The undercarriage was fixed and each leg was encased in massive 'trouser' fairings that also housed engine coolant tanks.

Students of aeronautical design will already have noticed that the Type 224 would not be able to fulfil its intended role as a high speed interceptor. The engine and its associated cooling system, plus the thick wing and fixed undercarriage, produced an unacceptably high drag coefficient. Flight testing revealed even more problems. Soon after the maiden flight in February 1934 it became obvious that the engine cooling system was the aircraft's weak point. Before the Type 224, liquid cooled engines had found favour in biplane designs. There the condensers had been mounted in the upper wing to provide a large surface for cooling the steam, which then condensed into water to be gravity-fed back to the engine to continue the cooling cycle.

To compensate for the lack of an upper wing, the Type 224's condensers were mounted in the trouser fairing. Cooled and condensed steam was pumped back up to a header tank mounted above the engine. Unfortunately for Supermarine, the cooling system was inefficient. Steam was fed back to the engine, guaranteeing that it would overheat. This could happen at any time during the flight test regime. The red warning lights would illuminate, requiring

The Supermarine Type 224 was to prove a blind alley in fighter development but it was still a monoplane without external bracing, which was then quite a novelty. The Type 224 was let down by its inefficient engine, cooling system and fixed trousered undercarriage, which slowed the aircraft down considerably. Eric Morgan Collection

the pilot to level out and allow the engine and cooling system to cool down.

While this was sufficient cause for alarm, it was the aircraft's performance that sounded its death knell. Having developed the speedy 'S' series of racers, Supermarine was disappointed to discover that the Type 224 could only achieve a top speed of 238mph (380km/h) at 15,000ft (4,600m). Even reaching this altitude was a struggle, because it could take up to eight minutes. Gloster won the contest to supply the RAF's next fighter with its SS.37, later to become better known as the Gladiator. The Type 224 went for further testing to the Marine Aircraft Experimental Establishment, Martlesham Heath. It was later passed to the Royal Aircraft Establishment, Farnborough where it was temporarily named Spitfire. The aircraft ended its days as a target on the Orfordness gunnery range.

While the Type 224 was failing to live up to expectations, a team from Supermarine was at the Air Ministry placing fresh proposals for a new design, owning more of a debt to the racing seaplanes, before senior officials. Fortunately, in the light of subsequent events, the Air Ministry was sympathetic and Specification 425A was issued to cover the new proposal. On paper the aircraft, designated the Type 300, was a vast improvement on its predecessor, having a thinner wing of reduced span and a retractable undercarriage. The design was considered capable of reaching 300mph (480km/h) in level flight, but the Air Ministry was unhappy with the specified Goshawk engine. Not only was it thought that the cooling system would be unreliable but also that the resulting aircraft would be unable to achieve the required top speed and manoeuvre adequately against enemy fighters.

The Type 300

Seeking a more suitable alternative, Mitchell and his team first considered the 800hp Napier Dagger. After careful study by the Supermarine board this engine was rejected in favour of the PV XII then under development at Rolls-Royce. By November 1934 this 27ltr engine had achieved a test-bench rating of 625hp. In flight this was increased first to 790hp at 12,000ft (3,700m) and then to 1,000hp. The Merlin had been born. Having chosen the engine to power the new airframe, Mitchell and his team refined the Type 300 design for

presentation to the Air Ministry. The Ministry responded by issuing Contract AM. 361140/34 on 1 December 1934. It called for one prototype to the revised specification F7/30, valued at £10,000. The main changes involved the engine mountings and also the wing leading edges from which the radiators and associated pipework were to be removed to make room for guns and their ammunition feeds.

The wing was also refined to produce the characteristic elliptical shape. This was seen as the best compromise between the lift and drag coefficients required for a highly manoeuvrable fighter. The wing now featured a gentle taper from tip to root. There was also a subtle twist, which meant the root would stall before the tip to give pilots ample warning of an impending stall. The wing root also housed the retracted undercarriage. Unlike the then-normal boom and web design, the Type 300's wing derived its combination of strength and lightness from a spar comprising shaped hollow sections of different sizes placed inside each other to create the tapered wing. Armament was initially to be four wing-mounted machine-guns, two per wing, but it soon became apparent that this would be ineffective against the all-metal bombers appearing in both Britain and Europe. The subsequent upgrade to eight Browning machine-guns was covered by Specification 10/35 issued in 1935.

Engine cooling continued to give cause for concern, especially as the Merlin generated enormous quantities of heat when running at full power. Evaporative cooling

was initially proposed, but it was quickly realized that this could prove to be the new fighter's Achilles heel. The alternative was to mount an air intake housing a cooling matrix under one wing. A further intake, smaller and circular in shape and mounted under the other wing, would cool the engine oil system. Designed by Frederick Meredith, the radiator featured an intake that forced air through the cooling matrix. The expelled air added a small amount of forward thrust, which overcame the induced drag of the matrix and its fairing. The cooling medium was switched to the more efficient ethylene glycol, which enabled the cooling system to be smaller and lighter than a water-based one.

While the main design team was ironing out the finer points of the new fighter's design, others were employed on extending the type's capabilities. The first idea was for a two-seat machine with a four-gun turret. This was abandoned as Boulton Paul was working on a similar design, which later became the Defiant. Another projected development was a two-seat trainer, which reflected expectations that the mettlesome new fighter might be tricky to handle. While this was recognized by the Air Ministry, a trainer version of the Spitfire was not to appear until the Mk IX, but these aircraft were only ever deployed by air arms outside Britain.

On 5 March 1936 the prototype Type 300 made its first flight with Vickers test pilot Joseph 'Mutt' Summers at the controls. By that time £20,765 had been spent on the project, of which £12,748 was

The start of it all: Supermarine Spitfire K5054. It seems hard to imagine that the evolution of this aircraft through various phases would lead to the Scimitar. Eric Morgan Collection

contributed by the Air Ministry and £7,500 by Rolls Royce with the manufacturer providing the balance. The aircraft had been built at Woolston and assembled at Eastleigh where taxying tests were undertaken. This first flight lasted about twenty minutes and the aircraft reached an altitude of no more than 5,000ft (1,500m). The undercarriage was locked down and Summers was restricted to gentle manoeuvres. On landing he told waiting company officials what they wanted to hear: that the Type 300 handled well and that it should be made ready for its next flight as soon as possible.

Spitfire!

The next flight came on 10 March. All of the systems were operated, enabling the pilot to report that flaps and undercarriage functioned correctly. Another flight the following day confirmed these results and enabled the handling to be explored further. Once the initial flights had been completed the aircraft was grounded for painting. When flying was resumed, Jeffrey Quill was the pilot in charge and his main duty was to check the Type 300's top speed. On 27 March Quill took it to 17,000ft (5,200m) and opened the throttle. The result was a disappointing 335mph (536km/h). The cure was to re-work the propeller, which enabled the speed to rise to 348mph (547km/h), closer to expectations. The Type 300 was then passed to Martlesham Heath, by which time the name 'Spitfire' had been bestowed upon it. This was not greatly to Mitchell's taste. This phase of flight development highlighted a major defect – one that would haunt both the Spitfire and the Seafire – a lack of forward visibility. This meant that while moving on the ground the aircraft had to be snaked from side to side.

Even as the prototype Spitfire was undertaking this test programme the Air Ministry had placed an order for 310 production Mk Is to Specification F16/36. This document laid down the changes required to upgrade the prototype to production standard, which included a strengthened and stiffened wing. This not only allowed for increases in top speed but also permitted the fitment of the proposed armament. Fuel capacity was increased from 75 to 84gal (340 to 380ltr). Flap travel range was raised from 57 to 85 degrees to improve stability during landing.

Delivery Begins

Supermarine had originally promised to begin delivery of production Spitfires within fifteen months of the contract being placed. But the delivery date of October 1937 was asking too much of the Supermarine workforce. The solution was for the company to take what was then the unprecedented step of subcontracting some of the manufacture to another company. General Aircraft Ltd, which was to play a significant role in the Seafire production programme, was contracted to manufacture tail units. This helped in the short term but the real answer was to disperse much of the manufacture from Supermarine's Southampton base. This was to pay off handsomely when the *Luftwaffe* attacked the town.

Once the war began in September 1939 it was obvious that the small production facilities available to Supermarine were inadequate for the task ahead, and a new manufacturing facility was established at Castle Bromwich. Managed by Morris Motors, it was intended that the factory would turn out aircraft just like cars. But this was not car manufacture. Constructing aircraft that were undergoing continuous modification meant that Castle Bromwich was producing only aircraft sections and

components at first. Eventually the factory refined its manufacturing processes to allow it to build other types including Seafires.

With the manufacturing drawings brought up to standard, the rate of manufacture increased rapidly. The first production aircraft, K9787, made its maiden flight on 15 May 1938 flown by Quill. His post-flight report mentioned the increased stability provided by the bigger flap range and also that he had discovered no significant handling deviations compared with the prototype. After completing company handling flights, the Spitfire went to RAE Farnborough for further flight testing. This revealed that it could not be flown above 400mph (640km/h) without the ailerons locking up, which was initially regarded as a benefit as it meant the airframe would be protected from overstressing.

The Spitfire represented a quantum leap from the earlier biplane fighters. It was also faster than the contemporary Hawker Hurricane, but the *Luftwaffe*'s new Messerschmitt Bf 109 had a slight handling edge due to the locking-up of the Spitfire's ailerons. Investigation revealed that the fabric covering was ballooning at speed, dictating the need to replace it with light alloy skinning. This modification, which improved the Spitfire's handling immeasurably, was applied to all new-build

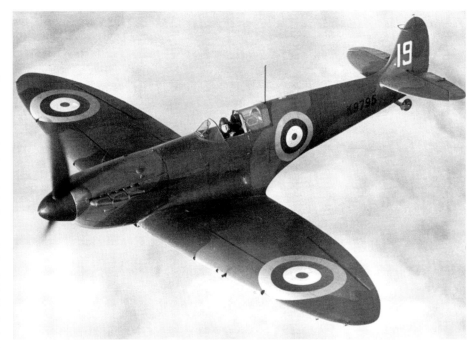

The first production version of the Spitfire was the Mk I with production Merlin engine and eight Browning machine-guns. BBA Collection

With Walrus and Stranraer seaplanes in the background, the Spitfire production line gets under way. Until some of the work was subcontracted out, the complicated wing construction meant that for a short period fuselages were stacked-up awaiting wings. BBA Collection

machines and retrospectively to earlier ones. There was also concern about the engine's inability to perform under negative 'g'. Rolls-Royce redesigned the carburettor; direct fuel injection had been considered but rejected because of a possible power loss.

Cannon armament was first tried on the Spitfire IB, but jamming of the breech mechanism rendered it ineffective. Further redesign work and extensive trials rectified the problems, although it had been recognized by both Supermarine and the Air Ministry that adding machine-guns to the cannons would result in a more versatile fighter. Deliveries of the Spitfire II to the RAF had started before a mixed armament fighter appeared. The main changes from the first production version included the Merlin XII engine, which featured a Coffman cartridge starter, and a pressurized water–glycol cooling system. The Mk II was built in two versions: 'A' with eight

Browning machine-guns and 'B' with two cannon and four machine-guns.

Developing the Spitfire

After the Mk II came the Mk V, which was to be one of the most numerous versions. First production aircraft were converted Mk Is and IIs. The major change was the up-rated Merlin 45, although Frame 5 needed to be strengthened to accommodate the new engine. The first Mk V (X4922) flew for the first time on 20 February 1941 with Jeffrey Quill at the controls. Production was split between three manufacturers: Supermarine, Westland and the Castle Bromwich factory. Two main versions were built. The Mk VA was armed with machine-guns only while the Mk VB mounted two cannon and four machine-guns. There was also the 'C', which utilized

the strengthened Universal wing and could therefore mount 'A'-type or 'B'-type armament, although the latter was the preferred option as it was a more flexible.

Once Fighter Command home-based units had been equipped with the Mk V it was the turn of those in the Mediterranean to receive the new fighter. But first there were extensive trials to develop an air filter system that would protect the engine from sand and dust. The result was the Aboukir system. Although it meant an 8mph (13km/h) speed penalty, it proved effective on both Spitfires and Seafires. Further modifications, which featured in subsequent versions, included a carburettor capable of continuous operation under all conditions. This was first applied to the Merlin 50, which appeared on the Mk V in late 1941. Successful trials resulted in a ground attack capability with a centreline crutch point capable of carrying 250lb and 500lb bombs.

Under-wing bomb mounts were later cleared for operational use.

Following the Mk V in the standard fighter role, came the Mk VIII and the Mk IX. The former introduced a retractable tail wheel, wing leading edge fuel tanks and also the Merlin 60 engine. This required slightly longer engine cowlings, which reduced the already marginal forward view available for landing and ground manoeuvring. Rotol Airscrews Ltd provided the answer with propeller assembly diameter reduced to the barest minimum. This also helped when the type went to sea. Like other versions of the Spitfire, the Mk VIII was required to act as a fighter bomber. But to carry a decent bomb load fuel had to be cut to keep weight within operating limits.

The Mk IX

The Mk IX had been intended as a stop-gap fighter pending mass production of the Mk VIII. But as the latter was more complex to build, the Mk IX became the predominant version; production exceeded 11,000 aircraft, not counting a further 1,100 powered by the Packard-Merlin engine. To assist in developing the Mk IX a pair of Mk Vs was despatched to the Rolls-Royce facility at Hucknall where they received Merlin 61 engines. As this was a more powerful and heavier powerplant the engine bay bulkhead and primary fuselage longerons were strengthened to compensate. While this was adequate for the trials aircraft, both the Air Ministry and Supermarine realized that the rest of the airframe would also need reinforcing. To absorb the extra power, a Rotol four-bladed propeller was installed, the whole being tested at the Air Fighting Development Unit at Duxford in April 1942. Reports from AFDU evaluators were positive in nature as the more powerful engine and propeller improved performance throughout the speed and altitude range.

Further airframes were also allotted to the Mk IX development programme. Some were used to test the four-cannon wing while others participated in Merlin 77 engine development, which required the use of a six-bladed contra-rotating propeller. Although these aircraft were eventually to chase high-flying Junkers Ju 86P bombers, whose attacks on the British mainland were largely unchallenged, much of the development work would find an outlet in production Spitfires and Seafires. During its

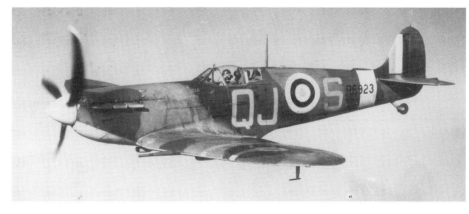

Originally destined to be a Mk I, this Spitfire was eventually completed as a Mk V with wing-mounted cannon. BBA Collection

While the Fleet Air Arm was pushing for carrier-borne aircraft, the Air Ministry came up with an alternative, a float-equipped Spitfire. Although the installation was a neat one, the floats hampered the aircraft's performance. BBA Collection

AB200 was built for the high altitude interception role and introduced the four-bladed propeller unit as standard. BBA Collection

The RAF wanted the Spitfire Mk VIII to be its standard fighter but production was complicated by its retractable tail wheel and, as a result, most were employed in the Far East. BBA Collection

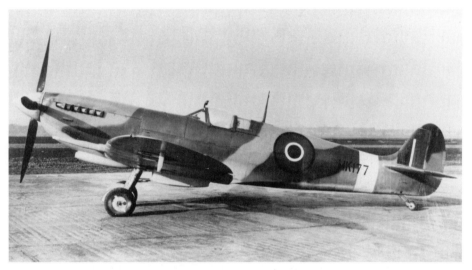

The Spitfire IX was the most-prolific variant and used a four-bladed propeller plus a combined wing-mounted cannon and machine-gun armament. BBA Collection

to avoid anti-aircraft defences while attacking ground targets. Further stress was placed on the wings during the high 'g' pull-outs immediately following low-level bomb release to avoid blast damage. The initial fix was external structural bracing applied to the affected area, although the long-term solution was found to be thicker stiffer skins as the internal structure was unaffected by vigorous handling.

Griffon Spitfires

More significant changes to both aircraft structure and engine were to follow. The appearance of *Luftwaffe* fighters able to outperform the RAF's Spitfires meant that Joe Smith, who had succeeded R.J. Mitchell as chief designer, was seeking ways of improving performance. The most obvious would be through increased engine power. The Merlin was close to the limit of its performance and Rolls-Royce was asked for a replacement. Fortunately for Spitfire development, the company had started developing the 'R' class engine just before the war. The result was the Griffon. Although its 36.7ltr capacity represented a considerable increase over the Merlin, the new engine's frontal area increased marginally – from 7.5sq ft (0.7sq m) to 7.9sq ft. Once Supermarine and Rolls Royce were sure that the Griffon could be installed into the Spitfire airframe the proposed new fighter was presented to the Air Ministry under Specification 466 in October 1939.

A Mk V airframe, then the main production variant, was selected to receive the Griffon – a single-staged supercharged Griffon RG2SM IIB driving a four-bladed propeller – and this became the first Mk XII (DP845). The aircraft made its maiden flight from the Supermarine airfield at Worthy Down on 27 November 1941. Once again Quill was in command. Handling was described as excellent, especially at low level, although it was noted that the throttle needed careful handling. Quill did, however, express concern about longitudinal stability because he found that sudden power applications resulted in corresponding trim changes. Had this been peacetime much time would have been spent in sorting out this defect. The chosen method was a warning entry in the pilots' notes.

Initial production Spitfire XIIs delivered to the RAF featured the standard 'B' wing with an armament of two cannon and four

production life, the Mk IX airframe underwent various changes. The most obvious was the replacement of the semicircular under-wing oil cooler intake with a rectangular one. The Mk IX was initially fitted with the 'B'-type wing, although this was quickly changed to the Universal type.

The rudder became more pointed in shape, the increased area helping to counteract engine torque. A more obvious change was a cut-down rear fuselage and the replacement of the original canopy assembly by a bubble-shaped unit, which improved all-round pilot vision. The Mk IX was also capable of carrying bombs under

the wings and on a centreline mount, which was also plumbed for a 90gal (410ltr) fuel tank. Production innovations included infra-red drying lamps to speed up external paint curing time from hours to minutes.

Mk IX flight testing was carried out at the Air Fighting Development Unit (AFDU), Duxford. Pilots were warned about a sudden nose-up pitch, which happened when bombs were released. More serious was wrinkling of the upper wing skins above the cannon and undercarriage bays. Interviews with pilots revealed that they had been putting the aircraft through a series of violent manoeuvres in an effort

The Royal Air Force and Supermarine were also aware that the Spitfire lacked range. The first attempt to cure this deficiency was through the addition of external tanks such as that shown here. The drawback was that the aircraft turned more tightly on the tank side of the aircraft. BBA Collection

The first version of the Spitfire to be equipped with the Griffon engine was the Mk XII. The first batch of aircraft were based on the Spitfire V with the second based on the Mk VIII. MB878 was from the second batch and carries a 500lb bomb on the centreline. BBA Collection

machine-guns. Much of the airframe was borrowed from the Mk V, although the retractable tail wheel came from the Mk VIII. The size of the cooling matrix fairing was increased too. The next production batch was based on the Mk VIII, which meant greater strength. Both versions featured clipped wingtips to improve roll control at low level. DP845 was retained as a test-bed and it was used to try out a variety of five-bladed propellers; such units were to feature in later versions of both the Spitfire and Seafire. It was also used to test the Griffon IV, whose increased power revealed that longitudinal stability was almost non-existent at full throttle.

Pointed Rudder Introduced

The solution was a larger and more pointed rudder, which was fitted retrospectively to other Griffon-powered aircraft. This also eliminated the aircraft's tendency to swing strongly on take-off, although the throttle still required careful operation to maintain correct take-off speed. Even so, the Griffon's opposite direction of rotation could cause the aircraft to swing violently to the right. There were further changes. Instead of the Merlin's 12-volt ignition system, the Griffon used the Coffman cartridge starter to bring the engine to life. In squadron service a tendency for the engine to cut out

under positive or negative 'g' required extensive experimentation and flight testing to arrive at a suitable carburettor modification.

The Fleet Air Arm had its first taste of Griffon power with the Spitfire XII. Early airframes, however, were fitted with 'A'-frame arrester hooks borrowed from the Seafire III production line. Both types were extensively tested at Arbroath by the FAA Service Trials Unit. Although a naval version of the Spitfire XII was not chosen for service use, the experience gained would lead to the Seafire XV.

Two-Stage Supercharging

Although the first Griffon-powered Spitfire was not the all-round success that had been intended, it did prove the concept of installing a bigger engine in the airframe. The weak spot, though, was the first version of the Griffon. With its single stage supercharger it was an excellent performer at low levels but struggled at altitude. This meant that interception above 15,000ft (4,600m) remained the province of Merlin-powered Spitfires. Bench testing of a two-stage supercharged Griffon began in 1943 and Supermarine supplied eight Mk VIII airframes to act as test-beds. The new unit was a revelation. It endowed the Spitfire with a spectacular turn of speed – 445 mph (712km/h) at 25,000ft (7,700m) – and a rate of climb of 5,000ft (1,500m) per minute. One aircraft from this batch was despatched to Rotol at Staverton for contra-rotating propeller development. These early units suffered from problems with the pitch change mechanism controlling the front three-blade unit, while the rear unit pitch was altered by a transitional bearing. This was another weak spot: the bearing exhibited a tendency to fail, accompanied by a loud bang. The result was a very sudden reduction in speed and the need to land as quickly as possible.

The other aircraft in the development programme were fitted with Rotol five-bladed propeller units, being designated the Mk XIV. In this initial form they were overpowered and unstable, rendering them unsuitable for front-line service. Changes to the engine were limited to the throttle friction damper and propeller control mechanism. As the up-rated Griffon had a greater power output, the fin and rudder were increased in both height and area to compensate. This reworked version was

The definitive Griffon-powered Spitfire was the Mk XIV, which introduced two-stage supercharging, a slightly changed wing planform and a strengthened undercarriage. BBA Collection

sent to the various test establishments, whose reports were positive especially where performance was concerned.

Up to 25,000ft (7,700m) the Griffon-powered machine behaved like its Merlin-engined counterpart, although the controls were slightly heavier. Above that height the Griffon-powered aircraft quickly outstripped its rival. A&AEE's final report recommended quantity production using the existing Mk VIII production line as the basis. To accommodate the Griffon 65 engine the Mk VIII structure was strengthened to compensate for the weight of the powerplant and that of the five-bladed Rotol propeller. Fixed armament included two cannon and a pair of 0.5in machine-guns in place of the earlier 0.303in weapons.

The fighter reconnaissance version of the Mk XIV featured a full complement of cameras just aft of the cockpit. There was also an additional rear-fuselage fuel tank, plus strengthened and improved under-carriage units. Further developments included modifications to permit the carriage of external fuel tanks and bombs, while safety improvements saw the engine oil tank relocated behind the fireproof bulkhead. This not only facilitated engine changes but also separated the oil tank from a potentially hot engine and the attendant fire risk. To cater for the bigger engine the under-wing radiators were greatly enlarged. That under the starboard wing was replaced by a box-like structure similar in size and shape to that under the other wing.

Although the Royal Navy was greatly interested in the Griffon-powered Seafire it was the RAF that fitted an arrester hook

and Rocket-Assisted Take-Off Gear (RATOG) to the aircraft to facilitate use from unprepared airfields in Europe after D Day. While neither feature was actually adopted for RAF use, both appeared on RN aircraft. Supermarine also proposed a bubble canopy version of the Mk XIV, which was approved for service. While useful in combat this innovation had one drawback: when jettisoned the heavy canopy assembly was likely to strike the rear fuselage and the leading edge of the fin, causing extensive damage. The solution was for pilots to avoid jettisoning the canopy when abandoning the aircraft.

As the Griffon-powered aircraft was as agile as its Merlin-powered sibling it, too, was plagued by distortion of the upper wing skin surfaces caused by violent manoeuvring. Instead of riveting external supports to

the upper wing skins, Supermarine strengthened the ends of the span-wise stringers under the upper wing skins. This cured the problem, although some aircraft did show signs of skin wrinkling; this was later traced to over-exuberant flying overstressing the airframe. Despite the enlarged rudder to counter engine torque, there were still reports of longitudinal instability. Investigation revealed the fabric-covered rudder to be stable throughout the flight regime, while a metal-covered assembly, complete with operating trim tab, caused much of the trouble. Disconnecting the trim tab and locking it in a fixed position removed the worst of the instability.

Spitfire XVIII

The Spitfire XVIII that followed was also based on the Mk VIII, although it required extensive modification and strengthening to cope with the proposed up-rated Griffon engine. This was the version of the Spitfire in which the characteristic wing planform was changed to a more elliptical shape. The method of construction also changed. A solid main spar replaced the previous riveted laminated square tubular booms, resulting in a stronger wing and one that was quicker to manufacture. Although the undercarriage units and their mountings were redesigned to cope with the increased weight, flight testing of the aircraft and its fighter-reconnaissance equipment revealed that further strengthening would be required before service entry. Testing also revealed that longitudinal instability had returned, now accompanied by propeller vibration. The remedy was an even larger rudder with

Later versions of the Spitfire XIV and XVIII introduced photographic reconnaissance capability and a Spiteful tail unit to improve longitudinal stability. BBA Collection

a broader chord and a new propeller unit. The arrester hook and RATOG were tested again but not adopted. There were two versions of this variant, the most prolific being the reconnaissance aircraft. The fighter-bomber was cleared for the available range of bombs and under-wing rockets. Two other versions of the Mk XVIII were proposed: a two-seat trainer and a target tug. Neither left the drawing board.

'Super Spitfires'

The final Griffon-powered variants are sometimes referred to as 'Super Spitfires', but as these three versions represented a significant departure it was originally intended to adopt the name 'Victor'. The F.21 appeared when Spitfire DP851 was fitted with a Griffon 61 engine. Its modified wings featured heavier-gauge skinning and a revised internal structure. Although this development airframe paved the way for the F.21, test flying revealed that the wing structure was too light for the task, as it twisted during combat manoeuvres. The answer was a complete redesign of the wing structure to cope with the increased loading. This resulted in an altered shape with a straighter trailing edge, which not only increased wing area but also improved high altitude performance.

The undercarriage bays had to be moved slightly outboard and were redesigned to allow for outer fairing doors. Although the size of the bays was basically unaltered, the legs themselves were slightly longer, necessitating a series of levers and cranks, plus a sequence of valves to contract the leg so that it would fit the bay. Complex it may have been, but this mechanism produced a clean under-wing surface and the resulting increase in overall speed was considered worth the effort. The lengthened undercarriage and increased undercarriage track also improved ground stability and provided greater propeller tip clearance. The standard Spitfire F.21 could have either the Griffon 61 or 64, both driving a five-bladed propeller. The F.21 also received the Griffon 85 with a six-bladed contra-rotating unit. Additional small fuel tanks were fitted into the wing leading edges. Armament comprised four 20mm Hispano cannon with part of the belt feed system hidden under blisters on the upper wing surface.

Initial flight tests of the F.21 with the contra-rotating unit showed that the Spitfire had evolved into a very stable gun platform.

The final series of Spitfires were the F.20s, which introduced further modifications to the aircraft. The most obvious ones in this view are the slightly forward-raked undercarriage and the outer doors to the undercarriage bays. BBA Collection

This later-build Spitfire F.21 is little different from the Seafire F.45, as it features the six-bladed contra-rotating propellers and the Spiteful tail unit also fitted the Seafire. Ray Sturtivant

The Spiteful represented Supermarine's last attempt to keep the Spitfire line alive. Although the fuselage was familiar, the wings were completely redesigned in planform. BBA Collection

Torque generated by the engine had been eliminated but the increased complexity of the propeller unit resulted in some initial unreliability. Eventually this was cured, but as the RAF did not adopt it, the unit's use was restricted to the Fleet Air Arm's Seafire FR.47. Without it, however, the F.21 was regarded as an unstable gun platform, although not dangerous to fly, and the tail surfaces were again increased in area to enable the F.21 to be cleared for service use.

Supermarine was also keen to refine the Spitfire's aerodynamic design and to increase the range of powerplants available. In the original wing the transonic centre of pressure was just aft of the leading edge. A proposed revamp would shift it closer to the centreline to produce a high-speed laminar flow design with a low drag coefficient. It also meant that the wing exhibited a consistent taper on both fore and aft edges. Not only did this change the shape of the wing but it also reduced its area from 242sq ft (22sq m) to 210sq ft (20sq m).

A semi-modified Mk VIII undertook limited initial flight trials at RAE, but as the changes were not really representative of Supermarine's intended new wing permission was sought to use the prototype F.21 as a test airframe. The resulting aircraft featured the new wings, complete with four cannon, reworked tail surfaces and a new designation of F.23. It was provisionally named Valiant. But the new Spitfire was not to reach production status. With the war in Europe drawing to a close the order for 438 aircraft was cancelled. The effort was not wasted, however, as the F.23 was used extensively in the Spiteful and Seafang development programme.

While the F.23 was a dead-end, Supermarine continued to push the F.21 design further. The result was the F.22, which was very similar to its predecessor except for the canopy and rear fuselage. The original high-back construction was cut down with a bubble canopy for the pilot. Internally the original 12-volt electrical system was replaced by a 24-volt one, which was to be featured in the remaining Spitfire and Seafire iterations. The F.22 with its improved tail surfaces was a much improved aircraft; as a fighter bomber it offered a stable bombing platform. The final Spitfire was the F.24, which offered minimal improvements over the F.22 apart from the ability to carry under-wing rockets.

The naval equivalent of the Spiteful was the Seafang, which featured a contra-rotating propeller, folding wings, an arrester hook and other naval fittings. BBA Collection

This side-on view of the Seafang 32 shows the clean lines of the type, plus the reconnaissance installation. BBA Collection

The final versions of the Spitfire were the F.22/24 machines. Featuring a bubble canopy and a cannon-only armament, they saw limited service. BBA Collection

R. J. Mitchell

Reginald Joseph Mitchell was born in 1895 in Stoke-on-Trent. His parents were both teachers and he had three brothers and two sisters. At school Mitchell revealed a flair for both mathematics and art, which led to an interest in engineering. In 1911, his schooling completed, Mitchell was apprenticed to a firm of locomotive manufacturers in his home town. This required attendance at night school classes where his flair for mathematics was commented upon. At the completion of his apprenticeship in 1917 Mitchell moved to Supermarine Aircraft, based in Southampton.

By 1918 Mitchell had met and married Florence Dayson, who was eleven years his senior and the headmistress of an infants' school in the Potteries. It was not long before he started making a favourable impression on his new employers, so favourable, in fact, that by 1920 he had been appointed chief designer. He was just twenty-five. Between then and 1936 Mitchell was responsible for twenty-four different aircraft designs ranging from large flying boats to light aircraft. His method of working was to develop an idea into a basic design before passing it to a member of his team to progress it to completion.

Supermarine was acquired by Vickers in 1928 and it was a condition of the purchase that Mitchell should stay with the company for the next five years. Initially, Vickers wanted him to work alongside its own chief designer, Barnes Wallis, but Mitchell was not keen and did not hide his feelings. Realizing that his genius would flower better without restriction, Vickers gave in.

Mitchell always showed great concern for safety and his only designs to raise concerns were the Supermarine S.4 racing aircraft – they revealed a wing flutter problem which proved difficult to cure – and the under-powered Air Yacht. While neither design saw Mitchell at his best, his Southampton and Stranraer flying boats proved good sellers and helped see Supermarine through the recession of the early 1930s. Under Mitchell's guidance Supermarine produced a series of high-speed floatplanes to contest the Schneider Trophy races. The eventual winner was the RAF High Speed Flight equipped with the Supermarine S.6B, whose success enabled Britain to capture the Trophy for all time.

The racers offered glimpses of the future for high speed aircraft. Mitchell incorporated some of the lessons he had learned in the Supermarine Type 224. But the Rolls-Royce Goshawk engine, the cooling system and the fixed undercarriage enclosed in cumbersome trouser fairings created a machine that was less than the sum of its parts. As a result the Type 224 has passed into history as an interesting oddity, having lost out to a Gloster-designed biplane later to be called Gladiator.

In the summer of 1933 Mitchell was diagnosed as suffering from rectal cancer and he underwent a colostomy that August. Even with today's medical techniques this procedure would result in a debilitating post-operative condition, but Mitchell was determined to return to work as soon as possible. In fact, such was the speed of his recovery and the depth of his determination that he started flying lessons in December of the same year. By the following July he had completed the course and gained his licence.

Disappointed with the Type 224, Mitchell had already begun work on its successor, the Type 300. This evolved into the Spitfire. The new design was also intended to be Goshawk-powered, but a much better alternative became available in the same company's Merlin. A significant result of the change was that the Type 300 would lose its leading edge radiators but retain the box structure that gave the aircraft considerable strength.

Although Mitchell was able to resume his career with Supermarine, his health was always a matter of concern. In 1936 the cancer returned. There was a brief spell in hospital in February 1937 after which he was allowed home. This time, though, he was forced to give up work, but he often went to Eastleigh to watch Spitfire flight tests. A visit to a clinic in Vienna followed in April but he was back home by the end of May, his condition deemed incurable. R.J. Mitchell died on 11 June 1937. He was forty-two.

Supermarine had lost its design genius but the Mitchell legacy was in safe hands. His successor, Joe Smith, for many years the company's chief draughtsman, proved more than capable of guiding the development of the Spitfire and its naval sibling throughout the war and into the following years. That the Spitfire remains an aviation icon symbolizing a nation's heroic defence at a critical time offers a fitting monument to Mitchell and all those involved in developing Supermarine's immortal fighter.

CHAPTER THREE

Shipboard Spitfires

The success achieved against the *Luftwaffe* by Royal Air Force Spitfire squadrons helped to highlight the growing gap between the performance of the Royal Navy's fighters and those they opposed.

Although based on a successful land-based fighter, the Sea Hurricane was essentially a stop-gap. The type served with distinction on the CAM ships, thirty-five of which were converted with rocket-powered catapults, and also the MACs, the armed merchant carriers, which were cargo vessels fitted with a flight deck. But encumbered with the equipment needed for naval operations and suitably strengthened for carrier operations, the Hurricane was hardly a sparkling performer. It also lacked the folding wings so necessary for carrier stowage. Even so, it was superior – at least in performance and agility – to the cumbersome Fairey Fulmar which sometimes had difficulty catching the faster German and Italian bombers.

Fighter Defects Exposed

In the early war years naval carrier forces were employed on anti-submarine duties, chasing German raiders and intercepting blockade runners. It was against this background that, in January 1940, the Admiralty requested a 'Sea Spitfire' with folding wings for service that October. Unfortunately for the Fleet Air Arm, the Admiralty was unable to persuade the First Lord, Winston Churchill, to push the project forward. At his request it was abandoned in March. In hindsight, given the events that began on 9 April, this was a gross mistake. When German forces started their invasion of Norway the defects of the Fleet Air Arm's fighters were cruelly exposed.

All the available fleet carriers were deployed to support naval and ground operations. But the maximum number of aircraft available for top cover was thirty, drawn from a pool of Skuas, Rocs and Sea Gladiators. Yet although they were out-

classed, these few fighters managed to break up numerous raids and shoot down some of the enemy aircraft without loss. RAF Gladiators and Hurricanes were also deployed to Norway to bring some relief to the hard-pressed carrier force.

By the end of May it was obvious that the Allied Expeditionary Force could not prevail in Norway and that evacuation was needed to save as many men as possible. As aircraft had to be retained for home defence it was proposed that as many of the RAF aircraft be recovered if possible. Although the RAF fighters were not equipped with arrestor hooks the Hurricanes and the Gladiators made successful landings aboard HMS *Glorious*. In a cruel twist of fate the carrier and her escorting destroyers encountered the German battle cruisers *Scharnhorst* and *Gneisenau*. All the aircraft and many of the pilots as well as the carrier's crew-members went down with the ship.

Although the Sea Hurricane joined the Grumman Martlet in Fleet Air Arm service, it was obvious that neither type was capable of further development. Because they originated from French and Greek contracts, the US-built machines were not equipped for carrier use and could only operate from shore bases. This prompted the Admiralty in late 1941 to press again for the Sea Spitfire. The response was positive – up to a point. The Royal Navy received forty-eight Spitfire VBs and 202 VCs, 50 per cent of the original request. The Air Ministry wanted to maintain a sufficient stock of Spitfires and further aircraft were required to meet Russian needs. In its response, the Admiralty stressed the importance of a viable fleet defence as the principal fighter, the Fulmar, was too slow and the Hurricane lacked wing folding capability.

Then, on 9 December 1941, the Defence Supply Committee displayed its grasp of the situation. It authorized production of sufficient fighters and other aircraft to fully equip RN carriers. Even though it would appear that the matter was settled, there was an acrimonious exchange of correspondence as the Admiralty and Air

Ministry blamed each other for the Fleet Air Arm's unsatisfactory equipment. A review of the fleet's aircraft requirements was completed by February 1943 with the result that the Seafire was chosen as the preferred fighter. The forthcoming Blackburn Firebrand was considered too large for use aboard current carriers, while the Merlin-powered Fairey Firefly was behind schedule. It was, in any case, being seen as an attack aircraft. The final outcome was that the fixed-wing Seafire IB was to be delivered as soon as possible for interim service, to be followed by the definitive folding-wing production machine. In the meantime, Spitfires were to be handed over for use in the training and evaluation role.

'Hooked Spitfire'

One aircraft, BL676, was fitted with slinging points and an arrester hook, earning itself the name of 'Hooked Spitfire'. Deck landing trials were carried out by Lt Cdr H.P. Bramwell DSC, commanding officer of the RN Fighter School. HMS *Illustrious* was selected as the trials vessel despite a damaged forward port hull and flight deck suffered during a collision with her sister ship *Formidable* in December 1941. Landing and take-off trials were carried out successfully before *Illustrious* was moved to Birkenhead. Further sea trials were undertaken off the Orkneys aboard HMS *Victorious* during March and April 1942. These trials, undertaken with a fully worked-up ship and experienced pilots, were to have far-reaching implications for future operations. The main complaint from the pilots was the lack of vision over the nose on approach as the line of sight below the horizontal was 4 degrees. This meant that, while they were trying to achieve a three-point landing, pilots were unable to see ahead. As this was considered unacceptable, a continuous curved final approach was adopted to enable pilots to keep the flight deck and the 'batsman' in sight until the wings were levelled out for touchdown.

BL676 was one of the original hooked Spitfire Vs used to train Seafire pilots in the art of deck landing. FAAM Yeovilton

These trials were considered successful enough for production aircraft to be ordered. The first was the Seafire IB, based on the Spitfire VB with the 'B' wing, while the Seafire IIC was based on the Spitfire VC with its heavier armament. The Seafire IB was intended as an interim aircraft, while the IIC was to be the main production version. This first version represented a straight adaptation of the production Spitfire VB and some early Mk Is required an 'A'-frame arrester hook on strengthened mountings at the juncture of the fuselage bottom longerons and frame 15. This point was 10ft (3m) aft of the main undercarriage units. The hook itself was some 6ft (1.8m) long and was attached to a hydraulic jack, which not only extended the frame into the airflow but also acted as a damper. As this was also a stress point, the local structure had to be strengthened. In the retracted position the frame was faired into the lower fuselage; when extended, it projected no more than 3ft (0.9m) below the aircraft's ground line.

With only the hook extending into the airflow this had little impact on the aircraft's top speed. Release was via a pilot-operated control connected to the retention jaws via a Bowden cable. Resetting the hook could only be carried out by the ground crew after landing. Further strengthening was applied to the port and starboard longerons and to the rear of the canopy, these areas being selected for the slinging points. Even so, it was not always possible for the Seafires to land-on. They had to be winched aboard

lighters and ferried to the ship. The remainder of the changes made were under the skin and concerned what in modern parlance would be called the avionics suite. This comprised a naval high frequency receiver-transmitter, a naval frequency Identification Friend or Foe (IFF) transmitter, a Type 72 homing beacon, plus a standard naval radio fit. Overall, the changes from the basic Spitfire only increased all up weight by 5 per cent, while the few slight protrusions into the air stream reduced top speed by 5mph (8km/h).

The Seafire IBs were converted under contract by Hamble-based Air Service Training Ltd, also undertaking Spitfire maintenance, and by Cunliffe-Owen Ltd, which was already involved in Spitfire sub-

contract work at Eastleigh. They turned out forty-eight and 118 modified machines respectively. Once the aircraft had been converted they were given new serial numbers, which had a tendency to conflict with production numbers. Confusingly, these Seafires were aircraft allocated after the initial batch had been agreed. The first forty-eight actually included three trials aircraft plus forty-five further ones drawn from RAF stocks. They were transformed into hooked Spitfires at RAF maintenance units. Although they featured the arrestor hook, radio and IFF equipment, they lacked slinging points and homing beacons.

They were not fully equipped for combat carrier operations either. As a result, these aircraft were used mainly in the training role

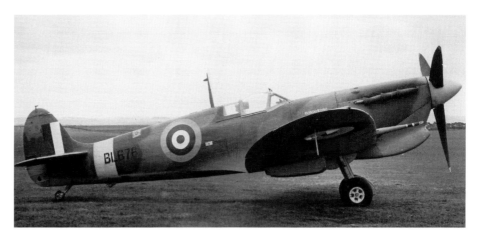

BL676, displaying the name Bondowoso, was used for a variety of trials including those of the tropical filter, shown here under the nose. BBA Collection

and the first Seafire IB was delivered on 15 June 1942 by Air Service Training. The company had been able to turn out these conversions quite quickly, which meant that their machines were delivered before those from Cunliffe-Owen. The first unit to be equipped with Seafires, No. 801 Naval Air Squadron, was assigned to HMS *Furious*. This vessel was unusual in that it had 'T'-shaped lifts, which meant that the lack of folding wings was not a hindrance; nor was the lack of a catapult for launching since the Seafire IBs lacked launch spools.

Further aircraft were requested by the Admiralty in late 1942 for use during Operation *Torch*, the landings in North Africa. These were to be sixty-five Spitfire VBs equipped with hooks but lacking launch spools, plus twenty retired Spitfires for flying training. All were required for delivery during September 1943. In case HMS *Illustrious* became available for this operation, the Admiralty increased its requirements by a further forty-eight hooked Spitfires with another eighteen for training. Sensing an opportunity for a major increase in its aircraft fleet, the Admiralty requested a meeting with the Ministry of Aircraft Production at which it demanded 240 aircraft. This was whittled down to 114, of which sixty-six were to be released for FAA use in early 1943. It was a critical period for British aircraft production as single-seat fighters were heavily in demand and the industry was struggling to cope. In addition, the British Purchasing Mission in the USA was struggling to obtain enough aircraft to fulfil Britain's needs at a time when the USA was rapidly re-equipping its forces. The situation was never fully resolved during 1943, but production was increased sufficiently to give each RN fighter squadron, whether on land or sea, enough aircraft to meet its operational needs.

The Mk II Appears

While the first Seafires were re-worked second-hand Spitfire Vs, the next version, the IIc and its low-level counterpart the L.IIc, were built from the outset as naval fighters. Supermarine-manufactured aircraft were based on new Spitfire Vs taken from the production line and rebuilt. Brand-new aircraft were produced under Contract B124305/40 by Westland Aircraft, which now became responsible for Merlin Seafire development. Both the Supermarine factory

This early Seafire was converted by Air Service Training at Hamble. Although similar to the hooked Spitfires, there are obvious differences: the external strengthening straps below the cockpit and similar plating on the lower aft fuselage. FAAM Yeovilton

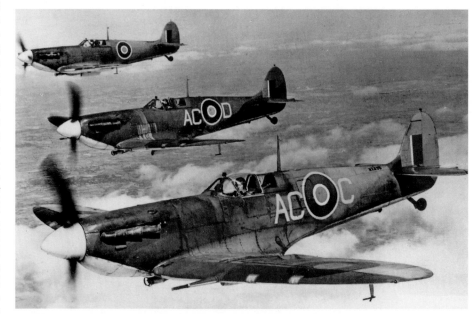

NX890 was a Seafire IB allocated to No. 759 Squadron based at Yeovilton as part of the Naval Air Fighter School. Two other aircraft from the same unit are seen lined up in echelon. FAAM Collection

A line of Seafire IBs with NX908 at the front receiving attention to its Merlin engine. FAAM Collection

Inside view of the pre-test flight shed at Westland showing Seafires being prepared for flight with Welkin high-altitude fighters in the background. BBA Collection

Castle Bromwich is the location and the scene is Spitfires undergoing final finishing. The management initially tried to build aircraft using car production methods but the growing number of modifications meant that it was not feasible. Eventually, the difficulties were resolved and the facility became a vital part of the Spitfire and Seafire story. BBA Collection

and the Castle Bromwich production facility were fully occupied turning out Spitfires and the addition of the Seafire to the production lines would have caused major disruption. Supermarine, however, delivered its small quota more quickly than Westland because the Yeovil-based manufacturer had first to tool-up and establish its production line. Cunliffe-Owen became its major subcontractor.

The major changes incorporated in the Seafire II series included arrester hook mounting spigots at fuselage frame 16 on either side, with a further pair mounted under the wing centre section for the launch spools. To strengthen the area around frame 16 an external fishplate was riveted along the mid-fuselage longeron from the forward cockpit bulkhead to the radio bay to compensate for the arrester hook. Further strengthening was applied to frames 9, 10 and 16, and to the fuselage longerons near the radio compartment. The forward pair of spools was mounted on braced frames riveted to the fuselage in line with the bottom longerons.

All of this extra strengthening was needed to counter the forces associated with carrier launches and landings. No less than 40,000 man hours were expended on redesigning the fuselage to accommodate the arrester hook, its mounting and additional strengthening. The Universal 'C' wing with its additional 25lb (11kg) of armour plate and mounting points for under-wing stores on the outer panels also required beefing up. To compensate for the increased weight, the undercarriage was redesigned and strengthened. The undercarriage units were also raked forward by 2in (5cm) in an attempt to reduce the aircraft's tendency to nose over.

The first prototype Supermarine Type 357 Seafire IIC, AD371, a converted Spitfire V, made its maiden flight in February 1942. By 25 February the prototype was at RAE Farnborough for evaluation. Carrier trials began aboard HMS *Illustrious* on 5 March. As delivered, the aircraft had an all-up weight of 6,490lb (2,950 kg). Although the Seafire initially performed well during take-offs and landings, problems become apparent later in the trials. During one catapult launch the aircraft swung slightly and the port wheel hit the deck coaming, causing the tyre to burst. The pilot completed the take-off and made a circuit of the carrier before landing, holding off the port wheel for as long as possible before making contact with the deck. But the

Seafire swung off the centreline and the radiator cowling was damaged.

After minor repairs a further nineteen catapult launches were undertaken before AD371 was returned to Worthy Down for inspection. The report was not promising. Buckling was found near the rear fuselage spools and there was more at frame 19 at the tail unit attachment point. During these trials the tailplane had become deformed, resulting in a tendency for the aircraft to twist to starboard, which required the application of full rudder. The pilot's headrest was considered to be too far back and the engine exhibited a tendency to cut-out on launching. All the defects were rectified, the major piece of remedial work – according to a Supermarine report of November 1942 – being a 50 per cent strengthening of the airframe.

The first production Seafire IIC ,MA970, – built by Supermarine and designated Type 358 – made its first flight from High Post airfield on 28 May 1942. It went to Worthy Down on 9 June for weighing, as the airframe now incorporated twenty Seafire and Spitfire modifications. A variety of armament options was also considered but the one favoured by the Admiralty – four 20mm Hispano cannons – was found to be too heavy for the airframe. This obliged their Lordships to accept the 'B' wing combination of two cannons and four machine-guns.

Westland's first Seafire IIC, LR631, did not appear until December 1942. After initial test flying it was transferred to Vickers' Worthy Down facility on 4 January 1943 for weighing and determination of its centre of gravity. As delivered, the airframe had a tare weight of 5,322lb (2,419kg), which increased to 6,978lb (3,172kg) for a normal take-off, although this increased to 7,272lb (3,305kg) with a 30gal (136ltr) overload tank. The aircraft was powered by a Rolls-Royce Merlin 46 driving a three-bladed Rotol Jablo propeller unit. It also featured a temperate climate air intake. As it was a later-build aircraft, some fifty-three Seafire and Spitfire modifications had been applied. During flight trials LR631 recorded a maximum speed of 363mph (581km/h) at 7,300ft (2,200m), which increased to 398mph (637km/h) at 21,000ft (6,400m). Rate of climb was determined to be 4,900ft (1,500m) per min at 4,800ft (1,500m) altitude which decreased to 4,050ft (1,250m) per min at 18,000ft (5,500m).

Production Tempo Increases

While Westland worked up to production status Supermarine delivered fifty Seafires by October 1942, just enough to equip four squadrons but with scant allowance for attrition. Westland's early build Seafire IICs

MA970 was originally constructed as a Seafire IIC, being utilized for the trials necessary to clear the type for naval service. Having completed this task, the aircraft was re-built as the prototype Seafire III. BBA Collection

MA970 was also used to test the four-bladed propeller and the tropical filter unit located under the nose. Somewhere along the way wrinkles have appeared in the lower fuselage skins. BBA Collection.

were equipped with Merlin 45 engines, whose most efficient operating altitude was 13,000ft (4,000m). Fortunately, operating experience had shown that many interceptions took place at lower altitudes. Obviously, a more efficient powerplant was needed for this kind of work and Spitfire I L1004 was fitted with a Merlin 32 engine rated at 1,645hp. Trials were undertaken during December 1942 and their success resulted in an immediate Admiralty request for Seafires to be fitted with this engine, which conferred a maximum sea-level speed of 316mph (506km/h), increasing to 335mph (536km/h) at 6,000ft (1,850m). While this engine produced the required improvements it also resulted in a conflict of interest; it had also been specified for the Fairey Barracuda, but some were eventually diverted to Supermarine. In production Seafires the unit drove a four-bladed propeller, which further improved the performance of an aircraft now designated the Seafire L.IIC.

Compared with the Merlin 32 the Merlin 46 featured a supercharger with smaller diameter blades, which enabled more power to be delivered to the propeller rather than being diverted to provide air for the engine at altitude. The Merlin 46 employed the Coffman cartridge-type starting system, which meant it was no longer dependent on an external electrical power source. As the increased weight of the Seafire had slowed it down in comparison with the Spitfire, various methods were sought to increase performance and manoeuvrability.

While there was an increase in top speed, the reduction in wing area cut maximum altitude to 20,000ft (6,150m). The loss of the wingtips also increased take-off and landing runs, especially under full military loadings.

A further consequence of the clipped wings was an increase in landing accidents; this was to lead to at least 30 per cent of the fleet being damaged. To counter this it was proposed to fit a tail parachute to slow the aircraft and stabilize it on landing. The design and testing of the parachute and its housing was undertaken at RAE Farnborough. During these trials the parachute exerted a tensile load of 1,200lb (545kg) with a proof load of 3,020lb (1,370kg) while the maximum loading was 4,040lb (1,830kg). As the parachute unit was required for use at sea, both it and its container were designed to be removable, which meant it required fitting before flight and removal afterwards. Trials of the system were seen as successful, but minor parachute hook release failures meant that it was shelved.

Only one other version of the Seafire IIC was produced. This was the photo-reconnaissance L.R.IIC, which was fitted with a pair of F.24 cameras, one a vertical 20in (51cm) unit and the other a 14in (35cm) oblique unit. As this model was not dedicated to reconnaissance work, armament was retained. Conversion of the first aircraft, MB194, was undertaken in July 1943 by Heston Aircraft Ltd, which also completed the remaining ones. As before,

weighing of the airframe and determination of the centre of gravity took place at Worthy Down on 14 July. The aircraft was found to have a tare weight of 5,310lb (2,413kg) with an all-up weight of 7,043lb (3,201kg).

RATOG Trials

While the Seafire was being delivered to operational units, reports highlighted a continuing problem during carrier deck landings. This resulted in stiffer undercarriage units, while Supermarine insisted on a reduction in propeller diameter with stocks of spare blades being retained to replace those damaged during landing. A further difficulty was the lack of catapults capable of launching a heavily-laden Seafire from some fleet and most of the escort carriers. An alternative launch method was provided by RATOG, the Rocket Assisted Take-Off Gear, which comprised two 5in (13cm) rockets. Each was 41in (104cm) long and weighed 66lb (30kg), of which 26lb (12kg) was cordite. RATOG mountings were fitted to the wing roots. Two aircraft, MB141 and MB307, were modified to test the rockets, initially at Worthy Down, before transfer to RAE Farnborough on 14 January 1944 for pre-service trials. Use of this system required the engine throttle be opened to full power, at which point the RATOG was ignited. The rockets burned for up to four seconds.

During the trials, various combinations of two, four and eight tubes were tried. MB141 was deployed aboard HMS Chaser but it was badly damaged in a crash-landing which killed the pilot, K.J. Robetson. The tests continued with the second aircraft, MB307, which had previously been used for the trials at Farnborough. The tests were not without incident. The rockets exhibited a tendency to ignite the fabric covering the rudder and elevators as well as the runway surface. Countering this required flashless powder for the rockets, flight control surfaces re-skinned in alloy and fire resistant runway surfaces.

Having completed trials on dry land, MB307 was flown out to Chaser to continue the development programme. Because of the RATOG system's inflammatory tendencies, personnel were warned never to initiate firing over the hanger deck. As Chaser was required to act as a ferry carrier for the British Pacific Fleet, the trials moved to HMS Slinger, which had been mined in the River Medway in February 1944.

Repairs had been carried during that month, the carrier returning to service in October when it arrived in the Clyde for training and work-up as well as RATOG trials. Both four and eight cluster units were tested. Use of the former reduced the take-off run with the ship's bow into wind to 270ft (83m), while the latter cut it to 230ft (70m). Aircraft weight was 7,250lb (3,295kg). Further Seafire trials concerned the Fleet Air Arm's need to rapidly re-arm the aircraft. Supermarine used a standard Seafire wing into which a modified hinged under-wing access door retained by quick release fasteners was installed. After stress analysis and practical trials this idea was rejected as the wing was structurally weakened and the door fastenings would have failed under load.

The final Seafire IIC, LR764, was delivered to Worthy Down for weighing and C of G checks on 18 October 1943. This machine differed considerably from the first example because it was powered by a Rolls-Royce Merlin 55 driving a five-bladed Rotol Jablo propeller unit. The aircraft recorded a tare weight of 5,219lb (1,145kg) and an all-up weight of 6,875lb (3,125kg). This aircraft was not to enter regular service as it was retained for trials, which included tests of the Seafire III tail unit at Boscombe Down.

The fixed-wing Seafires proved valuable but it was obvious that the next phase of development should be foldable wings. This would enable the aircraft to operate aboard the new fleet carriers, whose deck lifts were of the smallest possible size to reduce damage from enemy action. The first indication of the Admiralty's desire for a folding wing Spitfire had come when the Director of Air Material met Vickers representatives in November 1939. A full-blown proposal followed at the beginning of 1940 at a time when it was not considered desirable to divert airframes from the RAF.

Folding Wings Proposed

When the idea was resurrected, the Supermarine team made some minor revisions to the original drawings. At the same time, General Aircraft Ltd also put forward a proposal for folding Spitfire wings backwards instead of the concertina type favoured by the Admiralty and Supermarine. The idea was rejected due to the folding mechanism being heavier than that proposed by Supermarine, although the concept was a simpler one. Even so, Joseph Smith and the Supermarine design team faced a formidable task in fitting the folding mechanism within the Spitfire's thin wing while retaining its structural integrity and armament. The first production Seafire IIC, MA970, was flown to Worthy Down on 2 October 1942, where its wings were removed for conversion.

This entailed stripping the structure down to the basics before splitting it into the designated sections. Once the hinges, systems and skinning had been fitted, each wing mechanism was cycled before being returned to the aircraft. Further tests were conducted to confirm that the folding and locking units operated correctly. The hinges were mounted on the top web of the boom on both the front and rear spars. The locking point for the inner sections was located on the lower section of the spar booms, the locating pin featuring a gentle taper to facilitate insertion into the retaining lugs. When fitted, the folding wingtips were also hinged and locked manually. As they left a gap in the wing upper surfaces, fairing doors were provided to restore aerodynamic integrity. Operation of the inner hinge points and their locking mechanisms was undertaken using a locking lever mounted in each main undercarriage bay. Each lever was attached to a cable, which moved the pins into their respective lugs. Tapered spigots located in reinforced lugs helped locate the inner wing sections correctly.

Changes were also required to the gun heating ducting. To compensate for any minor mismatches between wing sections, hard-wearing felt pads were mounted on each pipe face. When the wings were fully deployed these pads made a joint to minimize air leaks. While the reduction in span to 13ft 4in (4.1m) meant that the Seafire III would fit comfortably on to the lifts proposed for the new carriers, each aircraft required five personnel to strike it down and prepare it for flight. Once the handling crew had become experienced in working the wing folding mechanism, they could perform the task in 45sec. Spreading the wings took 5sec longer. Wing folding reduced the torsional rigidity factor to 90 per cent of the original, although the Supermarine Design and Stress Analysis teams and the Admiralty were prepared to accept this for the benefits gained. Obviously, power wing folding would have been better but development time, plus the weight of the hydraulic system and associated jacks, would have been unacceptable.

Seafire III Development

It had been intended to use the Merlin 55 to power the Seafire III, which was designated the Supermarine Type 538. This engine was similar to the Merlin 45 except for a barometrically-governed automatic boost control to operate the supercharger as the aircraft gained altitude and reduce pilot workload. Absorbing the engine's 1,470hp output was a four-bladed Rotol R12/4F5 propeller, although some early-build aircraft were fitted with three-bladed units. Armament selected for the Seafire III

While not the clearest of images, this illustration shows a Seafire III allocated to No. 736 Squadron's 'B' Flight. It was normally based at Speke, although occasional trips were made to various carriers as part of the training process.
Ray Sturtivant

and late-build Seafire IIs was that of the Type 'C'. This reduced the number of cannon to two instead of the Admiralty's preferred four. The chosen installation, developed by Martin Baker Ltd, resulted in a smaller upper wing-surface blister, which increased top speed by 5mph (8km/h).

Westland Aircraft was the primary contractor for Seafire III production. Cunliffe-Owen was again the main subcontractor with many other smaller firms feeding into the production line. While design work and prototyping were undertaken as quickly as possible, establishing a production line was delayed by the creation of manufacturing jigs and machine tools. Even after these vital items had been delivered there were further delays in manufacturing the folding wing sections accurately. As a result, the first thirty Westland-built aircraft, plus the initial two from Cunliffe-Owen, were delivered with standard, single-piece Seafire II wings. They were eventually re-designated F.IICs to reflect their down-graded status. The second Westland-built aircraft, LR766, was delivered to Worthy Down for weighing and contractors flight trials on 8 June 1943.

While there, its internal and exterior paint finishes were thoroughly examined following reports that those applied by the factory were below the required standards and left the airframe open to corrosion. As this type of finish was not confined to one manufacturer an extensive series of photographs was taken with copies distributed to all those involved in applying final finishes to Seafire components. During its time at Worthy Down, LR766 was found to be unstable when the centre of gravity was 8in (20cm) aft of the datum. Thinking this Seafire might simply be a 'rogue' aircraft, Boscombe Down was asked if its Seafire III trials aircraft, LR765, was exhibiting similar tendencies.

Seafire III NF547 was allocated to No. 885 Squadron, based at Henstridge during May 1944. This view shows the method and detail of wing folding. FAAM Yeovilton

Although LR765 was originally designated as the Seafire III prototype, its lack of folding wings meant that it was later re-designated as a Mk IIC. BBA Collection

Instability Problems

As both aircraft were confirmed as unstable a solution had to be found before the type entered operational service. Getting the aircraft balanced required ballast weights in the rear fuselage. Initially, three were mounted in the nose to give the aircraft an all-up weight of 7,076lb (3,216kg) and a C of G datum of 8.1in (20.6cm) aft. But it was still out of limits. The next attempt saw weights fitted into the Seafire's tail, which produced an all-up weight of 7,218lb (3,281kg) and a datum point of 8.9in

(22.6cm) aft, just short of the required minimum. Further trials saw both MA970 and LR766 being loaded with weights, which placed the C of G trim to the required 9in (22.9cm) aft of the datum. MA970 behaved as before but LR766 was still slightly unstable. In a further effort to rectify this imbalance, the radio equipment was moved further aft, while MA970 donated its complete tail section to LR766 to see if an item known to be serviceable would make a difference.

Extensive test flying revealed that LR766 was still showing signs of instability. The final effort was to fit a 3.5lb (1.6kg) inertia balance weight to the elevator control circuit, which dampened the reaction of the

elevators. It was still obvious, however, that further investigation was needed. The first Cunliffe-Owen aircraft, NN333, was found to be suffering from exactly the same problem. The tail units of both LR766 and NN333 were given a thorough inspection but no fault was found. This directed the investigation to the one major difference between the Seafire II and Seafire III: the folding wings. Accordingly, a set of fixed Seafire II wings was installed on a Seafire III. This confirmed that there was an airflow problem over the wing fold joints. Seals at the wing fold joints filled the gaps and helped stabilize the airflow, but never really smoothed the disturbed airflow over the wing. Before its diversion to these investigations, NN333 had gone to Worthy Down on 25 October 1943 for weighing and C of G checks. This Seafire was fitted with a Merlin 55 with standard temperate-type lower engine cowling and nose ballast weights. Tare weight was 5,541lb (2,519kg), while fully loaded the aircraft weighed in at 7,197lb (3,271kg).

Three propeller units were destroyed in landing accidents during the trials, but film of the incidents revealed the cause. It was obvious that as the arrester hook made contact with the wire, the softness of the damper allowed the aircraft to gain a small amount of height before tensioning of the wire slowed it down. This forced it back on to the deck with the tail raised slightly to make contact between the propeller and deck inevitable. It was clear that a tail hook damper that would not throw the nose over was required. After much trial and error a suitable unit was available for manufacture. Further undercarriage modifications were required when the port undercarriage leg of Seafire III, LR840, collapsed on 24 March 1944 during its first landing aboard HMS

Major Modifications

While these investigations were in progress, Seafire III production was continuing and major modifications were incorporated as necessary. One of the first was the substitution of the Hispano Mk II cannon for the lighter Mk V. Wing strengthening was applied at a later stage and this permitted the carriage of four rockets with either 25lb or 60lb warheads, two per wing, or a single 250lb bomb under each wing. In addition a single 500lb bomb could be carried under the centre section. Further modifications were required to the gun heating system as pilots had complained of overheating. This was especially worrying as the highest temperatures were being recorded close to the ammunition boxes. The first attempt at a cure involved asbestos lagging. This proved ineffective; baffles in the ducting helped cool the air but the temperatures remained too high. The solution was to increase the cooling airflow to reduce the temperature to a safer level.

To enable the Seafire to operate in dusty conditions, some were fitted with the original bulky type of Spitfire tropical filter, which reduced performance. The Vokes Aero Vee unit was introduced at the 130th production aircraft and installed retrospectively. The plumbing and fitments needed for the carriage of external overload fuel tanks to increase range and patrol time were also featured on this aircraft. Modifications were also made to the main undercarriage legs as they showed a tendency to fail under extreme loads. Tests aboard the trials and training carrier HMS *Pretoria Castle* started on 12 February 1944 while the ship was cruising off the Clyde following repairs to damage sustained in a collision with HMS *Ravager*. The opportunity was also taken to eliminate arrester-hook bounce, which was causing some aircraft to miss the cables. Both spline and link oleo modifications were undertaken, with the spline-type performing slightly better.

Strenuous efforts were made to improve both the Spitfire and the Seafire. One focus of these efforts was the fuselage centre-line bomb and fuel tank carrier, seen here with a 500lb bomb in position. Eric Morgan Collection

Further development work saw the introduction of under-wing bomb carriers, although they were limited to carrying a 250lb load. BBA Collection

Indefatigable. Investigation showed that the Seafire had drifted slightly on landing, putting heavy and unexpected stress on the undercarriage mounting. This had sheared off, forcing the undercarriage leg inwards. Strengthening was undertaken as part of Modification 279. A stronger locking head lug was installed to helped counter side loads induced by the rolling of an aircraft carrier at sea.

As with the Seafire II, there was also a reconnaissance version of the Mk III, the first being MB194. Again, one vertical F 24 and an oblique F 24 camera were installed in the rear fuselage. The former could be fitted with either 5, 8 or 14in (13, 20 or 36cm) lenses, while the latter was restricted to an 8in (20cm) lens. Although the aircraft were built by Cunliffe-Owen, conversion work on the final 149 airframes was carried out by Heston Aircraft Ltd. The first, MB194, was despatched to Worthy Down on 14 July 1943 for weighing and C of G checks. This aircraft was fitted with a Merlin 32 engine driving a Rotol Jablo four-blade propeller, a temperate cowling, one F24 20in (51cm) vertical camera, plus a 14in (36cm) F24 oblique camera. The Seafire was found to weigh 5,310lb (2,414kg) tare, while fully loaded the figure rose to 7,043lb (3,201kg).

The Seafire LF.III came next with a Merlin 55M for improved low-level performance. The first aircraft, NF545, was flown to High Post from Westland's Yeovil plant for weighing and C of G checks, arriving on 31 March 1944. The checks revealed a tare weight of 5,457lb (2,480kg) and an all-up weight of 7,133lb (3,242kg). A later example of this variant, PP986, was despatched to High Post on 17 October for similar checks, weighing in at 5,449lb (2,477kg) tare, with a maximum of 7,221lb (3,282kg). Some of the extra weight was due to the gyro gun-sight fitted for trials alongside the standard reflector sight. To give an increased measure of quality control, three further Cunliffe-Owen Seafire IIIs went to High Post for weighing and C of G checks, these being NN390 (5,443lb or 2,474kg tare and 7,181lb or 3,264kg maximum), NN409 (5,443lb or 2,474kg tare and 7,172lb or 3,260kg maximum) and NN500 (5,517lb or 2,508kg tare, 7,201lb or 3,273kg maximum). The slight variations were due to the modifications that had been made to the airframes as production continued.

Overall, the Seafire III was reported to be a better performer than the Mk II. There

Having missed the arrester hook, Seafire III of No. 749 Squadron rolls at high speed into the safety barrier aboard the carrier HMS *Theseus* in June 1946. Such was the force of the final impact that the aircraft was written-off. BBA Collection

were constant concerns about longitudinal stability and pilot training was designed to reflect this. But it was not enough to stop pilots complaining that the Seafire III suffered from lateral trim changes as speed changed. They also continued to point out that the ailerons remained heavy throughout the speed range, while the rate of roll declined as the speed rose. After extensive testing the only cure considered possible was to raise torsional stiffness of the wing structure with extra stiffness provided by plating over the outer machine-gun bays. Roll rate improvements involved wingtip removal and aileron balance tabs.

Various aircraft were used for testing. PR314, for example, went to Boscombe Down in March 1945 for weapons loading and handling trials, which included the use of 200lb Mk II Smoke floats, 45gal (205ltr) slipper tanks, Mine A Mk VIII, 30lb Mk 1c bombs, 250lb Mk 111 bombs and 500lb AN-M64 bombs. A centreline mounting point was also tried. Another Boscombe Down trials aircraft was NN500, which arrived in November 1944. It was used to measure the leakage of carbon monoxide through the firewall access points into the cockpit and to find ways of reducing or eliminating it.

Seafire III PR265 is pictured outside the hangar at Henstridge. It ended up in French Navy service. Ray Sturtivant

Carrier Cruisers

As the Seafire gained extra range with additional internal and external fuel tanks, further ideas were put forward to increase its usefulness. Central to this was an increase in the number of ships equipped with homing beacons to help pilots find their way home and reduce navigation workload. This innovation led to the proposed carrier-cruiser, intended to provide additional air defence. The vessel would be based on a standard heavy cruiser with a 300ft (92m) flight deck complete with eight arrester wires. It would also retain its main armament.

As ever, when their Lordships came up with a new scheme, the Director of Naval Construction and his staff were asked to prepare the necessary outline drawings. At the same time, there were ideas for destroyer-sized carriers plus a redesign of the forthcoming Vanguard battleship. While the Fleet Air Arm accepted that more flight decks were needed, all three designs fell far short of the requirements for fighter operations, especially those by Seafires. Fortunately, further fleet carriers were on the stocks, while escort carriers were in quantity production in the USA to supplement those already in service.

Concerned about a possible shortage of pilots, the Admiralty asked the RAF to train Spitfire pilots for carrier operations should they be needed. The RAF responded by pledging up to 532 aircraft to be equipped for sea-going operations, together with a pool of 252 trained pilots. Eight squadrons – 64, 131, 141, 401, 402, 403, 412 and 416 – were selected. The chosen pilots were initially trained at their home bases using stretches of the runway painted to represent an aircraft carrier. Once this had been completed each unit was sent to Arbroath, which acted as the home base while deck landing training was conducted. While the pilots displayed the required proficiency, it was reported that they exhibited a tendency to land too fast. They also ignored the batsman's signals, preferring to rely on their own judgement. The programme progressed satisfactorily, but by the end of summer 1943 the tide of war was starting to move in the Allies' favour. The Admiralty sought cancellation of the programme, but the RAF decided to continue in case further sea-borne units were needed for attacks against the Japanese homeland. In the event, the Allied forces' overwhelming strength, together with the difficulty of transporting so many fixed wing aircraft to the theatre, put paid to the idea.

Sea Typhoon?

Although the Admiralty was generally pleased with the Seafire, it was still seeking other types to supplement it. Their Lordships were also aware that at the end of the war all Lend-Lease aircraft would either have to be returned or bought. Purchase was not considered a viable option as support costs would exceed those of British-built aircraft even if the airframes were offered at advantageous rates. The Admiralty's choices were Hawker's Typhoon and Tempest. Only the former was available for trials work as the latter type existed only in prototype form. The manufacturer was asked to prepare a preliminary design for sea-going versions with folding wings having greater area to improve handling at sea. Further fuselage modifications would be needed to absorb the forces involved in carrier operations.

As the Typhoon was a roomy aircraft, Hawker was able to convince the Admiralty that a naval version would be able to sustain a four-hour loiter or a six-hour endurance flight. To follow this up, the Admiralty requested the loan of a few aircraft to enable the idea to be developed. Accordingly, Typhoon DN419, the only aircraft available, was released to the naval station at Arbroath where it arrived on 8 February 1943. It did not last long. A crash-landing following an engine malfunction on take-off resulted in the aircraft being burnt out. The unexpected result of this accident was the cancellation of the entire programme by the Commander-in-Chief, Home Fleet. Denied the Typhoon's roomy cockpit, some Franks flying suits were requisitioned to help improve Seafire pilots' comfort, especially during long flights. Trials began in August 1943 with No. 807 Squadron aboard HMS *Formidable*. Although the suits were found to reduce fatigue, pilots complained that movement was difficult and that they could not enter their cockpits unaided. The suit was found to improve comfort during long periods in the air but it did not see widespread use.

Overall, some 1,220 Seafire IIIs were built, 870 of which came from Westland, while the remainder were manufactured by Cunliffe-Owen. First deliveries to the Fleet Air Arm began on 27 November 1943 when No. 894 Squadron received the type. Seafire IIIs were then delivered to Nos 887, 889, 801 and 880 Squadrons. Further units were equipped with the type, many of which saw service with the British Pacific Fleet, which was then fighting Japan in company with United States Navy task forces. This version remained in service until March 1946 when 887 and 894 Squadrons disbanded.

The Royal Navy had great hopes of the Blackburn Firebrand, which was intended to be its next fleet fighter, but the type encountered numerous engine and stability problems. BBA Collection

Seafire IIC Specification

The official specification for the Seafire IIC was issued on 15 August 1942 and signed by J.E. Serby on behalf of the Director of Technical Development. This reference document covered the manufacture of Research Aircraft No.3665, while the initial specification covered the conversion of Spitfire V airframes to Seafire IIC standard.

Each aircraft was to be constructed in strict accordance with the drawings and specifications listed in the construction schedule of 2 June 1942, except where they had been modified for the proposed naval role. There were two other specifications. DTD 1000 covered aircraft fittings and DTD 1003 the marking of aeroplanes and their individual items. The final camouflage was to be applied in accordance with ADM 332 and DTD Technical Order 144.

An extensive range of modifications, which had already appeared on the Spitfire list, was to be embodied. As the aircraft was required for naval duties, catapult spools and deck landing gear had to be added. Provision also had to be made for slinging and structural strengthening for catapulting purposes. Other modifications covered the provision of external 50gal (227ltr) fuel tanks, together with jettisoning arrangements as part of Mod. 436. Modification No. 438 also covered jettisonable external under-wing fuel tanks. Also included were an immersed oil heater, an R1147 radio, an R3108 instead of an R3002 radio, installation of a TR1196A radio (after the first thirty aircraft instead of the original radio set-up), deletion of the rear oxygen bottle and re-positioning of the economiser, deletion of the flare chute and associated controls, introduction of a free pistol mounting in the cockpit, plus the replacement of the original Mk IXF airspeed indicator by the Mk IXF* unit when it became available.

Items to be introduced when time and circumstances permitted included:

- tropicalization equipment
- provision for ballast on the port engine bearer
- provision for lashing points on the wings and undercarriage
- fuel tank strengthening attachments
- modified radiator shutter control
- strengthened seat to withstand the loading of a catapult launch
- adjustable headrest
- deletion of the tail mounting and ballast
- strengthening of the tail wheel oleo anchorage
- arrester release control improvement
- modified wheel fairings to clear loading chocks.

Extra equipment was also to be fitted for slinging gear, aircraft hold-down gear.

All alterations and modifications, except those issued under Special Order Only instructions, were to be applied to both the Spitfire V and the Seafire IIC, as applicable. After manufacture each aircraft had to undertake a test flight even though the early-build ones had already undergone a full flight test.

Before delivery the designated manufacturer or subcontractor had to furnish the Director of Technical Development (DTD) or his designated representative with certain details concerning the aircraft at least one week before delivery. These were applicable to the first, fiftieth and every 100th aircraft and included the tare weight, the weight when fully loaded and the location of the centre of gravity. If any aircraft was delivered without all equipment installed, an initial centre of gravity position was to be indicated while a correct datum point was required to be determined as soon as possible.

A subsequent DTD document dated 25 January 1943 amplified details of the requirements for Seafire IIC production by subsidiary companies or by subcontractors like Cunliffe-Owen and Westland. The aircraft were to be constructed in accordance with Seafire IIC drawings and schedules supplied via Ministry of Aircraft Production instructions dated 4 January. Outside of the basic airframe, engines, propellers, exhaust manifolds and other items, as specified, were to be supplied by the Ministry of Aircraft Production under embodiment loan terms.

Specifically highlighted was the interchangability of aircraft parts and structure sub-components. All were to be constructed using jigs to ensure accuracy. As well as manufacturing the initial run of components, the subcontractors were also to supply further additional parts to the Director General of Equipment's (DGE) office to enable them to be added to the Seafire spares schedule. To ensure component interoperability, the contractors were required to provide gauges, jig references and other agreed items to the DGE. As the subcontractors were not the designated design authority, any suggested changes to the components would be investigated; only the designers could authorize changes. Any proposed changes had to take into account interchangeability, operational considerations, safety and cost or date of delivery. As with the original specification, the contractors, on reaching their first, fiftieth and 100th aircraft, were to send the DTD a master schedule covering the equipment fitted to the aircraft, although there was a proviso requiring a conformity certificate should there be a lack of time to create a master schedule.

Flight testing of contractors' aircraft was required to be done by personnel from Vickers Armstrong (Supermarine) Ltd of Hursley Park, Winchester, the arrangements being controlled by the Ministry of Aircraft Production (MAP). Certain aircraft had to be delivered to A&AEE, as requested by the MAP. During the test flights the aircraft had be fully loaded with their centres of gravity fully aft. The external flight requirement was applicable only to designated point aircraft, the remainder being flown by the contractor's pilots. On completing the tests satisfactorily each aircraft received a certificate of general airworthiness (Form AM838). Every tenth machine had to be dived at full speed to check handling and behaviour, although this could be curtailed if the weather was unsuitable.

During flight testing, the Inspector in Charge of the Airworthiness Inspection Department (AID), in co-operation with other officials, could authorize extra segments of the full flight test, but not if it would delay delivery. This part of the schedule included at least one take-off at maximum boost; should more than one landing be made the undercarriage had to cycled fully. After take-off a full-throttle climb was to be maintained until boost started to drop off. Three minutes of level flight at full throttle was to be followed by five at maximum cruise and at maximum weak mixture. During these phases, the pilot was to exercise the controls, note all gauge readings and check the canopy and windscreen for optical clarity. Once all checks and testing had been completed the contractors were to provide facilities for the final in-depth examination of the first contract aircraft, as requested by the DTD or representative.

CHAPTER FOUR

Into Action

The landings at Salerno in southern Italy in September 1943 provided the Allies with their first major foothold on the European mainland to enable them to bring World War II to a conclusion. The operation also represented the first big test for the Royal Navy's Supermarine Seafires. About 100 aircraft from eleven Fleet Air Arm squadrons were deployed to provide air cover for the first four critical days of the operation.

But the Seafire had been blooded well before then. The type first saw action in November 1942 during Operation *Torch*, the Allied invasion of Vichy French-held North Africa. Seafires were again deployed in July 1943 for Operation *Husky*, the landings in Sicily.

It was at Lee on Solent on 23 June 1942 that No. 807 Squadron finally disposed of its outdated Fairey Fulmars and began re-equipping with the Supermarine Seafire. Originally a handful of Seafire IBs (including AB857 and AD926 together with BL514, BL858, BR561 and BR567) and hooked Spitfire VBs (W3967 and AD513) were taken on charge. Under the command of Lt A.B. Fraser Harris DSC RN, the squadron undertook a full work-up before moving to Yeovilton on 12 July 1942 for intensive flying training. This was followed by a move to Machrihanish on 24 August for weapons and air combat training combined with air patrol duties in support of forces operating in the Faroes gap. Working-up completed, the unit acquired new aircraft, which included MB343, MB357 and NX952. They were flown out to join the carrier HMS *Furious*, which had just completed a refit in the Clyde shipyards in April.

In July the carrier was declared ready for service with the Home Fleet. Her air wing comprised Nos. 801 and 807 Squadrons with Seafires, together with a flight of Fairey Albacores contributed by No. 822 Squadron. With this restricted air wing, *Furious* was involved in ferrying much-needed aircraft and supplies to Malta, two such trips being undertaken during August. No. 807 Squadron then prepared to accept more

aircraft to bring it up to full strength, the newcomers including MB372, MB374, NX898, NX903 and NX947.

Operation *Torch*

With the first Seafire squadron fully equipped, No. 801 Squadron traded in its Sea Hurricanes for twelve unmodified Spitfires. The switch came on 7 September 1942, which is regarded as the unit's official formation date, although a cadre of pilots operating under that unit designation had already acquired sea duty time plus valuable experience aboard *Furious* the previous month. The Spitfires were used purely in the training role at Stretton and included R6722, R7132, R7305, R7909, W3136, W3522, W3916, X4846, AA905, AD426, AD583 and AD584. The Seafire IBs, which included MB342, MB345, MB347, MB352, MB353, MB358, MB359, MB363 and MB364, arrived before the end of the month. Lt Cdr R. McD. Hall RN was appointed the squadron's CO and he remained in command while *Furious* and her air wing prepared for Operation *Torch*.

Originally named Operation *Gymnast*, *Torch* had resulted from Stalin's pressure on the Western Allies to open a second front to relieve his forces. US commanders initially favoured opening the second front in Europe, code-named Operation *Sledge-hammer*, but Churchill and his General Staff finally persuaded President Roosevelt that such a course of action would be disastrous. An assault on mainland Europe might have forced the Germans to divert resources from the Russian front but any benefits would probably have been short-term ones. An attack on French North Africa, on the other hand, would not only tie up the Germans but also give the Allies a chance to gain control of the Mediterranean and neutralize the Italian fleet as well as that of Vichy France tied up at Toulon.

In mid-October 1942 *Furious* departed British waters in company with HMS *Argus*

and headed for the Mediterranean. There, both ships were to form the Central Naval Task Group. In charge of the entire operation was General Dwight D. Eisenhower, with his headquarters in Gibraltar, while the naval commander of the Allied Expeditionary Force was Admiral Sir Andrew Cunningham. The force was divided into three elements. The western assault fleet, which comprised American units, had Casablanca as its objective, while the mixed British and American eastern force was to head for Algiers. The entirely British centre task force was directed to attack Oran. Robert Murphy, the American consul in Algiers, had given advice on the mood of the Vichy French forces and consequently it was considered advisable for the British forces to wear American Combined Task Force badges. Similarly, participating British aircraft were ordered to display American stars in place of their usual roundels. This would not only help avoid misidentification by trigger-happy US pilots but also conceal the aircrafts' nationality from Vichy personnel still bitter at the British attack on the French fleet at Oran in 1940.

While the task forces operated as three separate groups, the air assets were divided into two. One was commanded by Air Marshal Sir William Welsh and covered the area east of Cape Tenez, Algeria, while the other covered the area to the west and was commanded by US Army Air Force Major General James Doolittle. *Torch* began on 8 November and Seafires operating from *Argus* and *Furious* were ordered to provide air cover for the centre task force landings east and west of Oran. *Furious'* Albacores, supported by Seafires, were to attack the French airfield at La Senia with 500lb bombs at first light, while Sea Hurricanes from the Escort Carrier HMS *Biter* provided top cover. After the attack, the Seafires were to turn their attentions to the civil airport at Tafaroui, where Dewoitine 520 fighters were based.

Further out to sea, the fleet carriers *Formidable* and *Victorious* were to provide an air umbrella over the fleet, while their

The arrester hook fitted to Spitfire BL818 has failed to deploy, causing its undercarriage to collapse on landing. HMS Furious' deck landing party are shown taking the aircraft down to the lower aircraft deck. BBA Collection

As the nose tilts down, BL818's arrester hook finally lowers while the deck landing crews strain to control the aircraft's weight. BBA Collection

The Swordfish remained in the front line throughout the Battle of the Atlantic. It carried a variety of weapons including torpedoes, depth charges, bombs and rockets. BBA Collection

two accompanying battleships prepared to bombard the shore with their heavy guns and deter any hostile intervention. In the event the French scuttled their ships to prevent them falling into German hands, while the Italian vessels remained in harbour. The fleet also included a small liner converted to act as a command ship. Intended to control the landings and to direct aerial resources as required, this vessel had a full range of radio, radar and anti-aircraft guns, together with a complete command staff.

First Seafire Victory

The forecast weather was clear overhead with some cloud out to sea. Accordingly, the first strike sorties were launched at sunrise. Pilots were fully briefed on the location of anti-aircraft guns along the coast and around the strategic targets. It was hoped that what light there was at that hour would favour the attackers and keep defending aircraft on the ground. But the Albacores' slow pace meant that the French airfields were alerted, although the escorting fighters were able to take care of the defending fighters. The strike was successful, although at least one aircraft was shot down in flames. Seafires from No. 880 Squadron made amends for this loss by shooting down a Junkers Ju 88. But Sub Lt G.C. Baldwin RN, flying Seafire IIC MA986, had already become the first Seafire pilot to score a victory when he shot down a Dewotine D.520 near Oran. For this feat he was awarded the DSC. Although the central group landings were successful, post-attack debrief revealed some ineffective management of aerial resources, resulting in crews and aircraft either hanging around fruitlessly waiting for employment or flying repeated sorties without adequate rest.

The landings on the western beach were delayed by the appearance of a French convoy, which disrupted the minesweeping operations necessary to clear the way to the beach. Unlike later amphibious landings, Operation *Torch* suffered from inadequate pre-landing reconnaissance, as a result of which the landing craft were hampered by uncharted sand bars, which caused some damage. Despite this, the troops were landed safely and they secured the beach-head and the surrounding area in the face of slight resistance.

The same cannot, however, be said of Operation *Reservist*, which involved

HMS *Furious* began life in 1917 as a heavy cruiser. Converted into an aircraft carrier in 1925, the vessel served with distinction until being withdrawn from use, totally worn out, in October 1944. BBA Collection

With a battleship of the King George V class in the background, the deck handling party move this unidentified Seafire into position for take-off. As this view was taken before the take-off flap setting modification was introduced, wooden blocks have been inserted between the flaps and the wings. BBA Collection

With a fleet carrier, possibly HMS *Victorious*, and battleships of the King George V and Queen Elizabeth classes in the background, pilots discuss their next mission while their aircraft are prepared for flight aboard a light fleet carrier. Ray Sturtivant

securing Oran harbour to prevent the French fleet from interfering with the landings. The two destroyers carrying the troops involved were hit by multiple shells, forcing them to withdraw. This allowed the French fleet to clear the harbour and attempt to disrupt the landings; however, sufficient naval power had been made available to prevent this from being effective.

After two days of resistance by the defenders, French forces in the Oran area surrendered on 9 November after a bombardment by British battleships. But an unintended consequence of the North African invasion was that French forces in Tunisia pulled back to the Algerian border on the 10th, leaving the country open to German occupation. At first the French remained confined to camp, determined not to fight, but later they were ordered to attack the Germans. Despite outdated equipment, the French-led Tunisian soldiers put up such a spirited fight that they were rewarded with more modern British-supplied weapons. Once the French-administered territory had been secured the British pushed on towards Tunisia, being

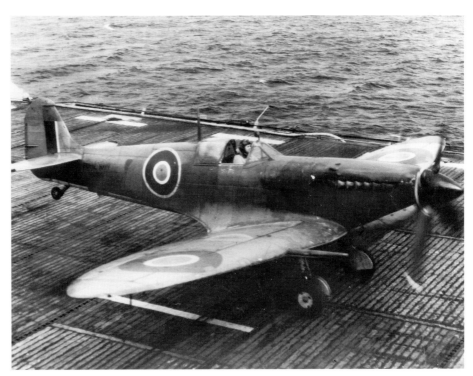

Roaring off the deck of an escort carrier, this Seafire IB already has its tail wheel up. As recommended in the Pilot's Notes, the canopy is fully open, being stopped from moving forward by the half-cocked access door. FAAM Yeovilton

finally stopped by German forces, which were later reinforced by others retreating westwards from Libya under the command of General Erwin Rommel, pursued by Gen Bernard Montgomery's Eighth Army. Under Operation *Vulcan* both the First and Eighth Armies combined in a massive assault against their German opponents. Once the air and naval support lines had been severed, this attack, together with the American capture of Bizerte on 6 May, forced the German forces to surrender on the 13th.

While Seafires operated from the fleet carriers involved in this action, the two participating escort carriers, *Biter* and *Dasher*, still had Hawker Sea Hurricanes aboard. Meanwhile, the unit allocated to HMS *Argus*, No. 880 Squadron, had disembarked its Sea Hurricanes at Stretton at the end of August 1942. The unit then received some Spitfire VBs, including W3756, for conversion training. With the initial work-up completed, the unit received Seafire IICs the following month, MB236, MB240, MB250, MB253, MB265, MB275 and MB297 being accepted. Having completed final training at Machrihanish, the unit, commanded by Lt Cdr R.J. Cork DSO, DFC, RN, was embarked aboard *Argus* on 16 October.

Operation *Perpetual*

After working up at sea with its new fighters the squadron was declared ready for operations by the time the ship reached the Mediterranean. During Operation *Torch* HMS *Argus* was hit by a 500lb bomb and near-misses had exploded close to the ship. Although the vessel was still able to operate, the damage sustained resulted in her return to the Clyde for repairs, but not before participation in Operation *Perpetual* on 11 November. This minor operation required the ship's fighters to provide combat air patrols in support of the assault on Bougie, Algeria.

Formidable and *Victorious* each deployed Seafire units. No. 885 Squadron's aircraft shared deck space aboard *Formidable* with two Martlet units and one operating Albacores. No. 885 had swapped its Sea Hurricanes for Spitfires at Machrihanish, a handful of hooked Spitfires being employed for deck training. They were replaced by Seafire IICs, examples being MB126, MB146 and MB156. Under the command of Lt Cdr (A) R. Carver DSC, RN, the unit

The pilot of this No. 768 Squadron Seafire IIC is receiving deck landing training aboard HMS *Argus* and, under the guidance of the deck landing control officer ('batsman'), his aircraft is prepared for another launch. Rick Harding Collection

deployed aboard *Formidable* on 28 October. *Victorious'* air wing comprised No. 809 Squadron (Fulmars), No. 882 (Martlets), Nos 818 and 832 Squadrons (Albacores) and the Seafire-equipped No. 884 Squadron. This unit had previously operated Fulmars until its move, on 21 August 1943, to Lee-on-Solent. There it acquired Spitfires (including P7316, P7902, AD135 and BL253) for training pur-

poses before moving on 25 September to Skeabrae to receive Seafire IICs including MA972, MA974, MA979, MA981, MA982, MA983 and MB121. When ready, the squadron, commanded by Lt Cdr T.B. Winstanley RN, went aboard *Victorious*. As both of these carriers were more recent than *Furious* and *Argus*, their access lifts were smaller so, lacking a wing folding facility, the Seafires had to be ranged on

Unusually, the pilot of this Seafire has not set his flaps to the take-off position, although the aircraft seems to be managing without difficulty. The photographer was obviously being cautious: the photograph was taken from the safety of the flight deck catwalk. FAAM Yeovilton

deck and parked on outriggers. Each vessel also carried a further half dozen aircraft in crates and these were off-loaded at North Front, Gibraltar. Further crated Seafires were also carried aboard the escort carrier *Dasher*.

Performance Concerns

Although the early Seafires participated in *Torch*, their performance gave rise to some concern. Just before the operation was launched, *Furious* had off-loaded some of her air wing to make way for thirty-one Spitfires VCs bound for Malta to reinforce the island's defence. Returning to Gibraltar the ship was attacked by a Junkers Ju 88, whose appearance wrong-footed the standing fighter patrol. Its leader, Lt Hall RN, was in the landing circuit while his wingman, Sub Lt Blanchard RNVR, had actually landed. After the Ju 88 had dropped its bombs – which missed the carrier – Hall gave chase but was unable to jettison his 30gal (136ltr) ventral tank. This reduced the aircraft's top speed to 310mph (194km/h), too slow to bring the attacker comfortably within range. Even so, Hall's fire caused some damage to the Junker's fuselage. Later in the day, another Ju 88 was able to escape a Seafire patrol comprising a IB and a IIC; the older aircraft proved the faster. Such engagements highlighted a major failing of the early Seafires: lack of speed, reducing the aircraft's effectiveness against the faster enemy bombers. The obvious answer was to press on with development of the more powerful Seafire L.IIC.

Gibraltar Convoys

Seafires provided air cover for two critical missions – starting on 19 April and 11 July – by HMS *Unicorn* to ferry aircraft to Gibraltar. *Unicorn* was an unusual vessel. She looked like an aircraft carrier but internally had been reconfigured to support a full range of aircraft maintenance services. This rendered the vessel incapable of supporting a fully operational air wing. On both trips, therefore, air cover was provided by one squadron, No. 887. This unit had originally been equipped with Fulmars before moving to Lee-on-Solent to acquire Spitfire VAs and Seafire IBs for type conversion. The operational complement of Seafire IICs, which included MA975/L, had arrived in March 1943. By this time,

the unit, commanded by Lt Cdr (A) Wiggington DSC RNVR, had moved to Hatston, although it had transferred to Machrihanish for final working up the following month. On completing the second Gibraltar mission, the squadron landed back in the UK, reaching Machrihanish in October.

When Convoy KMS.16 departed for Gibraltar on 4 June 1943, the escort carrier HMS *Battler* was assigned to provide combat air patrols with the Seafire L.IICs of No. 808 Sqdn commanded by Lt Cdr(A) Wallace RNVR. Before receiving the Seafires, the squadron had been equipped with Fairey Fulmars. They were swapped in November 1942 for a selection of Spitfires – both with and without hooks – for conversion purposes. The first nine Seafires arrived the following month and included MB302/3F, MB312/3D and NM970/3A. While supporting Convoy KMS.16, Sub Lt A.G. Penney RN, flying MB302, and Lt P. Constable RN, flying NM970, shot down a Focke-Wulf Fw 200 Condor on 24 June. At the completion of this escort duty, *Battler* returned to Britain, while No. 808 Squadron was detached for a rest, joining the escort carrier *Hunter* on 17 September.

Operation *Husky*

Having established themselves in North Africa, the Allies turned their attention to the invasion of Sicily, code-named Operation *Husky*. The British carriers assigned to the operation were *Formidable* and *Indomitable*, which formed part of Force 'H'. Aboard *Formidable* was the Seafire-equipped No. 885 Squadron, while the remainder of the air wing comprised Nos 888 and 893 Squadrons with Martlets with No. 820 Squadron's Albacores providing a strike element. By contrast, *Indomitable* had a full complement of Seafires with an air wing comprising Nos 807, 880 and 899 Squadrons and the Albacore-equipped No. 817. Formed at Hatston, the hostilities-only No. 899 began its training under the command of Lt Cdr(A) R.F. Walker RNVR. Like other units converting to the Seafire, No. 899 had previously operated Spitfires, both with and without hooks. Re-equipment with Seafire IICs (including MB244/6-Q) started in December 1942.

Husky opened on the night of 9/10 July 1943. Strong winds caused many of the airborne troops to land in the wrong places. This, however, helped to create an element

of surprise and ensure that the British forces were largely unopposed. The Americans met some opposition but achieved their goals with less trouble than expected. The entire campaign was completed by 17 August, being hailed as an emphatic Allied victory. It did, however, reveal a lack of air support, which allowed the Axis to withdraw substantial numbers of men, vehicles and stores almost unopposed.

To divert Axis attention from the Mediterranean theatre, the Royal Navy had launched Operation *Camera*, a sweep off the Norwegian coast, on 8 July. HMS *Furious* participated with the Seafires of No. 801 Squadron. Seafires were also involved in a similar operation on the 28th, code-named *Governor*. No. 894 Squadron was aboard *Illustrious*, while No. 887 Squadron flew from *Unicorn*. Another war-only front-line unit, No. 894 had been formed with Martlets in August 1942. Seafire conversion training began the following March at Hatston before the unit, under the command of Lt Cdr F.R.A. Turnbull DSC RN, went aboard *Illustrious*. Its complement of nine Seafire IICs included MB257, MB258, MB264, MB269, MB277, MB294 and MB303. After a quick trip to Iceland to give the air wing some cold weather experience, the carrier turned south to join up with *Unicorn*.

Salerno Landings

Winston Churchill had been keen on the Salerno landings because he was well aware that any invasion of northern Europe in 1943 would not succeed. The Prime Minister also wanted to build on the Sicilian invasion and also the growing Italian dissatisfaction for the war in general and Mussolini in particular. Churchill argued that an invasion of Italy would force the Germans to move more forces to that area and that it would lift the Italian threat to Allied Mediterranean convoys. This, he pointed out, would also allow supply convoys to sail to southern Russia and reduce the need for risky Arctic convoys.

Operation *Baytown* formed the opening move on 3 September. Units of the British 8th Army were shipped directly across the Straits of Messina from Messina to Calabria on the toe of Italy. They were unopposed. Montgomery called it a waste of time because his forces then had to hurry to Salerno to add their weight to the main invasion force. Meanwhile, the US 82nd

Airborne Division's Operation *Giant II*, a planned drop close to Rome, was cancelled when it became clear that the Germans had added two front-line regiments to the defence of the city.

The Salerno landings – Operation *Avalanche* – began on 9 September. But the opening phases had been badly planned and lacked a preliminary naval bombardment to soften up the defences. The Germans under Generalfeldmarschall Albert Kesselring put up such a stout resistance that at one stage the Allies were almost pushed back into the sea. The Italian surrender the day before was seen as a bonus, but it would be some time before any Italian forces would be available to support the Allied cause.

It was against this background that the biggest Seafire operation of the war in the Mediterranean took place. Two Royal Navy fleet carriers were deployed to provide air cover between 9–12 September. The force comprised *Illustrious* and *Formidable*, the aircraft support vessel *Unicorn*, plus the escort carriers *Attacker*, *Battler*, *Hunter* and *Stalker*. Aboard *Illustrious* was No. 894

Squadron, while *Formidable* had embarked No. 885 Squadron with Nos 809, 887 and 897 Squadrons aboard *Unicorn*. Other units were embarked as follows: *Attacker* – Nos 879 and 886 Squadrons; *Battler* – Nos 807 and 808 Squadrons; *Hunter* – No. 899 Squadron, plus 834 Fighter Flight; *Stalker* No. 880 Squadron with 833 Fighter Flight. The carrier fleet was divided into two distinct groups, the fleet carriers forming Force 'H' commanded by Rear Admiral C. Moody, while Force 'V' was under the command of Rear Admiral Sir Philip Vian, flying his flag in the anti-aircraft cruiser HMS *Euryalus*.

No. 809 had been a Fulmar unit before arriving at Stretton in March 1943 for conversion to Seafires. This culminated in the unit joining *Unicorn* in August with Major A.J. Wight RM in command. Also aboard was No. 897 Squadron, whose first Seafire experience had come in late 1942. Its main batch of aircraft arrived the following March when the unit transferred to Lee-on-Solent. It was finally declared ready with its Seafire L.IICs at the end of

July, by which time Lt Cdr(A) W.C. Simpson DSC RN had assumed command. Many of the units aboard the escort carriers were also new to the Seafire. *Attacker's* No. 879 Squadron had flown the Fulmar before transfer to Stretton in March 1943 for Seafire conversion, which was completed in June. The unit was aboard *Attacker* the following month under the command of Lt Cdr(A) R.J.H. Grose RNVR. No. 886 Squadron had also been a Fulmar unit but its conversion to Seafires had been completed at Turnhouse in June 1943 when it was commanded by Lt Cdr(A) R.H. Oliphant RN, who handed over to Lt Cdr P. Bailey RN in October.

Having departed the Clyde, *Attacker*, *Battler*, *Hunter* and *Stalker* arrived off Gibraltar on 9 August to embark their fighters. After joining up with *Unicorn*, the force participated in training exercises off Gibraltar, following which it sailed for Malta via Oran. It was during this period that doubts were raised about the standard of pilot training, the transit voyage having presented the squadrons embarked aboard

No. 879 Squadron suffered its share of landing accidents during its service on HMS *Attacker*. In this case, the aircraft has missed the aircraft ranged on the flight deck for take-off. Rick Harding Collection

the escort carriers with their only opportunity for deck landing practice. While Force 'H' was intended to provide general air cover for the British fleet off the Salerno beaches, Force 'V' was expected to give close-in air support at both low and medium levels. The two fleets sailed separately from Malta on 8 September. On the way, Force 'H' was attacked by German torpedo bombers during the night of 8–9 September. They missed their targets but during the attack one of No. 885 Squadron's Seafires, parked on an outrigger, was so badly damaged by blast from the anti-aircraft guns that it had to be written off.

As Sicilian bases were at least 200 miles (320km) from the beach-head, this restricted the on-station availability of land-based aircraft to thirty-six at any one time. This meant that sea-borne air power was vital to success. The first fighter patrols over the landing beaches were launched from *Unicorn* at 06.15hrs on 9 September. Their task was to provide high-level cover in the absence of land-based fighters. More fighters took off as the sun rose, to patrol the area at low level in support of USAAF North American A-36A Apaches (the ground-attack version of the P-51 Mustang), which were under the control of the fighter direction ship USS *Palomares*. The last Seafire returned to its carrier at dusk, thirteen hours after the first had taken off.

During this phase, each Seafire sortie lasted between eighty and eighty-five minutes, of which sixty minutes were spent in the combat zone with the remaining time being occupied by transit to and from the carrier. Due to their size only four Seafires could be launched from the escort carriers; *Unicorn* could launch eight at a time. Because of the tight timing involved, it required some slick handling to land-on an incoming patrol and launch its replacement. There were many landing accidents during these change-overs, many of which were attributed to a lack of pilot training. Eventually, seventy Seafires became inoperable. The main causes were collision with the barrier after missing the wire – excessive braking causing the aircraft's nose to tip over – and undercarriage failure on landing.

Losses sustained during the Tunisian and Sicilian campaigns, together with the continuing cost of operations in Russia, had sapped Axis air strength. Even so, the *Luftwaffe* threw all its available resources into repelling the invaders. As a result, Force 'H' experienced a torpedo attack on the night of 9 September. Another attack

Seafire IIC MB156 of No. 885 Squadron is seen preparing to leave HMS *Formidable* for its next sortie. Members of the deck party are stationed at the tail and wing tips. FAAM Yeovilton

came just after dawn. Both were unsuccessful. The handful of Junkers Ju 88s was intercepted by a Seafire patrol, forcing them to jettison their bombs without a shot being fired. Most of the *Luftwaffe* attacks, however, were mounted by bomb-carrying Fw 190s and Bf 109s. One of the biggest raids came close to midday when at least a dozen aircraft were spotted coming in from the north. Patrolling Seafires pounced and chased them away.

But while the Seafires were helping to keep Axis aircraft at bay, the situation was complicated by geography. At the rear of the beaches, and to the north, high ground created extreme clutter on the fleet's radar screens. This made both detection of attacking aircraft and the direction of fighters extremely difficult. The first indications of an attack often came when the attacking aircraft appeared above the beach. In an effort to counter this, some Seafire L.IICs, originally intended for duty over Capri, were diverted to act as airborne warning aircraft.

Seafire Success

At the end of a frantic day, carrier Force 'V' had completed 265 sorties. This was a creditable outcome but the pilots were

disappointed. Having intercepted many enemy aircraft, they had not been able to shoot down or even damage any of them. But they would have another opportunity. The original plan had called for carrier-borne aircraft to shoulder the burden of providing air support for the Allied ground forces for just one day. But Axis ground forces had put up a stiffer resistance than expected and one of the primary targets, Montecorvino airfield, was still the scene of intensive fighting. As this had been intended to form a key element in the Allied air support, the carrier fleet was required for further air support missions. As this possibility had been foreseen, extra supplies and stores for another day of intensive operations had been provided for the fleet.

The carrier force was now briefed to fly nearly 200 additional sorties. But with so many Seafires sustaining damage on the first day of operations, the force was now down from over 100 to sixty-five. Yet the carriers still managed to mount 232 sorties on 10 September. On that day the Seafires deterred at least forty attacks, forcing the intruders to jettison their bombs before reaching their targets. While the speed of the German fighter-bombers was reduced by their bombs, once free of their loads they were easily able to outrun the Seafires. This was emphasized by the attempt by Sub Lt E.J. Davies RNVR of No. 883 Fighter Flight to aid a patrol of USAAF Lockheed P-38 Lightnings under attack by *Luftwaffe* Bf 109s. The German fighters departed at high speed and Davies was unable to get within range. Greater success was achieved by the commanding officer of No. 897 Squadron, Lt Cdr W.C. Simpson RNVR. Leading a patrol of four Seafires, he spotted a patrol of Bf 109s flying at 12,000ft (3,700m) north of Salerno. In the ensuing battle, Simpson destroyed two German fighters, while his wing-man damaged another. One Seafire suffered minor damage.

By nightfall on the 10 September, Montecorvino airfield was in Allied hands. It remained dangerous to use, however, as artillery shells from both sides were screaming overhead. Even so, two Seafires were able to make diversionary landings there. These aircraft had been part of a group of four replacements from Sicily but unable to find their carrier in the haze. Montecorvino remained virtually unusable but US Army engineers had managed to lay a 1,000yd (920m) runway on a tomato-growing estate near Paestum. It would, however, not be until 12 September before it was ready for daytime use. Admiral Vian conceded that the sea-borne fighter force would have to remain in operation even though stores and ammunition were running low. Even more worrying was the lack of Seafires: losses to landing accidents were continuing. While the engineers worked around the clock to repair as many aircraft as possible, the fighter force was now at its credible minimum.

This meant that Force 'V' had just thirty-nine Seafires ready for a third day of operations. They were scheduled to fly 130 missions but in the event the day's final total was 160. During these sorties the Seafire pilots reported fewer encounters with German fighters, although they did meet a new foe: KG100's Dornier Do 217 bombers armed with radio-guided bombs. The primary mission of these aircraft was to attack the ships shelling German positions. Flown by experienced crews, the Dorniers managed to evade the defending fighters long enough to launch their bombs. Some ships were damaged but not badly enough to divert them from their purpose. Earlier in the month, though, KG100 had sunk the Italian battleship *Roma* with a radio-guided bomb just after it had surrendered to the Allies.

At dusk on 11 September, Force 'H' was withdrawn. Its primary purpose had been deterrence of the Italian fleet with a secondary role of supplementing the air support provided by the escort carriers. A total of sixteen fighters were provided for support purposes, these patrols being undertaken from dawn to dusk. Only one interception was made when a patrol of Martlets downed a Fiat RS.14 floatplane. As concerns grew about the vulnerability of the large carriers to both U-boat and air attack, their departure was seen as vital. They did not, however, take all of their aircraft with them. Eight Seafires and a similar number of Martlets were flown to *Unicorn* as the two fleet carriers departed. This brought the ship's air complement up to twenty-five, of which seventeen were Seafires.

Operational flying resumed at day-break on 12 September. Patrol activity was limited to three sorties as the emergency strip at Paestum was declared ready from midday. With all patrolling aircraft safely back aboard their carriers, the engineering parties worked flat out to prepare as many aircraft as possible for use ashore because land-based fighters from Sicily were not due for several days. A total of twenty-six Seafires, led by *Stalker*'s air wing commander, Lt Cdr J.C. Cockburn RN, was sent to Paestum. His force comprised two L.IICs from his own carrier, four from *Attacker*, plus five each from *Battler* and *Hunter*, with a further ten from *Unicorn*. All aircraft landed safely.

One suffered brake failure, which was soon repaired despite the primitive conditions. Refuelling involved the use of 5gal (23ltr) drums and hand pumps, while the pilots mucked in to service their own aircraft. The Seafires did not have to operate long in these conditions, as the dusty atmosphere was playing havoc with the unfiltered Merlin engines.

The first operation was conducted on 12 September, all aircraft being involved in a tactical reconnaissance sweep following reports – which proved to be false – of a German counter attack. The following day, twelve aircraft took off at dawn on medium altitude patrol supported by another four flying top cover. During these sorties the Seafires were bounced by a pair of USAAF A-36As, one of which was promptly shot down before the other was identified as friendly. The next sortie was undertaken in the early afternoon and involved twenty of the available Seafires. By the time they returned to Paestum nearly 100 Curtiss P-40 Warhawks had parked around the airstrip, prompting a move to Asa where the Seafires joined No. 324 Wing RAF and its Spitfires. Only one further patrol was flown that day. It was only eight aircraft strong, as the others were receiving much-needed attention from the RAF personnel.

The naval contingent flew only one more sortie from Paestum, on 14 September, when eight aircraft took off at dawn. On their return they were stood down for twenty-four hours while the RAF assumed

This overview of the Attacker class escort carrier HMS *Stalker*, shows its short flight deck and the location of the deck lifts. *Stalker* was commissioned in December 1942 and participated in operations in the Atlantic and Pacific oceans. Returned to the USN in December 1945, the carrier was rebuilt as a merchant ship, remaining in use until scrapped in 1975. BBA Collection

responsibility for fighter patrols. The next day the Seafires rejoined their carriers, flying via Falcone and Bizerta. During their time on dry land, the Seafires had flown fifty-six missions without loss to enemy action. But if their pilots thought their part in the Salerno operations had come to an end they were mistaken. German forces were still threatening to push the Allies from their beach-head. Strong resistance, plus effective air support, finally repulsed the Germans and resulted in final break-out. Until this was confirmed the escort carrier force was warned that operations might have to be resumed. In the event, the exhausted naval pilots and aircraft were spared further action and Force 'V' was disbanded. The Seafire's first major operation was over.

Salerno – the Reckoning

When all the reports were pieced together it was apparent that the Seafire force had shot down two enemy aircraft and damaged four others. The cost had been high: forty-two Seafires written off in accidents. The force had flown 713 sorties during which thirty-two aircraft had been totally wrecked upon landing. A further seventeen had sustained undercarriage failure, while another twenty-four had experienced severe wrinkling of the rear fuselage, a problem that would dog the type throughout its career. A further four aircraft were lost to engine failure with the remainder being lost to other causes, which included pilot error. Of the aircraft that returned to their parent carriers, many were rendered temporarily unusable due to the Seafire's propensity for propeller damage caused by hitting the flight deck on trapping the arrester wire. Although some spares were available aboard HMS *Unicorn*, they were soon expended and the carrier force had to find another way of keeping its aircraft flying. The answer was supplied by *Hunter's* captain, Capt H.H. McWilliam RN. After consultation with the carrier's engineering staff, it was suggested that each propeller blade be trimmed by 2 inches. This reduced the unit's 10ft 3in (3.2m) diameter by 4in (10cm). This change drastically reduced propeller damage without loss of performance.

The accident and write-off rate was attributed to a combination of the operating conditions and pilot inexperience. Many accidents had been suffered by pilots from *Indomitable* who had been sent to reinforce

This No. 807 Squadron Seafire III is pictured from the flight deck catwalk of HMS *Hunter* as it leaves for another patrol. Rick Harding Collection

Seafire LR.IIC LR691 of No. 807 Squadron has just crash-landed on HMS *Hunter's* deck. Damage appears to have been restricted to the engine and propeller but the centreline fuel tank has been torn from its mountings. Rick Harding Collection

the escort carriers, which had decks 30 per cent smaller than that of the fleet carriers and operated at least 10 knots slower. *Hunter's* pilots, however, had been drilled in the art of successful deck landings by the CO of 834 Fighter Flight, Lt F.A.J. Pennington RNZVR. As a result, few of them suffered 'deck pecks' during Operation *Avalanche* and the entire flight remained serviceable. The other carrier involved with the escort force was *Unicorn*, whose structure differed slightly from that of the

regular fleet carriers. This resulting airflow induced turbulence across the flight deck and led to twenty-one Seafires being badly damaged in landing accidents. Air currents forced the aircraft across the deck once the arrester wire had been engaged. In many cases, undercarriages collapsed with consequent rear fuselage buckling.

Another factor highlighted in the reports was that the carriers were concentrated in too small an area close to the shore. Even in favourable over-the-deck

Watched by a crowd of 'goofers', a Seafire of No. 867 Squadron is taken down to the hangar of the escort carrier HMS *Hunter*. Rick Harding Collection

wind conditions, the carriers were left with little room to manoeuvre. But when the wind speed dropped to almost zero the combination of emergency landings due to fuel shortage and restricted manoeuvring room increased the chances of accidents. Yet while the accident rate was alarming, the number of sorties flown by the force, even allowing for attrition, was impressive. A maximum sortie rate of 4.1 per aircraft was the highest achieved and was well above the expected rate of two per aircraft. Combat success, however, was disappointing. Although the Seafires were responsible for many of the attacking aircraft jettisoning their bombs prematurely, their lack of performance meant that only three enemy aircraft were shot down. During *Avalanche* Seafire air patrols were defensive in nature, whereas in Operation *Torch* the force was engaged in sorties that involved tactical reconnaissance and attacks on targets of opportunity.

While the escort carriers were achieving a high sortie rate close inshore, the two fleet carriers standing further out to sea were launching fewer air patrols as their task was high-level protection. As the early Seafires lacked folding wings, they had to be ranged on deck. This meant that the two carriers had to manoeuvre parked aircraft to clear the appropriate part of the deck for landings and take-offs. For *Formidable* this problem was soon reduced when many Seafires were flown off to reinforce the escort carriers, but *Illustrious* retained a full complement of ten aircraft. The continual shuffling around, plus the requirement for a standing patrol of two Seafires during daylight hours, meant that the deck crews were worked to the maximum. Overall, one lesson learned from Operation *Avalanche* was that while it had helped to develop future tactics, it had shown that reliance on a single aircraft type, even though it simplified maintenance and eased the spares position, was not a viable option. During this time, *Illustrious'* pilots tested a prototype 'g' suit, which was said to be like a personally tailored hot water bottle in the high Mediterranean temperatures.

Another day, another crash-landing: Seafire L.IIC LR642 of No. 807 Squadron ends up in a most undignified position opposite *Hunter*'s island. Close study of this picture reveals that the hook had failed to lower, which indicates that the pilot has actually made a good landing on such a short deck. Rick Harding Collection

Convoy Support

Although the Seafires had played a major role in both *Torch* and *Avalanche*, they did have more mundane tasks to perform during the *Avalanche* period. Nos 833 and 834 Squadrons formed the air component aboard escort carriers involved in convoy operations. The former squadron had lost most of its Seafires, however, which resulted in its pilots being absorbed into No. 880 Squadron whose Swordfish were moved to another unit. No. 834 Squadron transferred from *Hunter* to *Battler*, which then proceeded through the Suez Canal en route to the Indian Ocean and convoy escort duties.

In the Atlantic one of the first escort carriers to operate Seafires was HMS *Tracker* whose resident unit, No. 816 Squadron, operated nine Swordfish and six Seafires. The squadron had received its first Seafires in June 1942 at Fearn when its CO was Lt Cdr P.C. Nottingham DSC RN. After working up it traded its Seafire L.IICs for IBs, although its strength was increased to nine aircraft just before the move to *Tracker*. The ship accompanied three convoys during August, October and November 1943. Few Seafire sorties were flown and no U-boats were sighted.

HMS *Fencer* was similarly employed. She embarked a mixed unit, No. 842 Squadron, which had received Seafire IICs during July and August 1943 while based at Machrihanish. These aircraft were soon traded for six Seafire IBs, which were added to the nine Swordfish already on strength. With Lt Cdr L.R. Tivy RN in command the unit went aboard the carrier in October and its first duty was to escort the liner *Franconia* from the Clyde to the Azores, where an RAF transit base was to be established. The liner and her escort arrived on the 8th after an uneventful voyage and the airfield at Lagens was declared ready for operations two days later. Bad weather delayed the arrival of the RAF Coastal Command Hudsons and B-17 Flying Fortresses which had been intended to provide anti-submarine cover for ships in the area, so *Fencer*'s entire complement of Swordfish, plus two Seafires, were detached to undertake escort duties as an interim measure. The Seafires flew dawn and dusk patrols to escort the Swordfish. By 23 October the detachment had rejoined the carrier, which then set course for the Clyde. The additional work-up time afforded the Seafire pilots during this voyage had paid dividends, only one aircraft being damaged

in landing accidents in more than fifty sorties.

Because they were considered more suitable for such operations, Martlets began to supplement Seafires for convoy escort duties in November 1943. The first of the Grumman aircraft arrived aboard *Fencer* in November and the ship was employed on out-and-back Atlantic crossings between 27 November and Christmas Eve. During these operations the American aircraft flew the standing air patrols, while Seafires were held on deck-readiness. Yet it would be a Seafire which would see action with an enemy aircraft. On 11 December Sub Lt A. Sakhnovsky RNVR, piloting PA100/D of No. 842 Squadron, was scrambled from *Fencer* to intercept a shadowing aircraft that had been glimpsed through the mist and drizzle. Soon after take-off, the aircraft's radio system failed due to a lack of weather protection. Yet despite operating in limited visibility, Sakhnovsky managed to sight the marauding Condor through the clouds some 800yd (740m) ahead. He fired two short cannon bursts at extreme range and the four-engined German aircraft turned away from the convoy. Sakhnovsky was now left with the difficult task of locating and landing aboard *Fencer*, which he managed successfully.

Indian Ocean Operations

Tracker's employment on escort duties represented the Seafire's final Atlantic convoy. The ship's last Seafire departed at the end of December, although *Fencer* would retain her aircraft until March. Both ships were re-equipped with Wildcats, the RN having adopted the type's US name. This left *Battler*, now operating in the Indian Ocean, as the last escort carrier still operating Seafires as the primary fighter. This vessel spent the period between 16 October 1943 and 21 March 1944 on escort duties, with Bombay as home base. Operating a mixed complement of Swordfish, Seafires and Martlets, the carrier covered convoys AB18A, AB20, AB24A and AB27 between Aden and Bombay. These duties ended in January 1944. On the 16th *Battler* was involved in anti-submarine operations off East Africa and Madagascar. It was during this operation that a U-boat supply ship was encountered. But instead of applying the tactic developed in the Atlantic of launching fighters to suppress anti-aircraft defences, the carrier just launched a pair of Swordfish.

Although they damaged the support ship, two U-boats managed to escape. This represented the Seafires' final Indian Ocean trade protection operation. The aircraft disembarked from the carrier and flew to the South African Air Force base at Stamford Hill, while *Fencer* entered the dockyard at Durban for a much-needed refit.

By the end of 1943 American-built aircraft had largely replaced the Seafire. No. 801 Squadron aboard *Furious* was the only operational Seafire unit still in front-line service. The forthcoming Normandy invasion, combined with the desire for a Royal Navy presence in US-dominated Pacific operations against the Japanese, prompted the Admiralty to re-evaluate the Seafire's future role. The lessons of *Torch* and *Avalanche* were also taken into account in what emerged as two distinct plans. The first concerned the escort carriers, whose maximum complement of aircraft was set at around twenty. Embarking just one squadron aboard these vessels would simplify operations and reduce the number of personnel required to support the aircraft. The fleet carriers were to have smaller squadrons but the lines were not to be rigidly drawn to enable personnel and aircraft to be moved between units as required. The training regime was also to be expanded. As well as standard air defence duties, pilots were to be trained in tactical bombing and also ground strafing as the 20mm cannon had been found to be effective against ground targets.

Pilots specially trained in tactical reconnaissance were to join the carrier wings. They would be equipped with the camera-equipped Seafire LR.IIC. Training was undertaken by No. 718 Squadron, which had been re-formed on 5 June 1944 as the Army Co-operation Training Unit (later re-named the Army Co-operation Naval Operational Training Unit) at Henstridge. This unit had originally received nine Seafire IIIs, supplemented by six Spitfire PR.XIIIs for reconnaissance training duties. As well as schooling pilots in tactical air reconnaissance duties, the unit also provided air combat training, enabling pilots to graduate in a dual role. The result was not only better quality intelligence but also an ability to undertake attack sorties.

Enter the Mk III

It was also recognized that a faster, more flexible version of the Seafire was needed.

The Seafire III featured a more powerful engine as well as the much-desired wing-folding facility This would at last allow more aircraft to be carried aboard ship, as unused machines could be struck down below for storage and servicing. The result of all this reorganization was the creation of three carrier wings, Nos 3, 4 and 24. The first two units were designated for deployment aboard assault carriers and consisted of Nos 808, 886 plus 897 Squadrons and Nos 807, 809 and 879 Squadrons respectively, all operating Seafire L.IIC and LR.IIC aircraft. No. 24 Wing was intended to be a fleet carrier wing and only two units were allocated to it, Nos 887 and 894 Squadrons, both with Seafire IIIs as their main equipment.

Three further units were still equipped with various Seafire versions, these being Nos 801 and 880 Squadrons. The former still operated Seafire IBs, while the latter was equipped with IICs. Both were intended to form a carrier wing when enough Seafire IIIs became available. In October 1944 these squadrons finally received the later aircraft and joined HMS *Implacable* to form the 30th Naval Fighter Wing. No. 899 Squadron had originally been intended to equip with Seafire IIIs and become part of the wing. A change of plan resulted in the unit landing at Ballyherbert to swap its Seafires for a mix of hooked and standard Spitfire Vs. The unit's land-based sojourn ended in February 1944 when twenty Seafire IIIs were delivered and the unit embarked aboard HMS *Khedive* in April for service in the Mediterranean.

The vessel arrived in July. The following month, the squadron flew over 200 sorties in support of the landings in the south of France, code-named Operation *Dragoon*. Further sorties were flown in September against shore targets and shipping in the vicinity of Crete and Rhodes. At the completion of these operations, *Khedive* returned home for rest and recuperation. No. 899 Sqn resumed training until January 1945, when it was embarked in HMS *Chaser*. With her strength increased to twenty-four aircraft the ship departed for Ceylon. With no operations to perform there *Chaser* sailed to Australia. No. 899 Sqn disembarked at Scofields to became a Seafire training and reinforcement pool. During this period the squadron saw no active service, its pilots being gradually posted to operational in-theatre units.

Meanwhile, in October 1943 *Attacker*, *Hunter*, *Khedive* and *Stalker* were undergoing extensive modification to convert them

Caught just before touch-down, this Seafire III has its hook and flaps lowered while the pilot has throttled fully back in accordance with the instructions of the deck landing control officer, the 'batsman'. FAAM Yeovilton

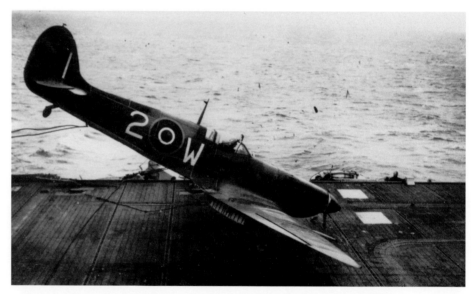

This is one of those pictures which have given the Seafire a bad name. Seafire III LR856 of No. 899 Squadron noses over and proceeds to destroy its propeller. This kind of accident was more prevalent aboard escort carriers. Pictured here is HMS *Khedive*. FAAM Yeovilton

from escort to assault carriers. In their original role these ships had been configured purely for fighter operations with extensive fighter direction and support for on-deck fighter operations. In their new role the ships would be working with amphibious forces and army units already ashore. The principal technical changes, therefore, involved improving ship-to-ship and ship-to-shore communications, complemented by better briefing and command facilities. Installing additional equipment in the

limited space available meant smaller aviation weapons magazines. It also meant that these carriers could no longer support anti-submarine or strike missions by types like the Swordfish and Grumman Avenger.

While the carriers were undergoing this conversion, the Dido class cruiser HMS *Royalist* was returned to dock after working-up to be fitted-out as a command ship. Changes included improved communications and extensive radar equipment, together with suitable accommodation for the force commander and his staff. In parallel with these conversions, Nos 3 and 4 Fighter Wings were also undergoing training for their new role.

Norwegian Operations

During December 1943, and throughout the opening weeks of 1944, only a few of the Royal Navy's aircraft carriers were at sea protecting convoys. The remaining ships were undergoing refitting and training for their projected roles in the invasion of northern Europe. As a practice run for the revamped carrier force, a dress rehearsal against German forces on the Norwegian coast was planned. Taking a central role was the veteran *Furious*, which sailed from Scapa Flow on 9 February 1944 escorted by two fast battleships, two cruisers and seven destroyers to participate in Operation *Posthorn*. *Furious'* strike component was provided by No. 8 Torpedo Bomber Wing, which comprised Nos 827 and 830 Squadrons, both with Fairey Barracudas. Fighter support consisted of fifteen Seafire IBs of No. 801 Squadron plus a further ten Seafire L.IICs of No. 880. The Barracudas landed-on first followed by the Seafires. But the fighter complement dropped by one when it was discovered that there was no room for the final aircraft, which had to return to Hatston.

Posthorn was intended to be a series of swift and decisive strikes against shipping in the vicinity of Stadlandet. As it was not possible to launch Seafires for night defence, the RAF was charged with providing night fighter cover. No enemy shipping was spotted during the passage until the merchantman *Ensland* was encountered off Vaagso. In response *Furious* launched ten Barracudas and twelve Seafires from No. 801 Squadron. As the Barracudas approached the merchantman a mixed force of Bf 109s and Fw 190s was spotted approaching from the rear.

Unfortunately for Sub Lt W.L. Horner RN, a radio malfunction combined with misty conditions meant that he was too late turning towards the enemy fighters and was shot down. Sub Lt Durrant RNZNVR engaged a pair of Fw 190s, while the flight leader, Lt L.D. Wilkinson RNVR, engaged two of the Messerschmitts. A fifth aircraft was engaged by Sub Lt G.W. Falcon RNVR. In the ensuing melee, Durrant managed to damage both of the Fw 190s before he was attacked by one of the Bf 109s that had

The primary strike aircraft during the Battle of the Atlantic was the Fairey Barracuda, but being difficult to handle it was not particularly popular with its crews. This example has suffered a tail-wheel failure on landing, leaving the handling crews with a clear-up job. FAAM Yeovilton

broken away from his leader. Wilkinson shot down the other Bf 109 and then dived after the other. Clearly realizing that the Seafires meant business and fearing that others might be in the vicinity, the Luftwaffe contingent broke away and headed for home. It was a wise choice. Another Seafire flight did indeed arrived to reinforce their squadron mates, who were now almost out of ammunition.

Meanwhile, the focus of the action, the *Ensland*, was hit by eight bombs from the Barracudas and broke in half. The Barracuda force returned safely and was followed home by the remaining Seafires. *Furious'* other Seafire squadron had not been idle. Its role had been to fly continuous combat air patrols to protect the naval force and to give warning of any enemy counter attack. *Furious* and her escorts were able to withdraw without encountering further opposition.

Attack on the *Tirpitz*

Seafires were also involved in Operation *Tungsten*, the Fleet Air Arm attack on the German battleship *Tirpitz* on 3 April. A large force of Barracudas armed with bombs and torpedoes was escorted by Corsairs, Hellcats and Wildcats, whose role was to keep defending German fighters at bay and to suppress anti-aircraft defences. As the

American fighters had longer range, the Seafire units performed the less glamorous role of providing air defence patrols over the fleet from *Furious*. The Seafires' next venture into Norwegian waters on 26 April involved a Dornier Do 18 flying boat being chased away, while another radar contact resulted in the Seafire patrol chasing shadows.

April 1944 saw No. 4 Fighter Wing, plus the carriers *Attacker*, *Hunter* and *Stalker* together with sixty Seafire L.IICs and LR.IICs being declared ready for combat service. In mid-May the force sailed for the Mediterranean, arriving in time to take part in Operation *Dragoon*, the invasion of southern France. For this operation the force was divided in two. Task Force 88.1 comprised the assault carriers *Attacker* and *Khedive*, already in-theatre, plus the fighter carriers *Emperor*, *Pursuer* and *Searcher*. Task Force 88.2 comprised the assault carrier *Stalker* together with the fighter carrier *Hunter* plus the American fighter carriers *Tulagi* and *Kasaan Bay*. The force commander was Rear Adm Sir Thomas Troubridge, flying his flag aboard the command cruiser HMS *Royalist*.

Dragoon and After

By 2 August 1944 the force was working up off Malta before departing to the designated attack positions for Operation *Dragoon*, which opened on the 15th. After its completion, the force arrived at Alexandria at the beginning of September for refitting and revictualing. On 25 August the entire British force departed for operations in the Aegean Sea, the target being German shipping and garrisons on the Greek islands. The attacks, code-named *Outing*, *Cablegram* and *Contempt*, were completed on 22 October and the fleet returned to Alexandria. Shortly afterwards, the bulk of the fleet departed for Britain via Gibraltar. *Attacker*, however, was retained to provide air support for Operation *Manna*, the re-occupation of Athens. It was not, therefore, until 10 November that the ship arrived in Devonport for repairs. During December 1944 all of the vessels involved in these operations were in various shipyards being prepared for their next task. This was to be in the Indian Ocean where they were to form part of 21 Aircraft Carrier Squadron, East Indies Fleet. From April 1945 the various carriers involved arrived to take part in the war against the Japanese.

In May 1944 the two squadrons aboard HMS *Furious*, Nos 801 and 880, began to re-equip with the Seafire III, which permitted a larger number of fighters to be carried in addition to the strike complement of Barracudas. By this time the Home Fleet had acquired another carrier. HMS *Indefatigable*'s air wing consisted of the Seafire-equipped No. 894 Sqn, plus No. 1770 Sqn with Fairey Fireflys and Nos 820 and 826 Sqns with Barracudas. Operation *Mascot*, a further assault on the *Tirpitz* in July 1944, was the force's first task. It was unsuccessful because the German smoke screen completely hid the ship from its attackers.

Operation *Turbine* off Norway in August was followed a few days later by Operation *Offspring*, which involved the carrier air group providing cover for minelaying aircraft from *Nabob* and *Trumpeter*. A short respite for revictualing ended on 22 August with further attacks on the *Tirpitz*. On 19 September *Indefatigable* undertook its last Atlantic operation, this being code-named *Divan*, off the Lofoten Islands. The carrier then joined the First Aircraft Carrier Squadron of the British Pacific Fleet.

While many Royal Navy carriers were departing for points east, not all the available squadrons went with them. The remaining units were quickly integrated into the Air Defence of Great Britain as well as preparing for the forthcoming invasion of Europe. In addition to Swordfish

Seafire L.III NF521 was allocated to No. 728 Squadron based at Hal Far, Malta for fleet requirements duties. BBA Collection

and Avenger units this meant that seventy-two Seafires and eighteen Hellcats, plus eighteen Spitfire LF.VBs manned by FAA pilots, were now available. This force was formed into eight squadrons, five operating Seafires, one Hellcats, four Swordfish and six Avengers. Many were stationed along the south coast of England.

D-Day Support

To support D-Day operations in June 1944 No. 885 Sqn, based at Lee-on-Solent, became part of the Air Spotting Pool of No. 34 Reconnaissance Wing, 2nd Tactical Air Force. Equipped with Seafire L.IIIs, the unit undertook bombardment spotting, fleet escort, offensive anti-fighter sweeps and anti-submarine patrols. Operating alongside, No. 808 Squadron provided similar services, although both units would return to naval control a few weeks later with No. 885 joining HMS *Ruler*, while the latter went aboard HMS *Khedive*. The spotting pool Seafires for Operation *Neptune* were under the command of Commodore E.C. Thornton RN. Nos 26 and 63 Squadron RAF, equipped with Spitfires, and the only US Navy unit to operate Spitfires, VCS-7, also joined his force. The two naval and RAF squadrons were assigned to provide support for Royal Navy vessels, while VCS-7 provided air cover for the Western Naval Task Force, which was mainly American in composition. D-Day stripes were applied

to the pool's aircraft on 3 June. The first sorties were undertaken in the early hours of the 6th when the first pair of Seafires took off to spot for the naval forces engaged in Operation *Overload/Neptune*. The much-anticipated invasion of northern Europe had begun.

The two aircraft had distinct roles to play. One acted as spotter for the big guns of the battleships and monitors, whose shells could reach up to 15 miles (24km) inland, while the second provided cover for the first. The spotting aircraft operated between 4,000 and 8,000ft (1,200 to 2,400m), with the covering fighter some 2,000ft (600m) above it. During the first day of the invasion the spotting pool flew 153 sorties. Three Seafires and a naval Spitfire were shot down, while the RAF and VCS-7 each lost an aircraft. The second day of the invasion saw the *Luftwaffe* taking such an interest in the spotters that its fighters made strenuous efforts to break through the top cover of Spitfires and P-47 Thunderbolts. Some were successful and Lt Cdr Devonald RN came under attack from eight Fw 190s. Having fought them off, Devonald was then faced with nursing his damaged aircraft back to base. Its engine eventually seized and he ditched alongside a tank-carrying ship whose crew rescued him.

The spotting teams continued to be harassed by the *Luftwaffe*, but the Seafires did achieve some success. On D-Day-plus two Lt H. Lang RNZVNR shot down a Bf 109. Other pilots managed to damage at

With another escort carrier in the background, HMS *Stalker* passes through the Suez Canal to join the British Pacific Fleet (BPF) with the Seafires of No. 809 Squadron on deck. BBA Collection

HMS *Atheling* was a member of the Ruler class of escort carriers, which entered service in October 1943, being allocated to the BPF as a fleet train carrier and spare flight deck. The vessel was returned to the USN in 1946, being sold on for conversion as a merchantman, a role it maintained until scrapped in 1967. BBA Collection

least one Fw 190. By 27 June the spotting pool was no longer required and its two naval units were allocated to other tasks. These included attacking midget submarines attempting to attack Allied ships anchored off the Normandy coast. On 15 July the Second Tactical Air Force released the naval units back to Fleet Air Arm control. During their support of the D-Day landings, six Seafires had been lost to anti-aircraft fire, three to enemy fighters, while two others were obliged to crash-land after suffering serious damage.

Back to Norway

While much of the world's attention was focused on the beaches of Normandy, the continued existence of the *Tirpitz* and the merchant shipping supporting the German forces in Norway was keeping elements of the Home Fleet occupied. On 1 June 1944 HMS *Furious* launched a strike force of eighteen Barracudas, supported by twelve Seafires and ten F4U Corsairs from HMS *Victorious* to attack a convoy off Aalesund. Such was the ferocity of the attack that seven of the armed escorts were rendered unusable while three of the cargo vessels were sunk. This was to be the last operation in Norwegian waters for HMS *Victorious* as the carrier was kept on standby at Scapa Flow during the opening stages of D-Day before departing for the Far East on 12 June. *Furious* made one final attack on the *Tirpitz* on 22 August 1944. Under the code-name Operation *Goodwood*, the attack involved the complete wing making another unsuccessful attempt to sink the German battleship. This thorn in the Allied side was finally dealt with by aircraft from No. 9 Squadron RAF whose Lancasters dropped Tallboy bombs on the ship, causing it to turn turtle. *Furious* undertook one more mission off the Norwegian coast in support of mining operations. On 15 September 1944 this venerable ship with such a distinguished history was finally paid off; her machinery and structure were worn out.

Furious was replaced off Norway by *Implacable*. Her first mission with Seafires aboard was undertaken on 26 October 1944. The units aboard were Nos 887 and 849 Squadrons, which together formed No. 24 Naval Fighter Wing, and the Barracuda-equipped Nos 828 and 841 Squadrons as No. 2 TBR Wing. Operation *Athletic* entailed strikes on Rorvik, Bodo and

During the D-Day operations, Fleet Air Arm pilots flew photo-reconnaissance sorties over the beaches and the gradually expanding battle fronts. Most sorties involved the Spitfire PR.XIII, the prototype of which, L1004, is seen here. Will Blunt Collection

Lodings, during which 27 tons of bombs were dropped in forty Barracuda sorties. Two days later the strike aircraft carried out the Fleet Air Arm's final airborne torpedo sorties. They sunk six merchant ships, damaged one and drove ashore and wrecked a U-boat. On the carrier's return to Scapa Flow at the end of the month the Naval Fighter Wing was disembarked.

Replenished, *Implacable* returned to sea on 8 November, having embarked No. 38 Naval Air Wing – which comprised Nos 801 and 880 Squadrons with Seafires – en route. After carrying out air support duties for minelaying operations off the Norwegian coast, the carrier undertook strikes off the Alster Islands. The Barracudas and the

Fireflys of No. 1771 Sqn sank two ships and severely damaged four others. The next day, 28 November, the carrier was badly damaged by heavy seas, forcing it to return to Scapa Flow for repairs. *Implacable* would undertake its final Home Fleet mission in December 1944 before entering Rosyth dockyard for a refit to enable the ship to join the British Pacific Fleet, by March 1945.

The successful invasion of Europe from the north and south, the growing offensive being mounted by the Russian Army on the Eastern front, plus the continued attacks on German shipping now meant that the Allies could turn their attentions to defeating the Japanese in the Far East.

After a heavy landing aboard HMS *Ocean*, this Seafire of No. 805 Squadron exhibits one of the type's main failings: structural failure between the tail unit and fuselage. Ray Sturtivant

CHAPTER FIVE

Anatomy of the Seafire

As the Seafire was based on the Spitfire it was inevitable that its construction would be similar to that of its counterpart.

The fuselage consisted of three sections each incorporating monocoque structures. The forward section housed the power-plant and engine bearers and terminated at frame 5, which acted as the main firewall. From there the main section of the fuselage extended aft to frame 19. This also provided the interface between the fuselage and the tail unit, which included the fin and tailplane mountings.

The primary frame (No. 5) was a solid structure comprising two aluminium skins with an asbestos lining in between. Attached to this were the forward wing spar mountings, the upper and lower mountings for the engine – Merlin or Griffon – and the auxiliary gearbox mounts. Just aft was the next vertical frame, No. 8, to which frame 7 was attached at a point two-thirds of the way up the frame, which was angled forward.

The space between frames 5 and 8 accommodated the two main fuselage fuel tanks with frame 7 acting as a flameproof bulkhead. Also mounted on frame 8 was the lower windscreen attachment. Further aft on frame 10 were the mountings for the rear wing spar and, further up, on the port

side, the leading edge of the pilot's access door. Frame 11 also incorporated the pilot's headrest and protective armour plate. It also marked the rearmost extent of the cockpit canopy's travel on high-backed aircraft. Between frames 11 and 12 was the

canopy's aft fixed portion, while the radio bay access panel was located at frame 15 with the accumulator access panel at frame 16. Between frames 17 and 18 in Merlin-powered aircraft was the emergency signal discharger.

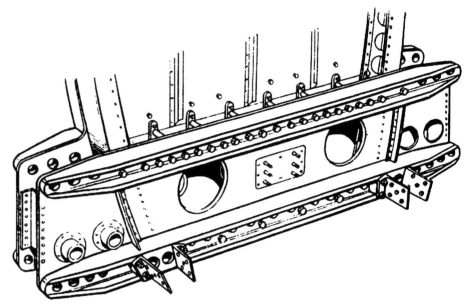

This close-up of the lower section of frame 5, plus the wing attachment points, reveals a substantial section. BBA Collection

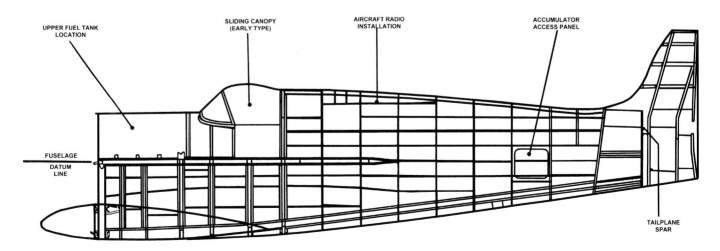

This side-on diagram illustrates the basic structure of the Spitfire and Seafire. Eric Morgan Collection

Mounted on to frame 5 was the Merlin engine with its accessories exposed. Also visible here is the light engine support frame and the cowling panel mounting framework. Chris Michel

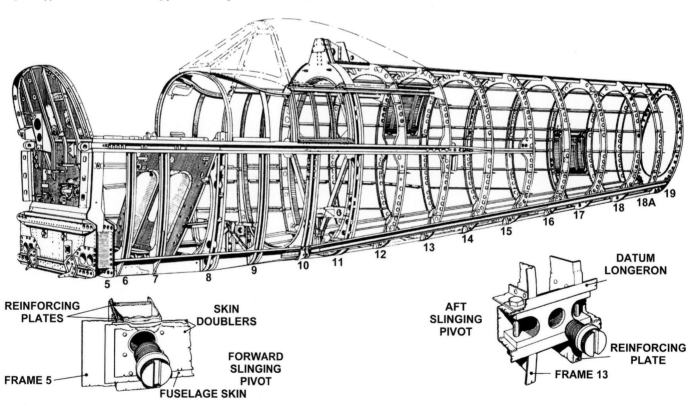

Installing the Griffon engine into the Seafire required a much stronger structure and reworked frame 5 engine supports. This diagram illustrates the Seafire XVII, although the main features, apart from the bubble cockpit canopy, were common to the Seafire XV. Eric Morgan Collection

Cockpit Section

During production the cockpit section between frames 6 and 10 was built as a separate unit. Assembling the main fuselage section required frame 5 and the cockpit section to be mounted in assembly jigs where they were joined together using the two bottom 'V'-section lower main longerons running from frame 5 to frame 14. The top engine bearer pick-ups were bolted to the ends of the side longerons, while the bottom pick-ups were bolted to the wing stub spar and bottom longerons. Once all these major items had been mounted into the assembly jig they were held rigidly in place to enable the intercostal stringers and plating to be riveted into position and complete the fuselage structure.

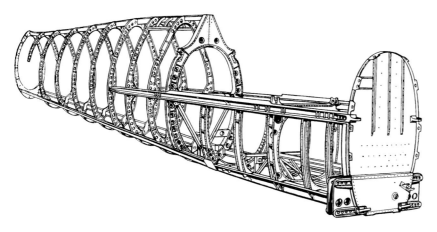

This view shows the layout of the frames, longerons and stringers that made up the Seafire's fuselage. Compared with the Spitfire, the Seafire featured additional strengthening of the longerons below the cockpit. Chris Michel

Fuselage Skinning

The thickness of fuselage skin plating varied between 24, 20 and 18 gauge, the thinnest material being towards the rear. At various points around the cockpit and engine bay, sections of armour plate protected the pilot and vital systems. Flush riveting was employed between frames 5 and 14; beyond that snap-head rivets were used. The skin plating up to the rear of the cockpit was joggled to present a flush surface. Further aft the skins were lapped to help speed production.

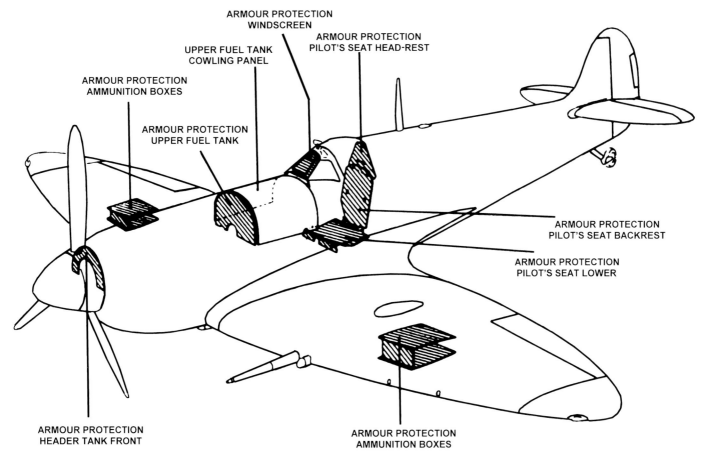

Armour plating was deemed a necessity for such aircraft as the Seafire to protect its vital components. This diagram illustrates the Seafire's protective armour. Eric Morgan Collection

One of the primary subcontractors heavily involved in Spitfire and Seafire production was Singer Motors. The company diverted part of its vehicle manufacturing capability to producing the mounting framework for the aircraft's engines. These were constructed mainly from tubular steel sections strengthened by a large rigid frame forming the central transverse member. This frame was built as a separate sub-assembly with its main bearers, which consisted of two cranked tubes, extending to the front mounting block. This then passed through the transverse frame, being attached to the bottom mounting fittings on frame 5. This was also assembled in a jig but in the upside-down position.

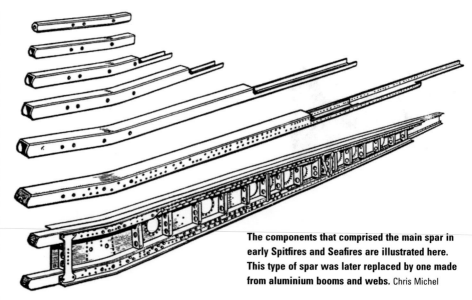

The components that comprised the main spar in early Spitfires and Seafires are illustrated here. This type of spar was later replaced by one made from aluminium booms and webs. Chris Michel

Fuselage Finishing

Once the fuselage had been assembled it was removed from the jig and placed in another to enable the wing root attachment points to be reamed out to the correct size to accept the mounting bushes. It was at this point that the wing root fillet panels were cut to shape and altered as required to fit the airframe. Once these actions had been completed the entire airframe was thoroughly cleaned to remove any extraneous material for the Quality Inspector's clearance. In the paint shop a layer of protective primer was applied, followed by the required camouflage finish.

Tail Unit

The tail unit was assembled as a separate section beginning at the interface with frame 19. This was connected to frame 20 by an 'L'-section former. Frame 21 formed the forward fin post, while frame 23 acted as the rear fin post. The intermediate frame, No. 22, provided the forward face of the tail-wheel bay on aircraft fitted with a retractable unit. On fixed tail-wheel machines, frame 22 formed the assembly's mounting point. Frame 23 doubled as the rudder mounting. A special jig was used to assemble the tail. The frames were placed into it first and then connected by a series of eight fin formers riveted in place. Once they were secured, longerons were riveted between frames 19 and 20, the whole section then being skinned with 22-gauge alloy.

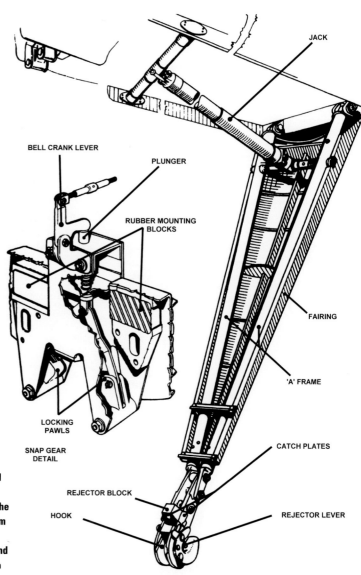

The early Seafires, including the first Griffon-powered machines, were fitted with an 'A'-frame arrester hook under the fuselage. This diagram also shows the mountings, damper and uplock. FAAM Yeovilton

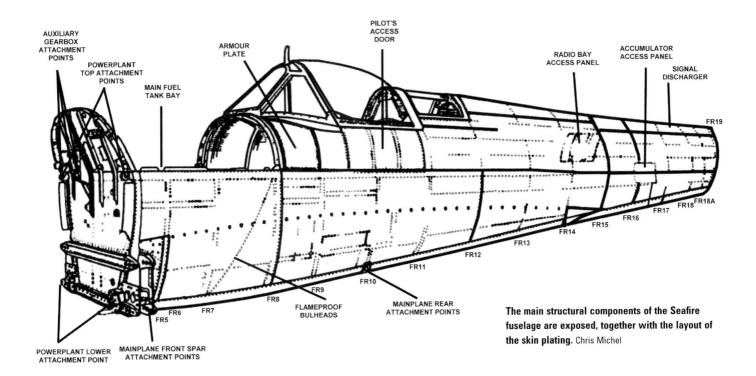

AUXILIARY
GEARBOX
ATTACHMENT
POINTS

POWERPLANT
TOP ATTACHMENT
POINTS

MAIN FUEL
TANK BAY

ARMOUR
PLATE

PILOT'S
ACCESS
DOOR

RADIO BAY
ACCESS PANEL

ACCUMULATOR
ACCESS PANEL

SIGNAL
DISCHARGER

FR19
FR18A
FR18
FR17
FR16
FR15
FR14
FR13
FR12
FR11
FR10
FR9
FR8
FR7
FR6
FR5

FLAMEPROOF
BULHEADS

MAINPLANE REAR
ATTACHMENT POINTS

POWERPLANT LOWER
ATTACHMENT POINT

MAINPLANE FRONT SPAR
ATTACHMENT POINTS

The main structural components of the Seafire fuselage are exposed, together with the layout of the skin plating. Chris Michel

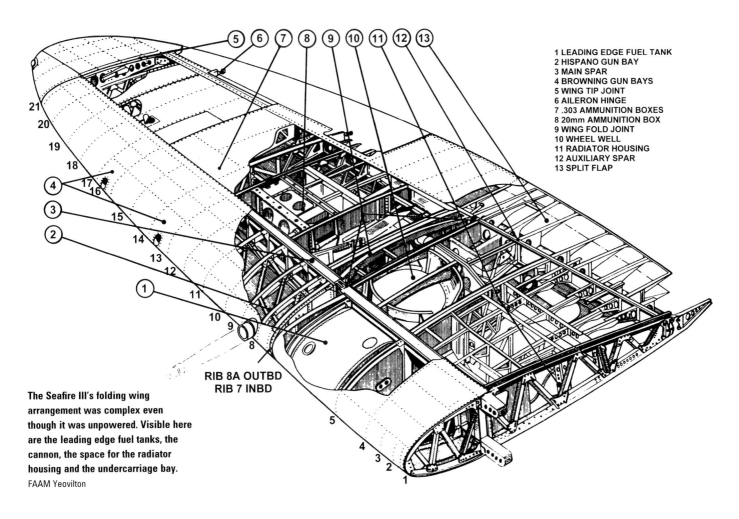

1 LEADING EDGE FUEL TANK
2 HISPANO GUN BAY
3 MAIN SPAR
4 BROWNING GUN BAYS
5 WING TIP JOINT
6 AILERON HINGE
7 .303 AMMUNITION BOXES
8 20mm AMMUNITION BOX
9 WING FOLD JOINT
10 WHEEL WELL
11 RADIATOR HOUSING
12 AUXILIARY SPAR
13 SPLIT FLAP

RIB 8A OUTBD
RIB 7 INBD

The Seafire III's folding wing arrangement was complex even though it was unpowered. Visible here are the leading edge fuel tanks, the cannon, the space for the radiator housing and the undercarriage bay.
FAAM Yeovilton

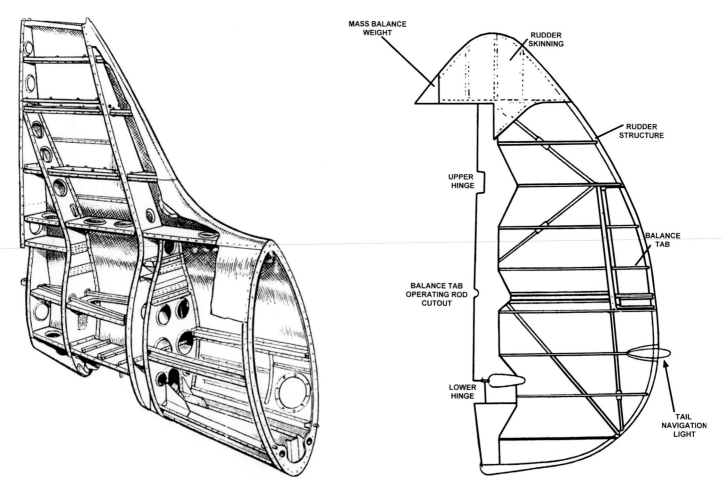

The tail unit was built as a separate component and incorporated the fin, together with the rudder and tail-plane mountings.
Eric Morgan Collection

Although this view shows the rudder of Griffon-powered aircraft, it should be noted that, apart from the tail navigation light, the layout and assembly was similar to that of all variants. BBA Collection

Tailplane

The tailplane comprised two spars joined by ribs. On the forward face of the front spar were attached the former ribs that defined the leading edge. The rest of its aerodynamic shape was determined by shaped wooden formers screwed to the intermediate ribs. The whole assembly was skinned with 24-gauge alloy. Once tailplane assembly had been completed, it was attached to the rear fuselage tail section. The complete assembly was then fitted to the fuselage. The rear flight control surfaces – the rudder and elevators – comprised a single spar to which nose ribs were riveted on one side with the trailing ribs on the other. All were built in jigs to provide a uniform shape and skinned mainly with alloy as fabric was prone to ballooning. Once the structure had been completed the hinge mountings were fitted,

while the elevators had the torque tube attachment forks added to their inner faces.

Wing Construction

Early-build Seafire wings were particularly complicated because at their core was the multi-section leading edge torsion box. With the leading edge ribs in place the entire section was 'D'-shaped and formed most of the wing's strength. In later aircraft the multi-section spar was replaced by a machined multi-section assembly. This aided manufacturing. Aft of the main spar was a secondary one, which, in the earlier aircraft, was of a lighter construction. It was beefed up in later-build machines, not only to improve overall wing strength, but also to permit a greater variety of external weapons to be carried.

The original spar consisted of extruded square-section booms of different sizes, each being fitted inside the other to form a tapered section. As there were many sections within this spar, the root was almost solid. At the tip the five tubes were reduced to one. As the booms moved out towards the wingtip the sections were shaped to help create the taper. This required part to be cut away to form a simple angle section. As these sections were precision items, their manufacture was undertaken by the Reynolds Tube Company. Reynolds not only assembled the entire spar but also added the required crank to create the specified dihedral angle, the unit being delivered ready for assembly. A single web plate, flanged top and bottom to form a channel section, was riveted to the rear of the boom.

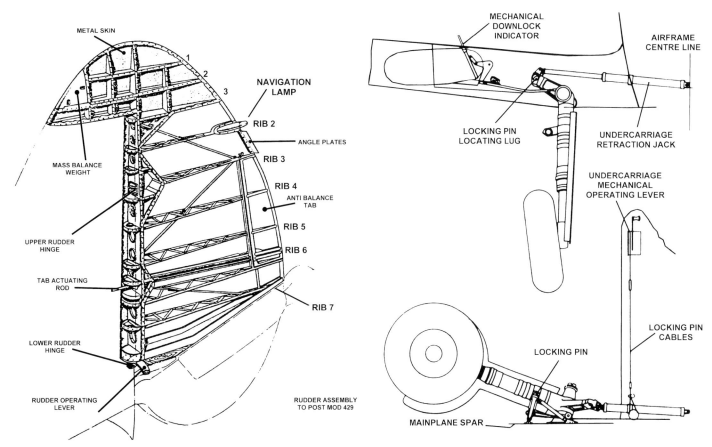

METAL SKIN

1
2
3

MASS BALANCE
WEIGHT

UPPER RUDDER
HINGE

TAB ACTUATING
ROD

LOWER RUDDER
HINGE

RUDDER OPERATING
LEVER

NAVIGATION
LAMP

RIB 2

ANGLE PLATES

RIB 3

RIB 4

ANTI BALANCE
TAB

RIB 5

RIB 6

RIB 7

RUDDER ASSEMBLY
TO POST MOD 429

MECHANICAL
DOWNLOCK
INDICATOR

AIRFRAME
CENTRE LINE

LOCKING PIN
LOCATING LUG

UNDERCARRIAGE
RETRACTION JACK

UNDERCARRIAGE
MECHANICAL
OPERATING LEVER

LOCKING PIN
CABLES

LOCKING PIN

MAINPLANE SPAR

The development of the Griffon-powered Seafire resulted in the re-location of the arrester hook. The sting-type hook was housed in a fairing under the rudder. FAAM Yeovilton

The undercarriage of the Merlin-powered Seafire was fairly simple as the leg was the only item that required powering. BBA Collection

An excellent view of a tubular main spar under construction at Airframe Assemblies on the Isle of Wight. Chris Michel

View of the wing showing the undercarriage bay, radiator mounting space, flaps and aileron hinge points. Chris Michel

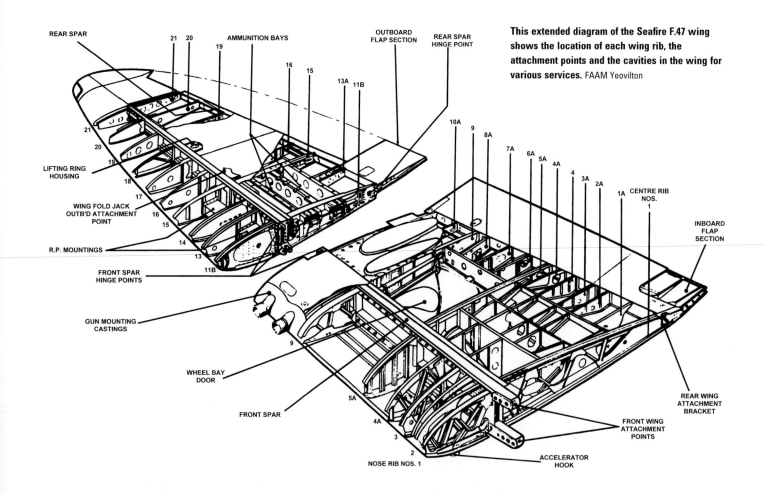

REAR SPAR

21 20

19

AMMUNITION BAYS

OUTBOARD
FLAP SECTION

REAR SPAR
HINGE POINT

16

15

13A 11B

21

20

19

18

17

16

15

14

13

11B

LIFTING RING
HOUSING

WING FOLD JACK
OUTB'D ATTACHMENT
POINT

R.P. MOUNTINGS

FRONT SPAR
HINGE POINTS

GUN MOUNTING
CASTINGS

WHEEL BAY
DOOR

FRONT SPAR

9

5A

4A

3

2

NOSE RIB NOS. 1

ACCELERATOR
HOOK

10A

9

8A

7A

6A 5A

4A

4

3A

2A

1A

CENTRE RIB
NOS.
1

INBOARD
FLAP
SECTION

REAR WING
ATTACHMENT
BRACKET

FRONT WING
ATTACHMENT
POINTS

This extended diagram of the Seafire F.47 wing shows the location of each wing rib, the attachment points and the cavities in the wing for various services. FAAM Yeovilton

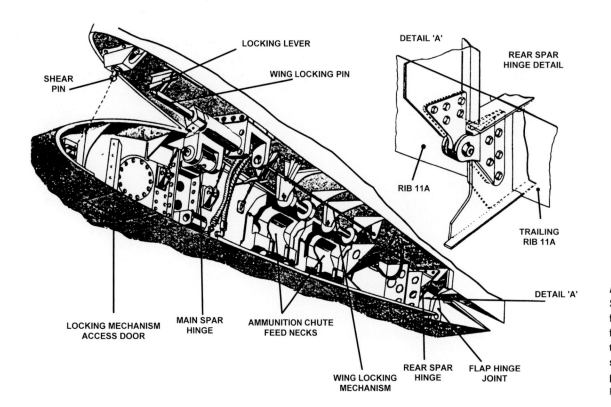

SHEAR
PIN

LOCKING LEVER

WING LOCKING PIN

DETAIL 'A'

REAR SPAR
HINGE DETAIL

RIB 11A

TRAILING
RIB 11A

DETAIL 'A'

LOCKING MECHANISM
ACCESS DOOR

MAIN SPAR
HINGE

AMMUNITION CHUTE
FEED NECKS

WING LOCKING
MECHANISM

REAR SPAR
HINGE

FLAP HINGE
JOINT

As shown here, the Seafire F.47's wing folding mechanism was far more complicated than the original manual system as a result of the power folding units.
FAAM Yeovilton

The leading edge skins were manufactured in two sections, butted together and joined by a nosing strip riveted under the inner faces. Spanwise strengthening was provided by intercostal 'Z'-section stringers to which the skins were riveted. The twenty-one nose ribs were of lattice and open girder construction. They not only provided a mounting for the nose skins but also formed part of the chordwise strengthening. The leading edge skin sections were manufactured from a single billet of 14-gauge alloy, which had been put through a stretching press to form it to the correct shape. As the wing required a completely smooth surface, countersunk holes were drilled in these skins. Solid rivets were then inserted into the holes and then milled down.

Once the cut-outs for the gunports had been made, the leading edge sections and rear spar could be placed in a jig for final wing structure assembly. With the structure framework in place the 2in (5cm) diameter undercarriage pintle pin was installed aft of the spar web. As the Seafires were cannon-armed, this eased wing manufacture because the gun bay was built as a separate structure in its own jig before being offered up to the wing structure. With the leading edge, undercarriage pintles and cannon bay in position, wing ribs Nos 1 to 21 were affixed to the rear face of the front spar. The rear spar could then be riveted in place in sections. With the rear spar in place the trailing edge ribs were riveted to the aft face of the rear spar and joined together at their outer tips by an alloy strip. The final items to be fitted before wing skinning were the radiator and wheel bays. Being the easiest to apply, the upper skins were riveted into place first, although the lower ones required greater preparation due to the awkward shape of the wing's inner sections. To maintain a sense of balance, Seafire wings were built in pairs by the same team and mounted in the jigs with the leading edges facing downwards.

With each primary section completed, it was time to install the internal systems. These included the electrical looms and their protective conduits, the aileron, rudder and elevator control cables, piping for the compressed air that operated flaps, guns and brakes, plus the landing lamps. Next came the lamps themselves, the aileron shroud panels and the main undercarriage legs. The last remaining internal installation was that of the gun heating system pipes. All connections intended to pass into the fuselage were left loose with temporary

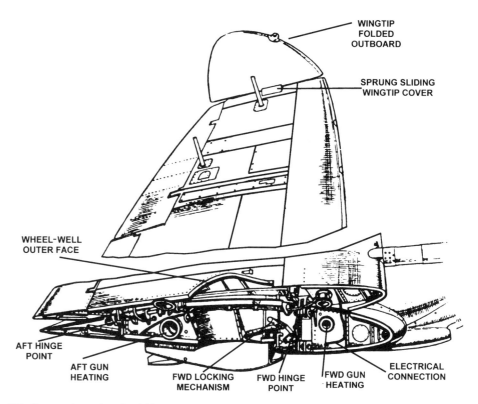

This diagram shows the wing fold arrangement and its major components, as fitted to the production Seafire III. FAAM Yeovilton

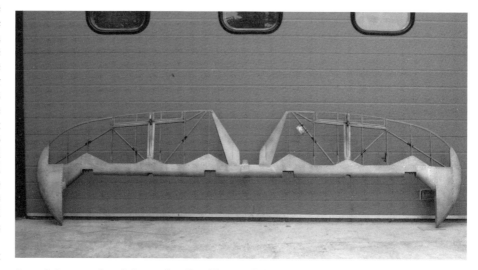

A set of elevators minus their covering alloy skins reveals the underlying structure. Also visible are the hinge points and trim tabs. Chris Michel

protective coverings. The final components to be fitted were the wingtip fairings and the remaining access panels. At this point the entire external surface was thoroughly cleaned and the wings passed for painting. Once they were ready for mating it was time for the fuselage to have its internal equipment fitted.

Fuselage Fixtures

To facilitate installation of its internal fixtures, the fuselage was mounted on two jacking points at frame 5. During this operation, support was provided by the forward wing attachment points and a shaped trestle placed at frame 18. As the

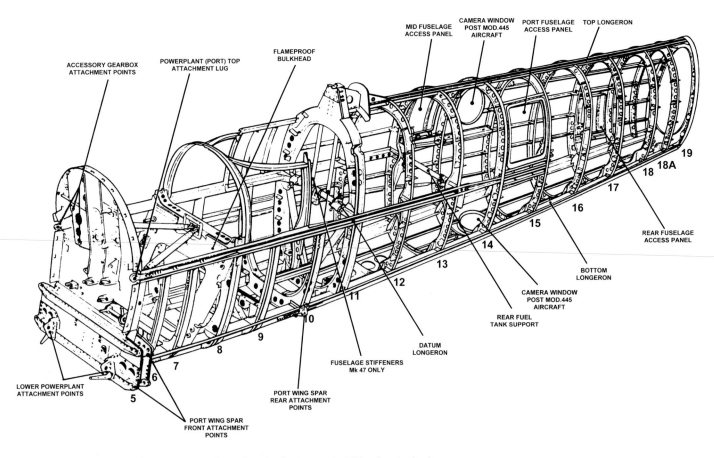

ACCESSORY GEARBOX
ATTACHMENT POINTS

POWERPLANT (PORT) TOP
ATTACHMENT LUG

FLAMEPROOF
BULKHEAD

MID FUSELAGE
ACCESS PANEL

CAMERA WINDOW
POST MOD.445
AIRCRAFT

PORT FUSELAGE
ACCESS PANEL

TOP LONGERON

19

18A

18

17

16

15

REAR FUSELAGE
ACCESS PANEL

14

13

12

BOTTOM
LONGERON

CAMERA WINDOW
POST MOD.445
AIRCRAFT

REAR FUEL
TANK SUPPORT

11

10

9

8

7

6

5

DATUM
LONGERON

FUSELAGE STIFFENERS
Mk 47 ONLY

PORT WING SPAR
REAR ATTACHMENT
POINTS

LOWER POWERPLANT
ATTACHMENT POINTS

PORT WING SPAR
FRONT ATTACHMENT
POINTS

Later Seafires utilized a similar structure to earlier variants but incorporated additional strengthening under the skin to absorb increased power and weapon loads. FAAM Yeovilton

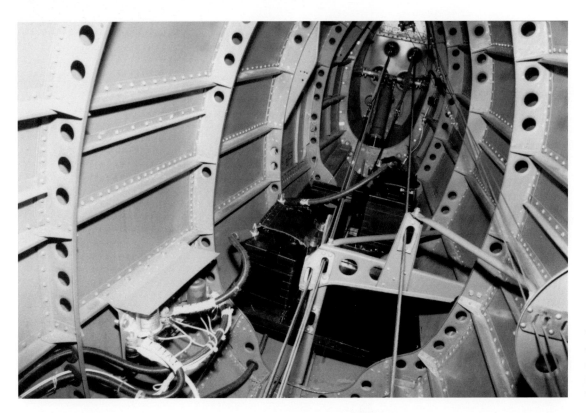

View looking back towards the rear fuselage frame showing the flight control runs, the trim cables and the batteries. Chris Michel

airframe was nose-heavy, a counter-balance weight in a canvas sleeve was hung over the tail. The first items fitted were the engine mounts. They were attached to the front face of frame 5, after which the cockpit fixtures and fittings could be installed. Once the cockpit was complete, the framework for the armoured glass windscreen and the screen itself could be fitted, together with the canopy. Armour plate was also installed to protect the upper fuel tank and around the pilot's seat where it joined that already around the ammunition boxes.

Before the seat was installed the flight control cables were connected to the rudder bar and control column, being held under light tension before fitting the flight control surfaces. The engine oil tank and the fuel lines were next, followed by the engine itself and the main fuselage fuel tanks. Once in place they could be connected up to complete fuselage system installation. The wings were now moved to the fuselage. Wheeled trestles not only provided support but also ensured that were offered up at the correct angle to the fuselage spar points. With the wings and their retaining pins in place and locked, the various systems could be connected and the flight control surfaces fitted.

To maintain a smooth aerodynamic flow, the wing fillet panels were fitted, the upper ones being bolted into captive nuts mounted on the support ribs located between the fuselage and the wing upper surface. The forward fairing wrapped around the leading edge, while fairing panels 2 and 3 were bolted to their matching ribs. The final two fairings, Nos 4 and 5, were treated as a single assembly and riveted together internally using a butt strap.

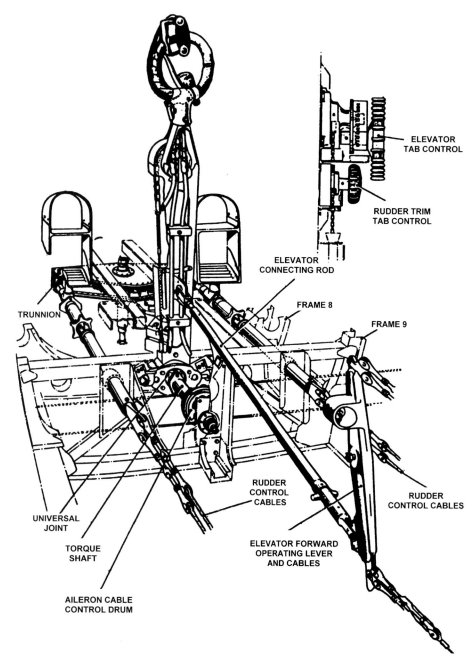

A Thorough Work-Out

Before being removed from its supports, the Seafire and its systems were given a thorough work-out. This enabled the under-carriage retraction sequence to be observed and the hydraulics, pneumatics and electrics to be tested. With everything checked, adjusted and inspected, the Seafire was taken from the assembly shop for fuel system leak checks before engine running. Where applicable, the wing folding mechanism was fully tested to ensure the mounting pins moved correctly and that there was no distortion or mismatch between sections. The operation of the arrester hook was the

This diagram illustrates the control layout for the elevator and the rudder and their relation to the spar under the cockpit floor. FAAM Yeovilton

final item to be checked before the aircraft was weighed and cleared for flight testing. That was the final step leading to the aircraft being declared ready for operational use.

The Seafire Mk.IB, II and III were described as single-seat low-wing monoplane fighters fitted with Rolls Royce Merlin 32, 45, 46, 50, or 55M engines depending on the variant and its role. Propellers could be of de Havilland or Rotol manufacture

and were either three- or four-bladed units, depending on the engine and role. Internal fuel was housed in two tanks in the forward fuselage, the top one containing 48gal (218ltr), while the bottom one had a capacity of 37gal (168ltr). The fuel system was so arranged that the upper tank fed into the lower one and then the engine. Both tanks' fuel cocks were mounted under the instrument panel. The engine oil tank had a capacity of 5.8gal (26ltr) and was located

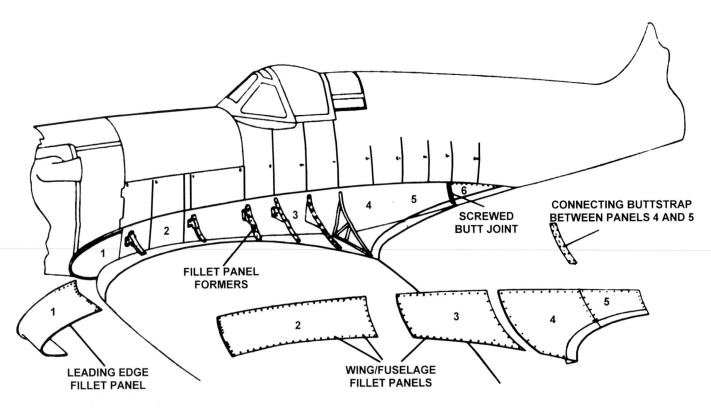

To ensure a smooth airflow between the fuselage and wings, a series of fairing panels was fitted. Their installation required specially shaped support brackets. Eric Morgan Collection

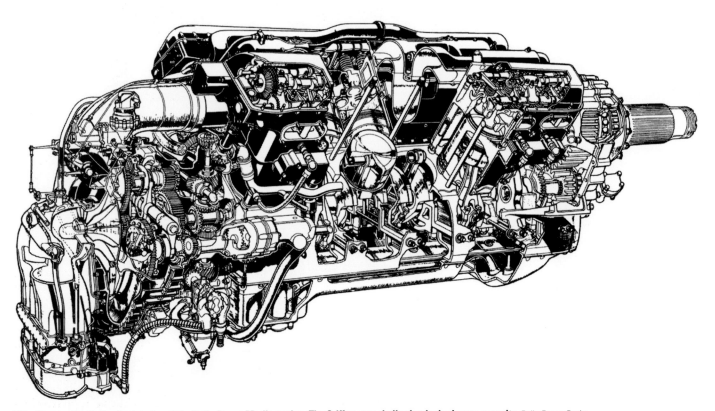

This diagram illustrates the interior of the Rolls-Royce Merlin engine. The Griffon was similar but had a larger capacity. Rolls-Royce Derby

This view, looking down into the cockpit, reveals the rudder pedals, the compass and the control column. Chris Michel

below the engine mountings. The oil coolers were mounted in tandem in an external fairing under the port wing.

Undercarriage Operation

The undercarriage was raised and lowered by an engine-driven hydraulic pump. An engine-driven air compressor fed by a pair of storage cylinders provided power for brake and flap operation. This system also drove the gun loading and breech mechanisms as well as movement of the landing lamps. The air cylinders were connected in series and held a maximum pressure of 200psi (14bar). Merlin-powered Seafires were fitted with a 12-volt electrical system charged by an engine-driven generator controlled by a switch above the instrument panel. In operation, the generator replenished an accumulator, which in turn powered the entire electrical system. A voltmeter placed to the left of the generator switch helped the pilot monitor the power supply.

Cockpit Controls

The Seafire inherited its spade grip control column from the Spitfire. On it were mounted the brake lever and the gun firing controls. The instrument panel, incorporating the basic blind flying panel, featured an airspeed indicator, altimeter, directional gyro, artificial horizon, rate of climb and descent indicator, plus the turn-and-bank indicator. A warning horn sounded when the undercarriage was locked up and the engine throttled back, although this could be cancelled by pushing a button on top of the throttle lever. It was also cancelled by advancing the throttle, although it would sound again once the control was pulled back. Initially there were only two flap positions: up or down. This rendered them unusable for take-offs, although careful use of shaped wooden blocks between the inner wing surface and the top flap skin could create an intermediate position for assisting departures. Engine starting could be either by the preferred cartridge method or, on earlier aircraft, by means of a hand crank whose handle was stowed behind the pilot's seat. The aperture for the crank was located in the starboard engine cowling panel.

The pilot's seat could be raised or lowered by a lever on the right-hand side. This was

The left-hand side of the cockpit, showing the gauges on the main pilot's panel, the engine control and some of the pipework.
Chris Michel

Another view of the port side of the cockpit showing the various trim wheels, engine controls and that famous spade-grip. Chris Michel

close to the release catch, which allowed the pilot to move within his harness without disconnecting it from the seat. To permit nocturnal operations the cockpit was fitted with lights, one each side, which illuminated the instrument panel and controls. A small adjustable flap on the starboard coaming above the instrument panel provided ventilation. The internal oxygen system was connected to a standard regulator mounted on the left-hand side of the cockpit and supplied the pilot's oxygen mask via a bayonet connector. An isolation cock was fitted to permit maintenance. A map case was mounted on the left-hand side. An external mirror provided rearward vision for the pilot.

Gun Controls

The Seafire was fitted with a reflector gun sight mounted on a bracket above the instrument panel. Two switches below the bracket controlled both the sight and the dimmer switch, which had three positions: 'off', 'night' and 'day'. Spare bulbs were carried in a holder on the right-hand side of the cockpit. The dimmer was normally set to day mode to provide full target illumination. Should the target background be too bright, a sun screen could be moved behind the windscreen to help and define the target with greater clarity. The low

wattage bulb used for the night position was controllable.

A G.42B cine camera was mounted in the port wing leading edge. Operation was via the gun firing button on the spade grip, but pilots had to remember to activate the system using a switch on the left-hand side of the cockpit. A footage indicator and aperture control switch were mounted on a plate near the throttle lever. The aperture switch allowed two positions to be selected, the smaller one being used for bright conditions.

Radio and Electrical Equipment

A combined radio transmitter-receiver was fitted, either the Type TR.9D or the Type TR.1133 transmitter used in conjunction with an R.3002 receiver. When the Type TR.9D was installed a Type C mechanical controller was fitted on the port side of the cockpit above the throttle lever. A remote contactor was located on the right-hand side with the master contactor mounted behind the pilot's headrest. A heating element was controlled by a cockpit switch, which was left in the 'off' position when the aircraft was on the ground and the cockpit unoccupied. The microphone telephone socket for connecting to the pilot's face mask was mounted on the right-

hand side of the seat. Many components and connections were common to the TR.1133 and the TR.9D but the Type C mechanical controller was replaced by a push-button electrical control unit.

Other equipment consuming electrical power included the navigation lights and the upper and lower identification lights, all controlled by the signalling switchbox mounted on the right-hand side of the cockpit. Besides the power switches, the switchbox also incorporated a Morse key. This meant that the lights could be set to 'Morse', 'off' and 'steady'. A landing light was located beneath each wing and controlled by a switch below the instrument panel. To ensure that at least one light was operable there were independent power circuits. With the control switch in the central position both lamps were in the up position and not illuminated. Moving it to either left or right controlled the port or starboard lamps respectively. Both lights were lowered pneumatically. A separate lever dipped their beam. To ensure that the airspeed indicator's pressure head did not freeze at altitude it was fitted with a heater controlled via a switch mounted close to the trim wheels. Once the aircraft was in the landing circuit the heater had to be switched off to conserve the battery's charge. A toggle control mounted on the left-hand side of the cockpit could be used to fire a signal cartridge from the top of the fuselage just aft of the cockpit.

Emergency Equipment and De-Icing Systems

The Seafire featured a variety of emergency equipment. This included the hood jettison mechanism, actuated by pulling a lever mounted inside the top of the hood. When moved forwards and downwards, the hood was disengaged from the rails and the pilot could force it clear of the aircraft with his elbows. For those aircraft not having this facility a crowbar was provided instead. A forced-landing flare was carried in a tube fixed inside the fuselage and operated via a ring grip mounted to the left of the seat. A first-aid kit was stowed aft of the wireless equipment and was accessible via a hinged panel on the port side of the fuselage.

The tank for the Seafire's de-icing system was mounted on the left-hand side of the cockpit directly above the bottom longeron. The fluid flow was controlled by a cock above the tank connected to a pump and

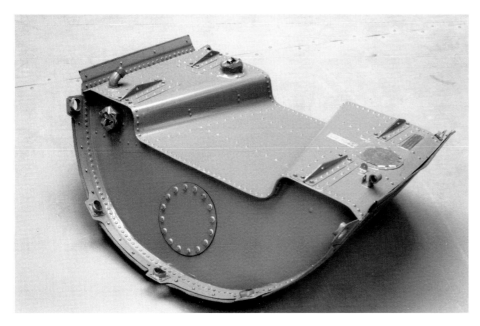

A brand-new upper fuselage fuel tank awaiting installation. Fuel from the upper tank fed into the lower and thence to the engine. Chris Michel

needle valve below the undercarriage emergency lowering lever. The fluid itself was pumped to a nozzle from which it was sprayed upwards over the screen's front panel. The pump plunger returned to the extended position by itself. When the de-icing facility was no longer required the cock could be turned off.

Redesigned Fuel System

The appearance of the final Seafire versions brought a redesigned fuel system. In the F.45 fuel was contained in two fuselage-mounted tanks and two interconnected wing leading edge tanks. The lower fuselage tank and those in the wings were self-sealing. In flight fuel from the upper fuselage tank was fed to the lower one while that in the wing tanks went via the upper fuselage tank, driven by air pressure and controlled by the pilot via a transfer cock. Fuel from the lower fuselage tank went directly to the engine through the main feed

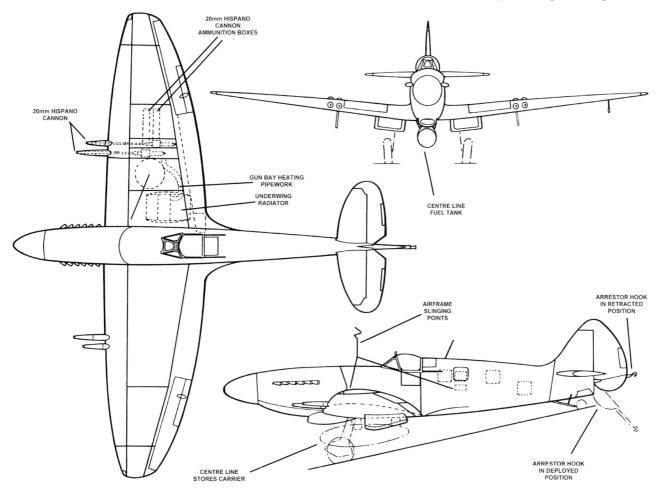

The location of the Seafire F.45's slinging points, essential items in lifting the aircraft aboard ship, are shown here. BBA Collection

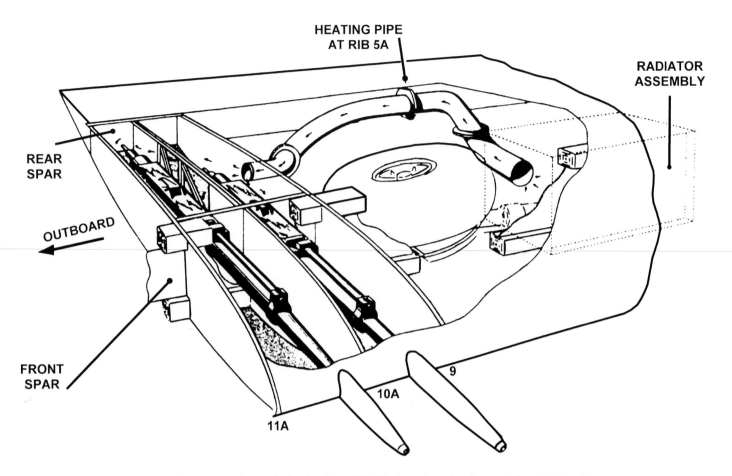

**HEATING PIPE
AT RIB 5A**

**RADIATOR
ASSEMBLY**

**REAR
SPAR**

OUTBOARD

**FRONT
SPAR**

9

10A

11A

Fighter gun-bays needed heat to stop the gun operating mechanism freezing at high altitudes and causing the guns to jam. FAAM Yeovilton

line. To stop the fuel boiling off at altitudes above 15,000ft (4,600m) in warm weather, the fuselage tanks could be pressurized. Pilots had to be aware if the self-sealing function was impaired, so this option could only be used when the fuel pressure warning light was illuminated. The upper fuselage tank held 36gal (163ltr) and the lower one 48gal (218ltr), while one pair of wing tanks contained 12.5gal (57ltr) and the other pair 5.5gal (25ltr) for a total of 120gal (545ltr). The Seafire 45 could carry a centreline mounted external 50gal (227ltr) tank. Fuel was fed directly to the main feed line and controlled by a cock, which kept the tank isolated until required for use.

The internal fuel capacity of the Seafire F.46 and F.47 was similar to that of the F.45 except that an extra 32gal (145ltr) tank was carried in the rear fuselage aft of the pilot's seat. The external tanks carried by these two variants were combat tanks, each capable of holding 22.5gal (102ltr), which fed into the main fuel feed line via an individual control cock. Fuel from the combat tanks was transferred to the upper

fuselage tank using air pressure from the exhaust side of the vacuum pump. To prevent overfilling, the upper fuselage tank had a control float to allow the transfer cocks to select wing or combat tanks irrespective of the contents.

The lower fuselage tank fuel cock was located just below the centre of the instrument panel. That for the external tanks was positioned on the right-hand side of the cockpit and was interconnected with the tank jettison lever. This meant that when the tanks were to be dropped, operation of the lever also ensured that the cock moved to the closed position. As Mk 46s and Mk 47s had rear fuselage tanks, a further control cock was located on the floor just forward and to the left of the pilot's seat.

The Seafire 45's fuel transfer cock was located near the throttle quadrant and it also regulated the supply of pressurized air to the external fuel tanks. Once the external tanks were empty the control had to be returned to the normal position to ensure effective pressurization of the internal tanks. By contrast, neither the Mk 46 nor the

Mk 47 had a main fuel system pressurization cock. This enabled the selector for external pressurization to be left open. Fuel transfer was effected by an electric booster pump located in the bottom of the lower fuselage tank and controlled by a cockpit switch. In later versions a second booster pump was fitted to the rear tanks, the controlling switch being marked 'main', 'off' and 'rear'. To confirm operation, there were press-to-test buttons.

A further priming pump was fitted to these final Seafire variants. There was also a control cock, the operating switches being located on the right-hand side of the cockpit below the instrument panel. It offered three selections: 'all off', 'main' and 'ground'. In the latter position the cock permitted high volatile fuel to be introduced into the fuel system for cold starting. When 'main' was selected the fuel was drawn from the bottom fuselage tank for engine starting, while 'all off' was only when priming the engine cylinders for starting. A fuel contents gauge on the right-hand side of the instrument panel displayed the combined total

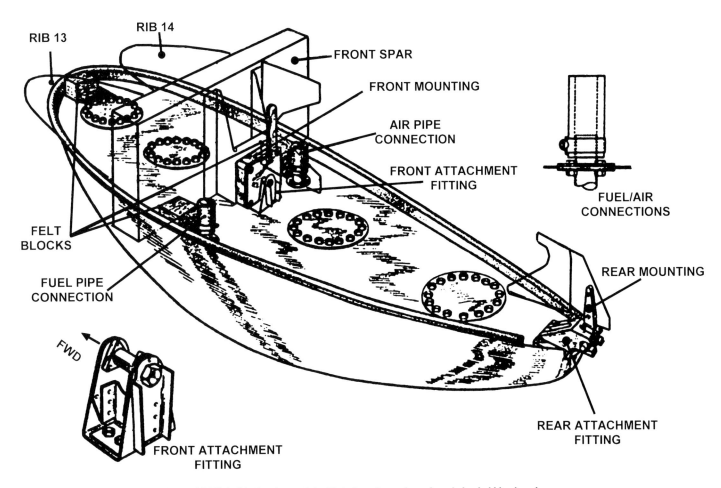

RIB 13

RIB 14

FRONT SPAR

FRONT MOUNTING

AIR PIPE CONNECTION

FRONT ATTACHMENT FITTING

FUEL/AIR CONNECTIONS

FELT BLOCKS

FUEL PIPE CONNECTION

REAR MOUNTING

FWD

FRONT ATTACHMENT FITTING

REAR ATTACHMENT FITTING

The wing combat tanks could hold 22.5gal (103ltr) of fuel and were faired into the wing undersurface, being held in place by an aft-mounted hook and two front attachments. FAAM Yeovilton

of both upper and lower fuselage tanks. A second gauge was installed in the Seafire 46 and 47 to enable the rear fuselage tank to be monitored. All gauges required electrical power to function but none was fitted to display the contents of the internal wing tanks and the external tanks. Warning lights illuminated when pressure dropped below operating minima. A low contents warning light came on only when there was enough fuel for thirty minutes' economical cruising flight. Both lights were located on the instrument panel.

The 9gal (41ltr) engine oil tank was located between the upper fuselage tank and the fireproof bulkhead. To reduce any risk of contaminants passing into the engine there was a filter in the feeder system. Oil leaving the engine was cooled by passing it through a matrix housed in the starboard under-wing radiator fairing. Gauges indicating oil pressure and temperature were mounted on the right-hand side of the instrument panel. Engine coolant was

supplied from a tank located above the reduction gear and fitted with a pressure relief valve. The radiator shutters were fully automatic and designed to open when the coolant temperature reached 115°C. Initially, a push button was mounted on the electrical panel for testing purposes, but on post-Modification 736 aircraft it was replaced by a two-position switch. This allowed the radiator shutters to be opened for taxiing, ground running and airfield deck-landing practice. Mounted on the right-hand side of the instrument panel was a temperature gauge to enable the pilot to monitor the temperature.

Hydraulic, Pneumatic and Electrical Systems

Seafire 40 series aircraft were fitted with hydraulic, pneumatic and electrical systems. The hydraulic system powered the main and tail wheels. Oil was carried in a reservoir

mounted on the fireproof bulkhead and passed around the system by an engine-driven hydraulic pump. A pipeline-mounted filter ensured isolation of possible contaminants. The pneumatic system was also powered by an engine-driven compressor. It supplied two reservoirs, which provided pressure to operate wing flaps, radiator flaps, air intake shutter, supercharger gear change and brakes. The reservoirs were pressurized to 300psi (21bar) and passed through a valve to reduce pressure to 220psi (15bar). Operating pressure for the braking system was reduced to between 80 and 90psi (5.5 and 6.2bar). On post-Modification 489 aircraft, brake operating pressure was increased to 140psi (9.7bar).

The Seafire 45's electrical system was rated at 12 volts DC, while that installed in the final two versions was re-rated to 24 volts DC. Power for both systems was supplied by an engine-driven generator, which charged the batteries. For use with an external power supply, a ground power

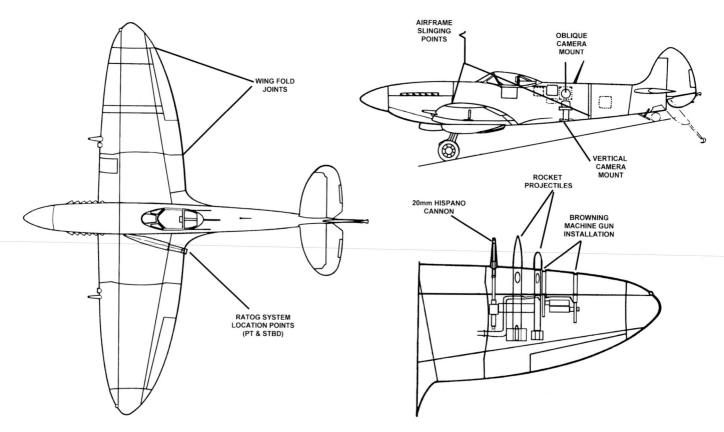

WING FOLD
JOINTS

AIRFRAME
SLINGING
POINTS

OBLIQUE
CAMERA
MOUNT

VERTICAL
CAMERA
MOUNT

ROCKET
PROJECTILES

20mm HISPANO
CANNON

BROWNING
MACHINE GUN
INSTALLATION

RATOG SYSTEM
LOCATION POINTS
(PT & STBD)

The Seafire FR.47 was equipped with cameras, their locations being shown in this diagram. Also visible are the rocket mountings. BBA Collection

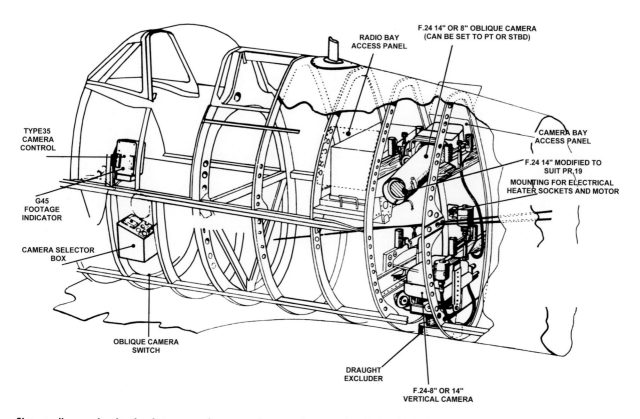

RADIO BAY
ACCESS PANEL

F.24 14" OR 8" OBLIQUE CAMERA
(CAN BE SET TO PT OR STBD)

TYPE35
CAMERA
CONTROL

CAMERA BAY
ACCESS PANEL

F.24 14" MODIFIED TO
SUIT PR.19

MOUNTING FOR ELECTRICAL
HEATER SOCKETS AND MOTOR

G45
FOOTAGE
INDICATOR

CAMERA SELECTOR
BOX

OBLIQUE CAMERA
SWITCH

DRAUGHT
EXCLUDER

F.24-8" OR 14"
VERTICAL CAMERA

Close-up diagram showing the photo-reconnaissance equipment and cameras installed in the Seafire. BBA Collection

socket was located on the port side of the fuselage just below and behind the cockpit. In the Seafire 45 the electrical master control was interconnected with the engine ignition switches. It needed to be selected to 'on' before the ignition switch could be selected to 'on'. On later aircraft the master switch was marked with 'ground' and 'flight' selections and mounted on the left-hand side of the cockpit together with most of the other electrical control switches and push-buttons. When the master switch was moved to the 'ground' position, all the electrical services could be operated and tested using an external power supply. In 'flight' mode the power was drawn from internal sources, so that the position had to be selected before engine start. Should there be a problem with the supply generator a red warning light illuminated to show that the batteries were not being charged.

Controls for Later Aircraft

As with the earlier versions, the Seafire 40 utilized a spade-grip control column. It incorporated controls for the brakes, gun firing, bomb and rocket projectile release, cine camera and gyro caging. The radio transmit push-button was also located on the grip. The rudder pedals had two foot positions, while the rudder bar itself was adjustable for different leg lengths via a star-shaped wheel on a sliding tube. Leaving the controls unlocked, particularly in gusty weather, could result in damage to both the surfaces and airframe. To prevent this happening the Seafire inherited the Spitfire's locking system. For the best results, the pilot's seat had to be placed in the highest position, after which two struts located on the right-hand side of the cockpit just behind the seat could be deployed. The longer one was used to lock the control column to the seat and to the starboard datum longeron, while the shorter one was connected to both the long strut and the rudder pedals to lock everything in place.

Trim tabs were mounted on the elevators and rudder. That for the elevator was controlled by a control wheel on the left-hand side of the cockpit. It moved intuitively and there was an indicator on the left-hand side of the instrument panel. Control of the rudder trim tab was exercised via a small hand-wheel just aft of the elevator trim control. Unlike the elevator, there was no indicator for the amount of trim in use but pilots were reminded that

Seen from overhead are the tail-plane, elevator, the rudder and its deflected tab, plus the castoring tail wheel. BBA Collection

The inner and outer view of the tail-plane; that on the right shows the trim tab access panel. Chris Michel

turning the wheel counter-clockwise would move the aircraft to starboard.

Undercarriage Operation

The undercarriage was operated by a selector lever moving in a quadrant mounted on the right-hand side of the cockpit. This had a gate at each end, plus an automatic cut-out coupled to the selector lever, which moved it to the idle position on completion of a retraction cycle. The selector lever was also coupled via chains and sprockets to the undercarriage locks, which were disengaged by direct action of the lever. This also closed the automatic cut-out. Before selecting undercarriage up

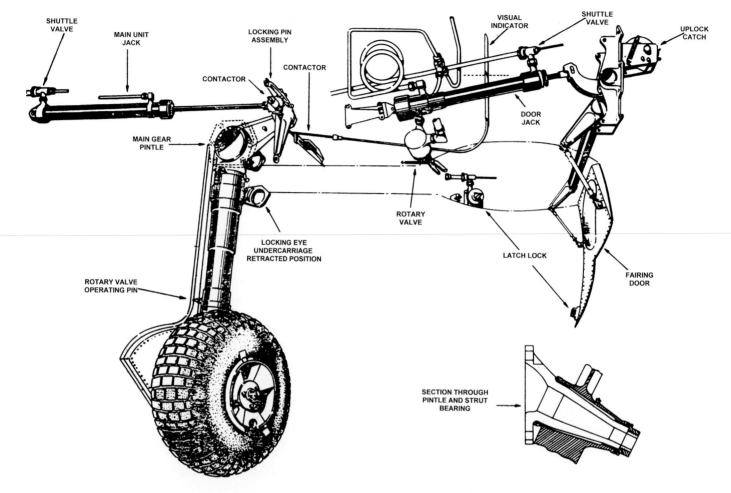

When the Seafire 40 series was developed it was decided to add fairing doors to cover the wheels, resulting in a more complex undercarriage operating system. FAAM Yeovilton

or down it was imperative that the hydraulic system was delivering the required pressure to relieve the locks of the weight of undercarriage legs. If not, the locks could be difficult to withdraw, causing the selector lever to jam. Raising the undercarriage required the lever to be moved downwards to disengage it from the slot. It was then moved inwards and through the gate to allowed full movement through the quadrant. At the end of its travel the lever had to move outwards through the upper gate.

When the undercarriage was up and locked the lever would automatically spring back into the upper slot. Lowering the undercarriage required the lever to be held forward for two seconds after which it could be moved through the upper gate then backwards in one smooth movement. The lever then needed to be moved outwards through the lower gate. When it was released, and the undercarriage was down

and locked, the lever automatically sprang into the lower slot. An indicator in the quadrant showed whether the undercarriage was in the down, idle or up position, depending on the position of the hydraulic valve. 'Up' or 'Down' was only shown when the undercarriage was making the appropriate movement; 'idle' was shown when the lever was in either slot at the end of the quadrant. When the aircraft was parked, it was possible for the indicator to show 'down', although once the engine was started the lever would return to 'idle'. Should this not happen it was possible that the engine-driven hydraulic pump had failed.

Should difficulty be encountered in lowering the undercarriage in flight, the Seafire pilot could operate CO_2 bottles to blow it down. Semi-transparent windows, marked 'up' on a red background, and 'down' on a green one, provided an indi-

cation of undercarriage position. On the Seafire 45 this indicator could be switched on and off by the master switch. In other versions the indicator was energized by use of the ground flight switch. On all three variants there was a secondary indicator light to indicate the position of the tail wheel, although this was restricted to green for down and locked and out when the tail wheel was up and locked. On many variants there was a secondary indicator system, consisting of indicator rods that protruded through the wings when the undercarriage was fully down.

Operating Flaps and Arrester Hook

The split flaps had just two positions, up or down, although they could be set to 18 degrees by spring-loaded pins. Early

The undercarriage unit of a Merlin-powered Spitfire, which was very similar to that of early-build Seafires. Chris Michel

When the Griffon engine was installed, the Seafire required structural strengthening, together with a stronger undercarriage. BBA Collection

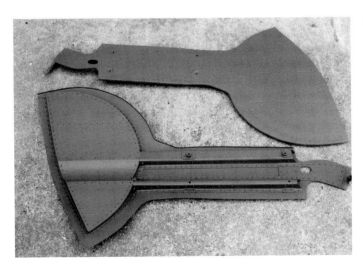

The inside and outside faces of the aircraft's main undercarriage doors, which were attached to the undercarriage legs. Chris Michel

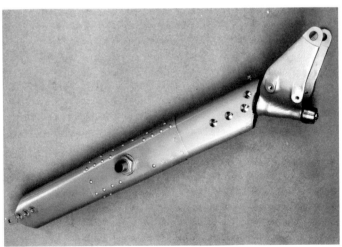

Both fixed and retractable tail-wheel legs shared one characteristic: the fork was designed to castor on the ground for easier manoeuvring. Chris Michel

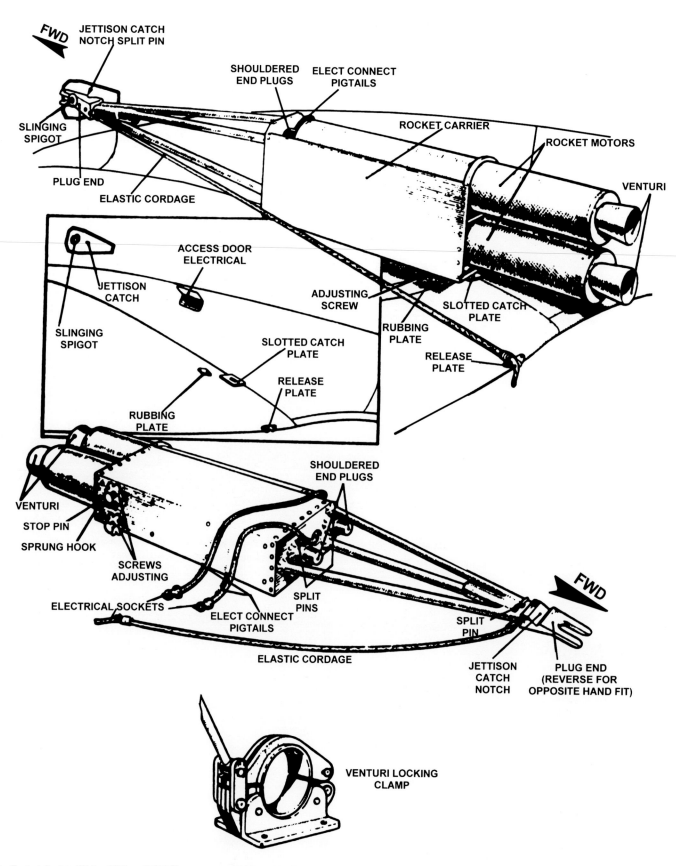

FWD

JETTISON CATCH
NOTCH SPLIT PIN

SHOULDERED
END PLUGS

ELECT CONNECT
PIGTAILS

ROCKET CARRIER

ROCKET MOTORS

VENTURI

SLINGING
SPIGOT

PLUG END

ELASTIC CORDAGE

ACCESS DOOR
ELECTRICAL

JETTISON
CATCH

SLINGING
SPIGOT

ADJUSTING
SCREW

SLOTTED CATCH
PLATE

RUBBING
PLATE

SLOTTED CATCH
PLATE

RELEASE
PLATE

RELEASE
PLATE

RUBBING
PLATE

VENTURI

STOP PIN

SPRUNG HOOK

SCREWS
ADJUSTING

ELECTRICAL SOCKETS

ELECT CONNECT
PIGTAILS

SPLIT
PINS

SHOULDERED
END PLUGS

SPLIT
PIN

FWD

JETTISON
CATCH
NOTCH

PLUG END
(REVERSE FOR
OPPOSITE HAND FIT)

ELASTIC CORDAGE

VENTURI LOCKING
CLAMP

The Rocket-Assisted Take-Off Gear (RATOG) system was developed to lift heavily loaded aircraft off the deck of an aircraft carrier without catapults or for use in cases of catapult failure. Although tested by France's Aeronavale, it was not adopted as it was considered unreliable. FAAM Yeovilton machines utilized the wooden blocks first seen on Merlin-powered Seafires. The flaps were controlled by a three-position lever located on the instrument panel's top left-hand side. This lever was marked 'up', 'air off' and 'down'. After the flaps were lowered the pilot selected 'air off' to cut power to the circuit.

Control of the sting-type arrester hook was via a release handle to the right of the pilot's seat. This had to be pulled upwards by approximately 1.5in (3.8cm) to release the hook. Before ground operation, personnel nearby had to be warned to stay clear as the hook moved with great speed. A green light on the left-hand side of the instrument panel illuminated when the hook was deployed. Pilots, were, however, warned that it might not light up even with the hook out and down until speed was reduced to 110mph (176km/h).

On the Seafire 46 and 47 there was provision for Rocket-Assisted Take-Off Gear (RATOG) with a cockpit-located master switch and push-button. The master switch, fitted with a sliding lock and nut, was located at the bottom of the left-hand side of the instrument panel, while the igniting button was on top of the throttle lever. A 'T'-handle had to be pulled out fully to jettison the RATOG units. Wheel brakes were operated by a control column-mounted lever, which was retained in the 'on' position for parking by a locking clip. A triple pressure gauge fitted to the instrument panel indicated air pressure between zero and the maximum of 300psi (20.6bar). Normal operating pressure was 80psi (5.5bar) and 140psi (9.7bar) after Modification 489.

Griffon Engine Controls

The Griffon engine required numerous controls to manage its performance and behaviour. The combined throttle and mixture control lever operated in a quadrant. Mixture control was fully automatic, which reduced pilot workload. A friction-adjusted lever on the inboard side of the quadrant held the lever in position. Pulling the lever backwards reduced friction but a sudden pull could have the opposite effect. Engine speed was managed via a throttle quadrant-mounted lever, which governed the range between the maximum of 2,750 rpm down to 1,800rpm. A fuel cut-off, used to stop and start the engine, was mounted on the outboard side of the throttle quad-

As the Griffon engine was larger, heavier and more powerful it needed a much stronger support beam, as shown here. BBA Collection

A close-up view of the exhaust stubs of the Griffon engine, plus the fastenings for the cowling panels. BBA Collection

rant. This was spring-loaded and had to be set forward to allow the carburettor to deliver fuel to the engine. Cutting the fuel supply required the lever to be pulled fully back and through the gate to hold the valve shut.

The supercharger was controlled by a switch, which had to be set to 'auto-normal'. The supercharger change gear control was operated by an electro-pneumatic ram, which engaged and disengaged high gear

automatically via an altitude sensor. The alternate switch position for the pilot's switch was 'MS', which kept the supercharger in low gear at all altitudes. The system was also fitted with a test button on the electrical panel. This allowed high gear to be selected during engine run-up; in flight a red warning light illuminated to indicate high gear engagement. The test button only functioned when the supercharger switch was set to 'auto normal'.

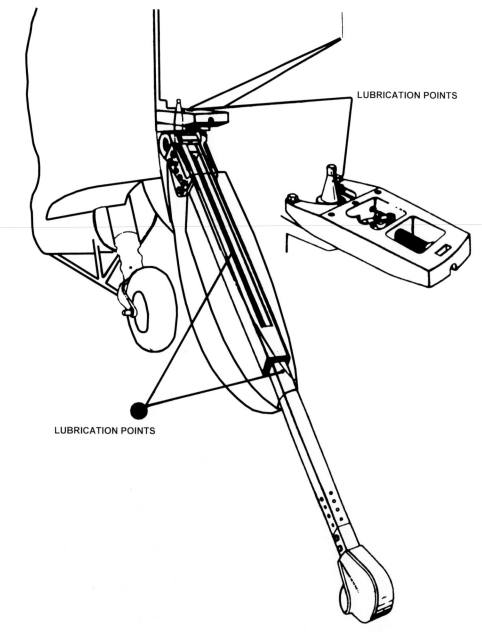

LUBRICATION POINTS

LUBRICATION POINTS

The sting hook and its rudder fairing shown in the fully-down position. In an attempt to reduce the damage caused to aircraft with 'A'-frame hooks, the sting-type was given some lateral movement. BBA Collection

Canopy Operation

On the Seafire 45 the cockpit hood was operated by a hand-grip on the canopy itself, while that on the Mks 46 and 47 was opened by a crank handle on the right-hand cockpit wall. This crank had to be pulled towards the pilot before it could be operated. It allowed for intermediate positions because releasing the handle permitted the ratchet to engage the drive mechanism. Should the handle fail to engage it had to be rocked backwards and forwards until the mechanism engaged. Before take-off and landing the canopy handle had to be in the locked position to prevent inadvertent movement of what was a heavy assembly. Opening the canopy from outside was done via a push-button mounted just under the starboard hood rail. This disengaged the lock and allowed the canopy to run freely.

On all three variants the cockpit access door had a two-position catch, which set it partly open and prevented the canopy from closing completely. This was operated as a safety measure for take-off and landing. As the Seafire 46 and 47 featured a drive mechanism, care had to be taken when winding the canopy shut to ensure that the access door was properly shut. If not, the canopy could become jammed or even derailed. Keeping the door in the interim position was highly recommended for emergency landings, to enable the pilot to leave the aircraft as quickly as possible.

Final-build Seafires included a windscreen de-icer with a fluid reservoir located on the lower right-hand side of the cockpit. This system also required a control cock, pump and needle valve to control the flow of the fluid, which was pumped as a spray to the base of the windscreen, even distribution relying on the passing airflow. To prevent inadvertent operation, the plunger was locked down by a catch, with the operating cock returned to the off position.

Weapons Operation

The Seafire's guns were fired pneumatically by a selective push-button mounted on the control column spade grip. On the Seafire 45, pressing the upper section of this button fired the outboard guns, pressure on the lower section selected the inboard guns, while pressing the centre resulted in the discharge of all four. With the introduction of the Seafire 46 and 47 the upper section

Supercharger cooling was achieved by an intercooler radiator mounted ahead of the coolant radiator under the port wing. The carburettor air intake filter prevented the engine from ingesting foreign objects and was operated by a lever with two positions: 'normal intake' and 'filter intake'. This lever was mounted on the left-hand side of the cockpit forward of the elevator trim tab control. The 'filter' selection was for ground running, take-off and landing and when operating in sandy or dust-laden conditions.

The starter button was mounted just above the main fuel cock and was shielded to prevent inadvertent operation. When pressed, this button not only ignited the starter cartridge but also energized the booster coil. Five starter cartridges were provided and selecting a fresh one required careful operation of the re-indexing control at the bottom right-hand corner of the instrument panel. There was one cockpit light on either side, controlled by dimmer switches in the centre of the instrument panel.

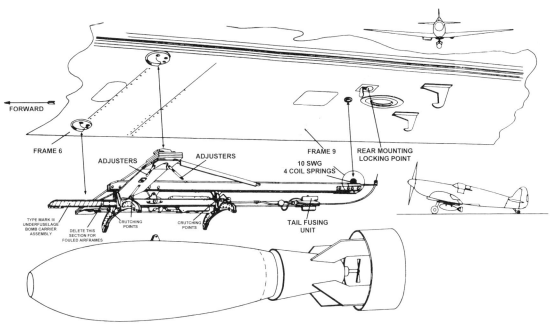

FORWARD

FRAME 6

ADJUSTERS   ADJUSTERS   FRAME 9   REAR MOUNTING
                                      10 SWG   LOCKING POINT
                                      4 COIL SPRINGS

TYPE MARK III
UNDERFUSELAGE
BOMB CARRIER   CRUTCHING   CRUTCHING   TAIL FUSING
ASSEMBLY   POINTS   POINTS   UNIT
          DELETE THIS
          SECTION FOR
          FOULED AIRFRAMES

Both Supermarine and the operators were aware that the Spitfire and Seafire needed increased capability. Centreline and under-wing bomb mountings were developed as a result. The centreline mounting also featured plumbing for an external fuel tank, which increased the type's range. FAAM Yeovilton

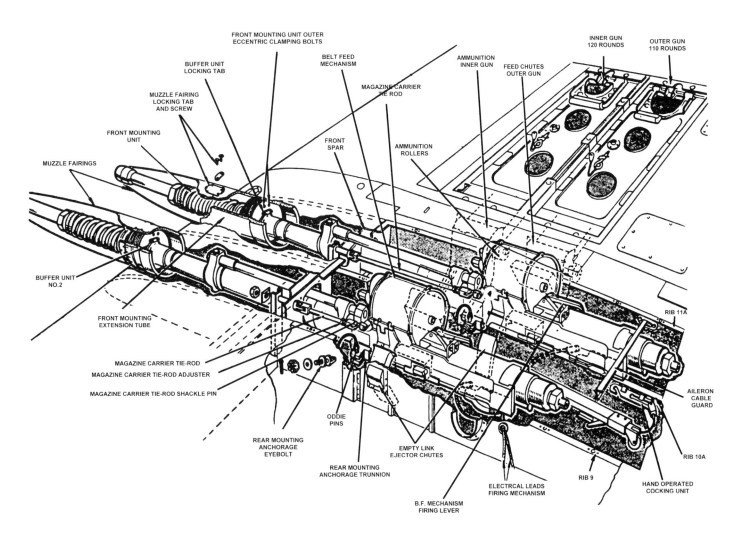

FRONT MOUNTING UNIT OUTER
ECCENTRIC CLAMPING BOLTS

BUFFER UNIT
LOCKING TAB

BELT FEED
MECHANISM

MUZZLE FAIRING
LOCKING TAB
AND SCREW

MAGAZINE CARRIER
TIE ROD

AMMUNITION
INNER GUN

FEED CHUTES
OUTER GUN

INNER GUN
120 ROUNDS

OUTER GUN
110 ROUNDS

FRONT MOUNTING
UNIT

FRONT
SPAR

AMMUNITION
ROLLERS

MUZZLE FAIRINGS

BUFFER UNIT
NO.2

FRONT MOUNTING
EXTENSION TUBE

MAGAZINE CARRIER TIE-ROD

MAGAZINE CARRIER TIE-ROD ADJUSTER

MAGAZINE CARRIER TIE-ROD SHACKLE PIN

RIB 11A

AILERON
CABLE
GUARD

ODDIE
PINS

REAR MOUNTING
ANCHORAGE
EYEBOLT

REAR MOUNTING
ANCHORAGE TRUNNION

EMPTY LINK
EJECTOR CHUTES

ELECTRCAL LEADS
FIRING MECHANISM

RIB 9

RIB 10A

HAND OPERATED
COCKING UNIT

B.F. MECHANISM
FIRING LEVER

This diagram illustrates the layout of the wing cannon, together with ammunition feeds and ejectors in the wings of later Seafire variants. FAAM Yeovilton

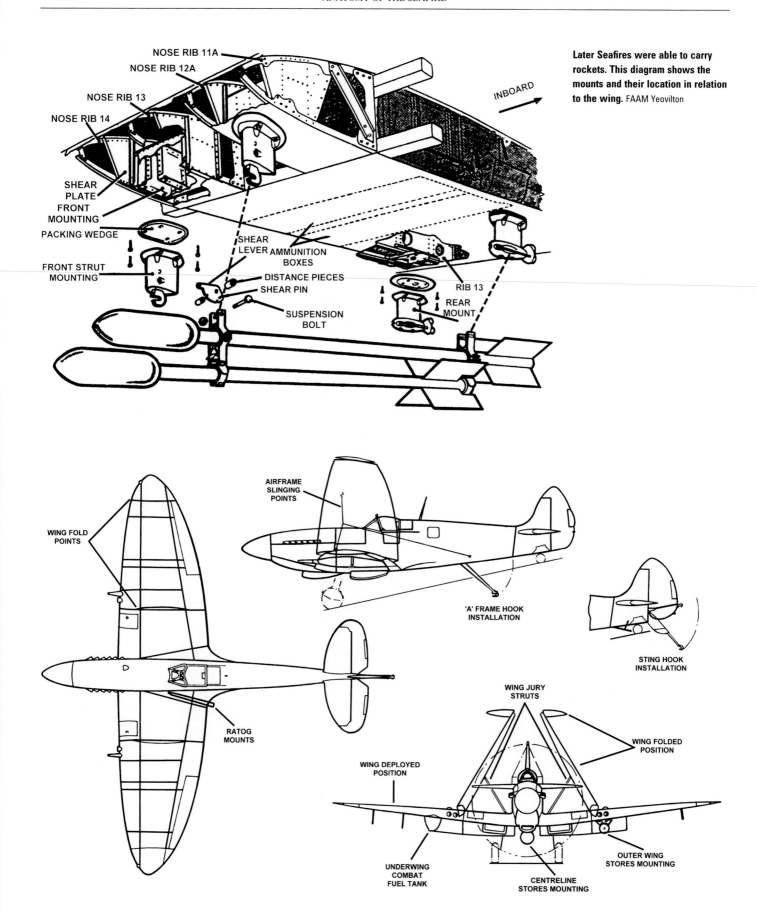

NOSE RIB 11A
NOSE RIB 12A
NOSE RIB 13
NOSE RIB 14

SHEAR
PLATE
FRONT
MOUNTING
PACKING WEDGE

FRONT STRUT
MOUNTING

SHEAR
LEVER
DISTANCE PIECES
SHEAR PIN

SUSPENSION
BOLT

AMMUNITION
BOXES

RIB 13
REAR
MOUNT

INBOARD

Later Seafires were able to carry rockets. This diagram shows the mounts and their location in relation to the wing. FAAM Yeovilton

WING FOLD
POINTS

AIRFRAME
SLINGING
POINTS

'A' FRAME HOOK
INSTALLATION

STING HOOK
INSTALLATION

RATOG
MOUNTS

WING JURY
STRUTS

WING DEPLOYED
POSITION

WING FOLDED
POSITION

UNDERWING
COMBAT
FUEL TANK

CENTRELINE
STORES MOUNTING

OUTER WING
STORES MOUNTING

This diagram illustrates the Seafire XV's wing fold arrangement, supporting struts, arrester hooks, fuel tank locations and RATOG mounts. BBA Collection

fired all four guns, while the lower section either released bombs or fired the rocket projectiles. Bomb controls included the distributor, fusing and selector switches, which were mounted on the left-hand side of the cockpit, just forward of the door. In the Seafire 45, bomb release was achieved by pressing a button mounted on the top of the throttle lever.

In the Seafire 46 and 47 the throttle button was used for RATOG ignition, while the bomb release was moved to the spade grip. The rocket projectile controls also released the bombs. There was a master switch with others for auto selection, pairs salvo and firing control. When the master switch was set to 'RP' and the pairs salvo set to 'pairs', operation of the firing switch launched the rockets in pairs. When the switch was set to 'salvo' and the selector set to '1' or '3', pressing the switch fired the bottom rack of rockets. With the selector then set to '2' or '4', the top tier of rockets could be fired.

Weapons were aimed by a ranging gyro gunsight, the control for which was incorporated into the top of the throttle lever. The gunsight master switch was located on the bottom left-hand corner of the instrument panel, while the gunsight dimmer switch was on the right-hand cockpit wall. On the Seafire 46 and 47, the control to enable the sight to be used for aiming the rockets was mounted just ahead of the bomb control panel. The push-button for caging the gunsight during violent manoeuvres likely to cause toppling was mounted on the control column spade grip.

A cine camera was mounted in the leading edge of the starboard wing. On some Seafire 45s it was operated by pressing either the top or bottom of the gun firing push-button. On later aircraft control was via a separate spade-grip mounted push-button. On the Mk 46 and Mk 47 aircraft the cine camera was operated either by pressing the top half of the gun-firing button or by a control panel push-button. To enable them to operate in the photo-reconnaissance role, both the Seafire 46 and 47 could be equipped with vertical and oblique cameras. Operating switches were located on the forward part of the bomb-control panel. The vertical camera was protected against mud splashes by a panel that could be jettisoned after take-off.

Repairing Damaged Airframes

As the Seafire displayed a propensity for nose-down crash-landings on carrier flight decks, there had to be a procedure for dealing with damaged aircraft. Airframes that could be reclaimed were assigned a repair category as follows:

- Cat A: capable of being repaired by operating unit
- Cat AC: beyond local repair
- Cat B: requires transfer to repair unit.

Further categories were:

- Cat C: relegate to ground instruction
- Cat E: write off
- Cat E2: suitable for scrapping.

At sea, aircraft in the last category were summarily dealt with. The remains were simply manhandled to the side of the ship and dumped overboard.

CHAPTER SIX

Flying the Seafire

As the earliest versions of the Supermarine Seafire were based on the same company's Spitfire Mk V, the aircraft were hardly unknown quantities when they entered service with the Fleet Air Arm. As a result of the early development, the Merlin-powered Seafires were considered to be generally stable in flight about all axes.

These variants, the Mk IB, Mk IIC and the Mk III, were powered by versions of the Rolls-Royce Merlin, which included the 45, 45M, 46, 50, 50A, 50M.55 and 55M, all of which burned 100 octane fuel. Performance was similar whatever the powerplant. This meant that the maximum take-off power-setting to climb to 1,000ft (300m) was 3,000rpm with boost set at plus-12psi (0.8bar). This was reduced to plus-9psi (0.6bar) and 2,850rpm at maximum climb rate, while a further reduction to plus-7 (0.5bar) and 2,650rpm was available at maximum rich continuous setting. Should the engine be run at the weak setting, the boost was reduced to plus-4psi (0.3bar). Combat settings, limited to five-minute bursts, allowed for a maximum of 3,000rpm at plus-16psi (1.1bar), which was raised to plus-18psi (1.2bar) for 'M'-suffixed power-plants. The lower limit for combat boost was 2,850rpm.

Engine oil temperatures had to be monitored throughout the flight envelope. The average of 90°C increased to 105°C in combat. Coolant temperatures also varied. At maximum climb it reached 125°C, falling to 105°C at continuous settings, although this could rise to 115°C for short periods. In combat mode it increased again to 135°C. Before take-off, engine oil temperature had to be at least 15°C with coolant at 60°C. The normal range for engine oil pressure was between 60 and 80psi (4.1 to 5.5bar), with a minimum for safe flying of 45psi (3.1bar).

Fuel System Management

Fuel system pressure had to between 8 and 10psi (0.6 and 0.7bar). Other system requirements included maintaining straight

This view of the cockpit through the entrance door shows the compass, gunsight and seat straps wrapped around the control column. Chris Michel

and level flight with a 90gal (409ltr) external tank attached. This restriction did not apply to the 30gal (136ltr) tank. The Seafire could also carry 170gal (773ltr) tanks as well as smaller ones containing just 29gal (132ltr), one of which could be slung under each wing. In either case, straight and level flight had to be maintained when they were attached.

Pilots were warned not to select the rear fuselage tank and the external tank to 'on' simultaneously because this could allow air to be drawn into the fuel system. This restriction applied even after the external tank had been jettisoned as, when left open, the external connection could act as an efficient fuel venting system. The bulky 170gal container could only be jettisoned in straight and level flight, but there was no such restriction covering the smaller under-wing tanks. With external tanks of any size fitted, the aircraft had to be started, warmed up and lifted off to a safe height of approximately 2,000ft (600m) before the main tanks could be switched off and the external ones selected. With the 170gal tank, the Seafire was limited to an indicated airspeed (IAS) of 185mph (296km/h) level flight, which decreased to 170mph (272km/h) when it was empty.

Once the external tanks were empty the engine would start cutting out, at which point the rear fuselage tank had to be selected. At this point the pilot faced two choices. Should maximum range be required, the external tank had to be jettisoned at once, but if needed for further use the pilot had to be aware that still-air range was reduced by 120 miles (190km). Under certain circumstances the external tank had to be jettisoned before it was fully empty. The drill then was to select main tanks 'on' before switching the external one to 'off' and jettisoning it. The rear fuel tank could be selected when needed. Once it was empty the engine would cough slightly, at which point the pilot was advised to switch to the main fuel system.

The tank contents and fuel consumption had to be carefully monitored to wring the most out of the limited capacity. Internal fuel capacity was 75gal (340ltr), 48gal (218ltr) in the top tank and 37gal (168ltr) in the bottom one. This could be increased to 175gal (796ltr). Additional internal (90gal/409ltr) and external (30gal/136ltr and 170gal/773ltr) tanks took the total to 284gal (1,290ltr). Varying the fuel loads also meant changes to the quantity of engine lubricant carried. With the two normal internal tanks full, 5.8gal (26ltr) of oil was usually sufficient. This was raised to 8.5gal (39ltr) with an additional 90gal (409ltr) of fuel or 14.5gal (66ltr) of oil with maximum fuel.

Fuel consumption varied depending on mixture settings. Rich mixture at 3,000rpm with boost at plus-9psi (0.6bar) resulted in a rate of 88gal (400ltr) per hour. With the power reduced to 2,850 rpm at the same boost setting, it dropped to 84gal (382ltr) per hour. At 2,650rpm with plus-7psi (0.5bar) boost, consumption fell to 67gal (305ltr) per hour. Pilots were warned that these values applied to straight and level flying. Where appropriate, weak mixture settings covered the range between plus and minus 4psi (0.28bar) at heights from 6,000 to 20,000ft (1,850 and 6,150m). When flying at minus 4psi boost at 650, 2,400, 2,200, 2,000 and 1,800rpm, consumption was 39, 36, 34, 31 and 26gal (177, 164, 155, 141 and 118ltr) per hour respectively. At minus 2psi (0.1bar) boost at the same rpm boost settings, fuel consumption rose to 43, 40, 38, 35 and 31gal (195, 182, 173, 159 and 141ltr) respectively. At zero boost settings using the same rpm settings, consumption rose to 47, 44, 42, 39 and 35gal (214, 200, 191, 177, 159 and 141ltr), while at plus-2psi boost it increased to 51, 48, 46, 43 and 39gal (232, 218, 209, 195 and 177ltr). The final setting of plus-4psi at the same power took consumption to 56, 53, 51, 47 and 43gal (255, 241, 232, 214 and 195ltr) per hour.

Having been initiated into the complexity of the fuel system, the novice pilot then had to master engine handling and management. Before starting, the fuel cock levers had to be set to 'on', the throttle to 0.5in (1.3cm) open, the propeller speed control to 'fully back' if a de Havilland unit was fitted or 'fully forward' for Rotol or de Havilland Hydromatic units. Radiator shutter setting was 'open'.

Starting the Engine

In very cold weather, pilots were recommended to use high volatility fuel for priming. The hand-operated primer had to be pumped until an increase in resistance was felt. This confirmed that the suction and delivery pipelines were full of fuel. The ignition and starting magneto, if fitted, were turned on before the starter and coil buttons, again if fitted, were pressed. Each starting cycle was to last no more than twenty seconds, with an interval of thirty seconds between each attempt.

During the starting cycle the pilot was expected to work the priming pump as rapidly and as vigorously as possible. The recommended number of strokes was four at a temperature of 0°C with high volatility fuel or twelve for normal high octane fuel. Standard fuel could not be used at minus 10°C and below. As the temperature dropped, the number of priming strokes increased. In low temperatures it was recommended that the pump be operated until fuel reached the carburettor. Once the engine was running the booster coil button – or the starting magneto switch as appropriate – was released and the priming pump screwed down. The engine was run as slowly as possible for half a minute, after which power could be set to fast tick-over to warm it up. With aircraft fitted with de Havilland 20-degree propeller units, the propeller speed control had to be pushed fully forward after a minute's running.

During ground running, the canopy always had to be locked fully open with the access door handle set at half cocked and the brakes applied with pressure maintained at 120psi (8.3bar). After warm-up was complete it was recommended that the aircraft's tail be held down by two men before the throttle was advanced. The first operational engine test required the boost setting be at 'weak', after which the propeller pitch-change mechanism could be cycled and the throttle opened fully to check take-off boost and rpm. With rich mixture selected it was time to check each magneto in turn. Magneto drop should not exceed 150rpm.

To ensure maximum range, the boost setting in climb had to be at plus-9psi (0.6bar) at 2,850rpm with the mixture set to rich, if appropriate. To attain maximum range, pilots were instructed to balance height and speed, so that below 8,000ft (2,500m) indicated airspeed should be close to 160kt (180mph or 288km/h). From there to 15,000ft (4,600m) speed dropped to 142kt (160mph or 255km/h), while above this height speed declined to 133kt (150mph or 240kph). At low altitudes the speed could be raised to 178kt (200mph or 320kph) without detriment to fuel consumption. Where a mixture control was fitted, a weak setting was recommended with boost at plus-4psi (0.28bar), as richness increased automatically. Engine speed could be reduced to around 1,800rpm to maintain the desired velocity, although pilots were instructed to ensure the generator was charging correctly. Should speed increase beyond 1,800rpm, they were advised to reduce boost and cut speed to the desired limit.

If speed decayed drastically the aircraft would stall. At this point, one wing dropped, irrespective of flap position. If the pilot attempted to recover by pulling the control column back, the Seafire would spin. Stalling could also occur during a steep climb or during a looping manoeuvre; a high-speed stall could be induced as a result of elevator sensitivity. When this happened the entire aircraft would shudder violently and there would be a clattering noise. This would be followed by a lateral flick. Should the pilot not instantly put the control column fully forward, the aircraft would enter a rapid roll from which a spin could result.

Pilots had to remember a set pre-take-off drill: 'TMP'. 'T' stood for trimming tabs, which required the elevator to be set to one division down with the rudder trimmed to starboard. 'M' meant mixture control: rich, if appropriate. 'P' stood for propeller speed control: fully forward. For take-offs from land, the flaps were to be 'up' and the radiator flap 'fully open'. At the end of the runway, or on the flight-deck, the pilot had to open the throttle slowly to the rated boost position.

After brake release any tendency for the Seafire to swing was countered by application of coarse rudder. Should the aircraft be leaving a short runway, or with a full load of fuel and weapons, the throttle had to be pushed through the gate to take-off boost. Once airborne, the undercarriage was raised using the selector lever. Pilots were instructed to hold it hard against the quadrant until the indicators confirmed that the undercarriage was up and locked. Until the aircraft had reached 124kt (140mph or 224km/h) the Seafire was allowed to ascend slowly before entering any period of sustained climb.

During climb from sea level to 10,000ft, (3,000m), Merlin Seafires were not to exceed 150kt (170mph or 272km/h), while between there and 16,000ft (5,000m) the not-to-exceed speed was 140kt (160mph or 250km/h). Between 16,000 and 21,000ft (6,500m) this value reduced to 130kt (150mph or 240km/h). From that altitude to 37,000ft (11,000m) the speed reduced by 9kt (10mph or 16km/h) per 5,000ft (1,500m) increment. Above 37,000ft maximum climb speed was not to exceed 100kt (115mph or 180km/h).

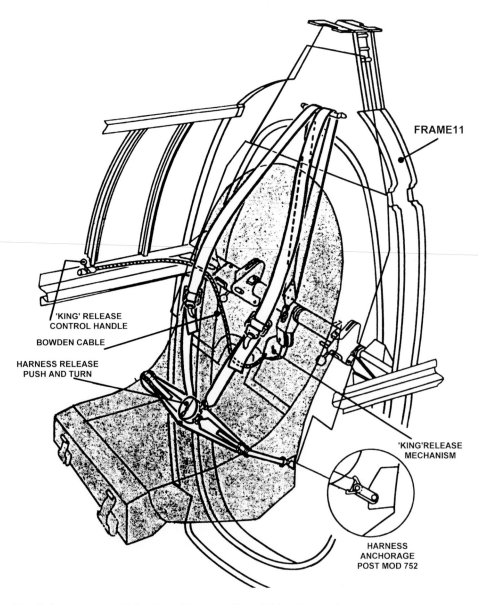

FRAME11

'KING' RELEASE
CONTROL HANDLE

BOWDEN CABLE

HARNESS RELEASE
PUSH AND TURN

'KING'RELEASE
MECHANISM

HARNESS
ANCHORAGE
POST MOD 752

The pilot's seat was mounted on frame 11, as were the restraining straps and release mechanism. FAAM Yeovilton

With the canopy open and the door set at the recommended half-cocked position, this Seafire IB leaves for another sortie. Will Blunt Collection

In normal flight it was recommended that the radiator shutter be kept in the minimum drag position. When the aircraft was prepared for landing with undercarriage and flaps down, there was a markedly nose-down trim change. During the landing phase at a loading of 6,400lb (2,900kg) the stalling speed with everything retracted was 65kt (73mph or 117km/h); with everything out and down, speed dropped to 57kt (64mph or 102km/h). Should the pilot be forced to make a power-off landing, the propeller speed control had to be pulled right back and the radiator flap set to the minimum drag position. Both actions were required to increase gliding distance. During combat manoeuvres, on the other hand, pilots were advised to use climb rpm to cover any sudden power requirements. The Seafire's maximum diving speed was 400kt (450mph or 720km/h), while at the other end of the range, speed with undercarriage lowered was limited to 140kt (160mph or

MB141 took part in RATOG trials at Farnborough. These tests cleared the system for ship-board use and MB141 participated in further trials. FAAM Yeovilton

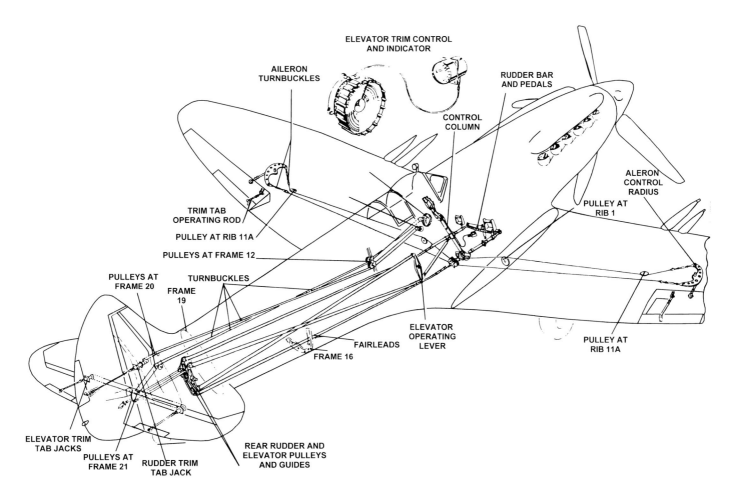

This diagram shows the flight controls and their associated runs, together with the turnbuckles and supporting fairleads. Eric Morgan Collection

The deck parties are working flat out to spread the wings of these Seafires before a sortie. Note the support struts still lying on the wings. BBA Collection

250km/h). This was similar to the flaps-down limit, although it fell by 18kt (20mph or 13km/h) if landing lights were extended.

Performing Aerobatics

Spinning was permitted with written permission from the squadron commander or chief flying instructor. Pilots were warned not to start a spin below 10,000ft (3,000m) and that recovery had to begin above 5,000ft (1,500m). Speed had to be above 130kt (150mph or 240km/h) before recovery was initiated. Aerobatic limitations included looping, which required an entry speed of 260kt (300mph or 480km/h) for inexperienced pilots. This could fall to 220kt (250mph or 400km/h) for those more experienced. Rolling could be undertaken between 200kt (180mph or 290km/h) and 260kt (300mph or 480km/h). During rolls the nose had to be kept at approximately 30 degrees above the horizon. The manoeuvre itself required the roll to be barrelled to keep the engine running. When undertaking a half roll off a loop, the entry

speed had to be kept between 280kt (320mph or 510km/h) and 310kt (350mph or 560km/h). An increase to 400mph was required for an upward roll, but pilots were warned that flick manoeuvres were not to be undertaken under any circumstances.

Diving

Because the Seafire became tail-heavy in a dive as speed increased, the aircraft had to be trimmed before the nose was pushed over to avoid any risk of excessive speed in recovery. Once the dive had been completed and speed was decaying after pull-out, forward trim was wound back. As the aircraft exhibited a tendency to yaw to the right, correction had to be applied by application of the rudder trim tab.

Approach and Landing

The approach and landing called for serious thought by Seafire pilots. The first actions during the approach involved opening the

cockpit canopy fully and setting the handle on the cockpit side door to half cocked. Pilots were recommended never to put their arms out of the cockpit and into the airflow. With early airframes speed had to be reduced to 120kt (140mph or 220km/h), after which the landing mnemonic had to be applied. First came 'U' for undercarriage, which had to be selected 'down' and confirmed in the locked position via the indicators and green lights. This was followed by 'M' for mixture control: set to 'rich', but only if the appropriate control was fitted. 'P' indicated that the propeller control had to be placed fully forward. The final action in this sequence was to select flaps 'down'.

During the approach with flaps down and the engine running, the minimum speed was 120kt (85mph or 136km/h). This increased to 85kt (95mph or 150km/h) with flaps up. In a glide approach, speed was to be held between 80kt (95mph or 144km/h) and 90kt (100mph or 160km/h) with flaps up. When the pilot was ready, the undercarriage could be lowered, the operating lever having been pushed fully forward for about two seconds to allow the weight to be eased from the locking pins. This would allow them to turn freely when the lever was pulled back – smartly to the down position and left there – to select 'undercarriage down'. The lever was not to be forced through the gate because, when it had completed its full range of travel, the undercarriage would spring the lever through the gate. The hydraulic valve indicator would then return to the idle position.

If the undercarriage lever would not go all the way through the gate, it had to be pushed forward for two seconds, which was normally enough to release the locking pins. A smart blow usually freed a jammed lever. If not, more drastic action was needed and pilots were recommended to put the aircraft into a dive and invert it. It was possible for the undercarriage to appear down and locked but without the green indicator light being illuminated. In such cases the recommended action was to hold the lever fully back for a few seconds. Should this action fail, the undercarriage had to be cycled again. The last resort was the emergency blow-down system. This required the selector lever to be in the 'down' position with the aircraft in a nose-down attitude or even inverted to free the locking pins.

Lowering the Undercarriage

Pilots were warned that lowering the undercarriage too late during the approach could result in insufficient engine speed to drive the hydraulic operating pump. This would prevent the lever moving through the gate into the fully down and locked position. With the lever outside the gate, there was a risk that the undercarriage would collapse on landing. If the lever had not passed through the gate, it was necessary to go-around and attempt another landing, the required speed being 105kt (120mph or 190km/h). This was also the speed for landing in low visibility with flaps lowered. The radiator shutter was to be fully open to keep engine coolant temperature at 100°C, while the propeller speed had to be set to cruising rpm.

Flaps were raised before the aircraft was taxied to its designated parking spot. With those fitted with the de Havilland 20-degree propeller unit, the speed control had to be pulled fully back while the engine was revved sufficiently to change pitch to coarse. With the aircraft parked the engine was to be run at 800 to 900rpm for approximately two minutes, after which the slow running

Having made a successful trap, this Seafire XVII will run out to the end of its landing before being disconnected from the arrester wire. FAAM Yeovilton

cut-out was pulled and held until the engine stopped. The fuel cocks and ignition were then turned off.

After ground school and Operational Training Unit, novice pilots were then required to undergo flying training from a training carrier. Here an additional set of actions was required. Before take-off pilots were instructed to avoid warming the engine up for prolonged periods as radiator temperature was not allowed to exceed 100°C. Once lined up for take-off, pilots were instructed to lower the flaps to 18 degrees, if the Seafire had been subject to Modification 63, or otherwise fully. Ground crew then had to insert shaped wooden blocks between the wing and the flap, after which the flaps were raised to grip the block. When the aircraft was safely in level flight, the flaps were fully lowered to release the blocks, then raised fully up.

Before landing-on, pilots were instructed to reduce speed to 125kt (140mph or 225km/h) and deploy the arrester hook. At this point the radiator light indicator had to be checked for a green light. With aircraft flying with others, pilots were asked to check that their formation mates had also deployed their hooks. With all checks completed the cockpit canopy had to be locked open, the access door handle set to partly cocked with brake pressure at a minimum of 120psi (8.3bar). Vital pre-landing drills involved 'U' for undercarriage

down and locked, 'P' for propeller control – fully forward – hook down and green light illuminated, and flaps down. Approach speed was 70kt (80mph or 130km/h), reducing to 65kt (75mph or 120km/h) on final approach. The nose had to be kept high and, to keep the flight deck in sight, the aircraft had to be crabbed slightly from side to side. Just before touch-down it was straightened up to avoid excessive strain on the main undercarriage mountings.

For catapult launches the cockpit canopy had to be locked open and pilots were advised to hold their heads firmly back against the headrest. The vital drills were 'T' for trim tabs, elevator neutral and rudder fully to starboard; 'P' for propeller control – fully forward – fuel cock lever 'on' and bottom tank contents checked; the flaps fully up and radiator flap fully open. The control column then had to be held centrally and the rudder bar moved about one-third of the way to starboard. To counter any tendency to swing, coarse rudder was recommended.

Ditching

In the event of major trouble, pilots were advised to take to their parachutes. If this was not possible and ditching was inevitable, the first action was to jettison long-range fuel tanks, which had to be done

during straight and level flight. Flaps were set fully down to reduce speed, but pilots were warned not to attempt a ditching unless the undercarriage was fully retracted. If the engine was still running, power was to be applied to help force the tail down, while keeping speed as low as possible. The canopy had to be jettisoned and pilots were strongly advised to adjust their straps as tightly as possible to minimize impact injuries. Finally, it was recommended that the aircraft be set down along the swell. In the case of Mk III Seafires, the only Merlin-powered variants with folding wings, there were additional pre-ditching checks. Pilots had to ensure that the wings were properly spread and locked and that the small access doors under each wingtip were similarly secured. The round red indicator rod mounted just inboard of the main wing fold joint had to be checked to ensure it was flush with the wing upper surface.

With a fully-raised tail trestle in position, BL687's arrester hook can be fully extended. It was recommended that all personnel stay well clear during this operation. FAAM Yeovilton

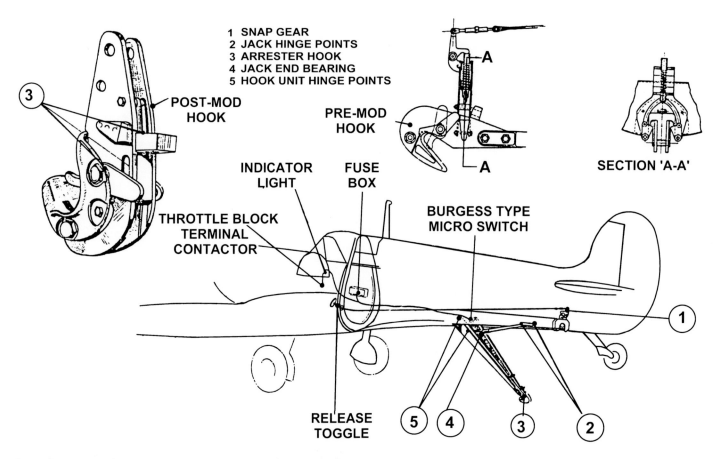

1 SNAP GEAR
2 JACK HINGE POINTS
3 ARRESTER HOOK
4 JACK END BEARING
5 HOOK UNIT HINGE POINTS

POST-MOD HOOK

PRE-MOD HOOK

SECTION 'A-A'

INDICATOR LIGHT

FUSE BOX

BURGESS TYPE MICRO SWITCH

THROTTLE BLOCK TERMINAL CONTACTOR

RELEASE TOGGLE

The 'A'-Frame arrester hook, together with the operating switch and mechanism. BBA Collection

Griffon Seafires

Although they shared the same parentage as the Merlin-powered aircraft, the Griffon Seafires differed considerably. Only three versions of the final Seafire family were built and each differed from the others in many ways. The Mk 45, powered by a Griffon 61 driving a five-bladed Rotol propeller, had a high-backed fuselage, non-folding wings and a 12-volt DC electrical system. The F.46 and FR.46 had a Griffon 87 driving a six-bladed contra-rotating unit, a modified fuel system with added plumbing for external fuel tanks, and an electrical system up-rated to 24-volts DC. The rear fuselage was cut down for better pilot vision, while an enlarged tail unit improved stability and handling. The F.47 and FR.47 were similar to the F.46 except that their wings could be folded for carrier stowage. In the first batch of aircraft, the wings had to be folded manually, but most featured a hydraulically powered mechanism. The final two variants were capable of using RATOG gear and, although only the Seafire 47 was designed for carrier operation, all had sting-type arrester hooks.

With 40-series Seafires, pilots were advised to take great care in managing the fuel system. For the F.45 the tank use sequence began with the pilot ensuring that the engine was started using the lower tank. The fuel transfer cock had to be set at 'normal' to ensure that the contents of the upper tank would feed into the lower one. This was the preferred selection for take-off and the initial climb-out. During this phase the booster pump had to be switched on for take-off and landing. This also had to be done during tank switch-over, when the fuel pressure warning light illuminated or when there were signs of fuel starvation. The booster pump also had to selected to 'on' when the aircraft was climbing to higher altitude. It was not to be operated on the ground unless the fuel cut-off switch was in the 'cut off' position, because there was a risk of the engine being flooded and even of fire.

Fuel System Management

Once the upper fuel tank contents had dropped into the red it had to be switched off and wing tanks selected. After five minutes the selector had to be returned to the normal position, and the next pair of wing tanks selected for another five minutes. The selector could then be returned to normal. If these actions were not taken the main wing tanks would not pressurize correctly. When an external fuel tank was carried, change-over from the lower fuselage tank was to be done at a safe height. At that point, the drop tank cock had to be selected to 'on' with all other fuel cocks and the booster pump set to 'off'. There was a possibility of delay in fuel reaching the engine as the external tank emptied, and this required the lower fuselage tank cock to be turned on before the external tank cock was switched off.

Fuel system management in the Seafire 46 and 47 required the engine to be started using fuel from the lower fuselage tank.

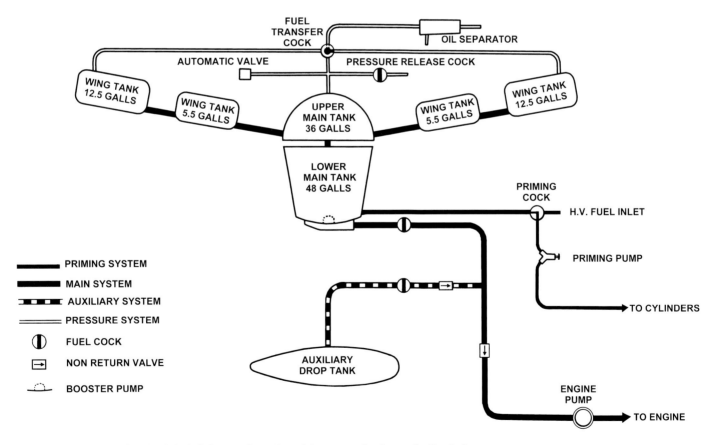

Layout of a late-build Seafire. As this included extra wing tanks and, later, a rear fuselage tank, pilots had to be aware of the need to manage their fuel with care. BBA Collection

Caution was needed when the rear fuselage tank booster pump was selected to 'on' as the lower fuselage tank cock had to be 'off'. It was possible for fuel from the rear tank to be pumped into the lower one, which could cause excess fuel to be vented. Pilots had to be aware that fuel in the rear tank had to be used as soon as possible to avoid adverse movement of the aircraft's centre of gravity. Despite this warning, use of the lower fuselage tank for starting and take-off was mandatory to cope with carburettor spill-back in the upper tank.

Should the rear fuselage tank not be in use, the fuel transfer cock had to be set to 'wing tanks' to allow fuel from the wings to feed into the upper fuselage tank. This selection sequence was supposed to continue until the main fuel contents gauge indicated 70gal (318ltr), which meant the wing tanks were drained of usable fuel. The pilot then switched the selector cock to 'normal'. When the rear fuselage tank was full, the start and take-off sequence was normal. Once a safe height had been reached, the rear tank cock was set to 'on' with that for the lower one set to 'off'. To ensure that fuel from the rear tank was fed to the engine, the booster switch had to be set to 'on'. When the fuel tank was virtually empty, the process had to be reversed to allow fuel to flow from the wing and fuselage tanks as normal. When the aircraft was fitted with wing combat tanks and full wing and fuselage tanks, the operating sequence was to use the rear one first, then the external tanks, followed by the upper and lower fuselage tanks.

Before entering the cockpit, pilots were required to make the usual external checks, paying special attention to the arrester hook, which had to be fully retracted. On Seafire 45 aircraft only the hood jettison pins had to be fully home. In the cockpit, pilots had to check that the gun firing button was set to 'safe', the bomb master switch was 'off' and, on Seafire 46 and 47 aircraft, the RATOG switch was also at 'off'. Engine ignition switches had to be 'off', the undercarriage lever at 'down', flap selector at 'air–off' and fuel cut-off at 'cut off'. Pneumatic system pressure was to be at the maximum of 300psi (20.7bar), while flying controls had to display full and free range.

After all the switches had checked as being correctly set, engine power was applied and all gauges and indicators monitored to ensure correct operation. These included the undercarriage indicator – green and 'down' – and the tail-wheel

light – showing 'down'. The fuel contents gauge had to be checked, with the rear tank and external tank cocks 'off' and the transfer cock set at 'normal'. The booster pump had to be 'off'. With initial checks completed the hood jettison control was checked for correct stowage and the canopy tested for free movement. On the Mk 45 the overhead handle had to be deployed, while on the Mks 46 and 47 the winding handle was to be tested. The canopy was to be stopped just short of the closed position, at which point the pilot was required to push the lower forward edges outwards to ensure the canopy's correct engagement with its rails. The canopy was then returned to the fully open position.

Starting the Engine

Engine starting required the lower fuselage tank fuel cock be set to 'on' and the throttle opened by 1in. The rpm lever was placed fully forward, the supercharger change gear switch set to 'auto normal', the air intake filter selector set to 'filter in operation', while, if fitted, the radiator shutter switch was to be set to 'open'. The Coffman starter had to be indexed to bring the next cartridge into position. As these cartridges were temperature-sensitive, the No. 4 Mk 1 was normally used in temperatures above 5°C, with the No. 5 Mk 1 being preferred for lower values.

The fuel cut-off lever was then set at 'cut off' for ten to fifteen seconds, after which the booster pump was set to 'off' and fuel cut-off lever pushed fully forward. At this point, the priming selector cock had to be set to 'main' before the priming pump was operated, until fuel reached the priming nozzles. This was indicated by an increase in resistance. Use of the priming pump was needed when the engine was cold.

For engine starting the appropriate button was pressed and held to energize the booster coil. Should the engine fail to start with the first cartridge, the engine had to be re-primed, although this would not be required if the initial priming had been overly generous. Under normal circumstances, no further priming was needed except when a new cartridge was selected or when temperatures were high. In lower temperatures, the opposite action was required. Continuous priming was therefore necessary even after engine start. Once the engine was running smoothly the buttons could be released, the primer screwed down and the selector cock set to 'all off'. The

engine had to be allowed to warm up until the oil pressure steadied, after which it could be opened up to 1,200 to 1,400rpm and held there until everything was thoroughly warmed up. During this process pressures and temperatures had to be checked before the pneumatic systems were tested by raising and lowering flaps and radiator shutters.

Magnetos were tested before the engine was run at a faster rate. Once the oil temperature had reached 15°C with the coolant temperature at 40°C, the propeller unit could be cycled through its complete range by pushing and pulling the operating lever twice through its quadrant. With the lever fully forward, the rpm had to be checked to ensure that it was within 50rpm of the normal value. With the engine running correctly the supercharger could be tested to check that rpm dropped in high gear and boost rose in low gear. After the test, original ratings were to be restored.

When at static boost, the electrical generator was checked for correct functioning, the visual indication being that the warning light went out. Next on the checklist were the magnetos. Should one show a drop exceeding 100rpm without vibration the test was to be done again at a higher power to see if that cleared the problem. But if the engine still misbehaved it was to be shut down for further investigation. After rectification of a magneto problem the aircraft would require full-power engine runs. Given the Griffon engine's power the tail had to be securely tied down, although at sea further tie-downs could be used. Under these conditions the throttle had to be opened fully, during which the take-off boost and rpm were checked as quickly as possible. At take-off power each magneto was tested in turn. Should either exhibit a 100rpm drop, the engine had to be shut down for further investigation.

Once the aircraft has been confirmed as fit for flight, the pilot then had to ensure that the brake pressure readings were correct and that pneumatic system pressures were within limits. With the brakes confirmed as operable the pilot could proceed to the runway, although he had to be aware that on the ground the Seafire was distinctly nose heavy. This required care with the brakes. Pre-take-off checks included ensuring that elevator trim tabs were set at neutral for the Mk 45 and at two divisions nose-up for Mks 46 and 47 aircraft. The rudder had to be set fully left with the Seafire 45. With aircraft equipped with contra-rotating propellers, the rudder tabs were set to neutral. Now correctly trimmed, the rpm lever could be set fully forward.

With the Seafire 45, the lower fuel tank cock was set to 'on', with the transfer cock at 'normal'. The drop tank cock and booster pump were 'off' and 'on', respectively. In addition to these actions, the rear tank cock in the Seafire 46 and 47 was to be at 'off' with the booster pump set to 'main'. Flaps were at 'up', the lever being at 'air-off', while the air intake control was to be set at 'in operation'.

Take-Off

On take-off the throttle was opened slowly to plus-7psi (0.5bar) boost. With the Seafire 45, a sudden power increase could exacerbate its tendency to swing strongly to the right. This could lead to excessive tyre wear on paved surfaces. Once airborne, boost could be increased to plus 12psi (0.8bar), although the lower setting was more than adequate for the take-off run. The Seafire

46 and 47 could take off under full power as there was no swing, but pilots were recommended to hold boost at plus-12psi. After take-off, a quick dab on the brakes was required to stop the wheels spinning before retracting the undercarriage. At 1,000ft (300m) the carburettor air intake control was set to 'normal intake' – unless conditions were dusty – with the radiator shutters moved to 'closed'. This set the system to automatic. On the Seafire 46 and 47, the rear fuel tank could be selected once the aircraft had reached 2,000ft (600m).

With the aircraft cleaned up, it could be climbed from sea level to 25,000ft (7,700m) at a constant speed of 150kt (170mph or 270km/h), although above this height the speed had to be cut by 3kt (4mph or 5km/h) per 1,000ft. If the aircraft was in a combat climb the supercharger would automatically change to high gear at 11,000ft (3,400m). Under normal conditions – 2,600rpm at plus-9psi (0.6bar) boost – the maximum rate of climb was best obtained by delaying the gear change until boost had dropped to plus-6psi (0.4bar).

Handling in the Air

Handling of later Seafires varied. They were described as being stable around all axes, although when climbing at low airspeeds longitudinal stability decreased in the Mk 45. During landing and take-off, changes in trim affected behaviour. Undercarriage retraction prompted the nose to rise and the reverse happened when it was lowered. Flap movement was similarly accompanied by a trim change in the same direction of movement. The radiator shutters also had an effect, with closure bringing the nose up. Handling was described as generally light and effective throughout the speed range, all trim tabs being effective. There was one exception: sudden application of the rudder or trim tab in a high speed dive caused the aircraft to skid violently.

Stall warning limits were 80 knots (90mph or 140km/h), with everything retracted and operating at a normal service load, and 85kt (95mph or 150km/h) at full load. As the undercarriage and flaps increased drag, the stalling speeds came

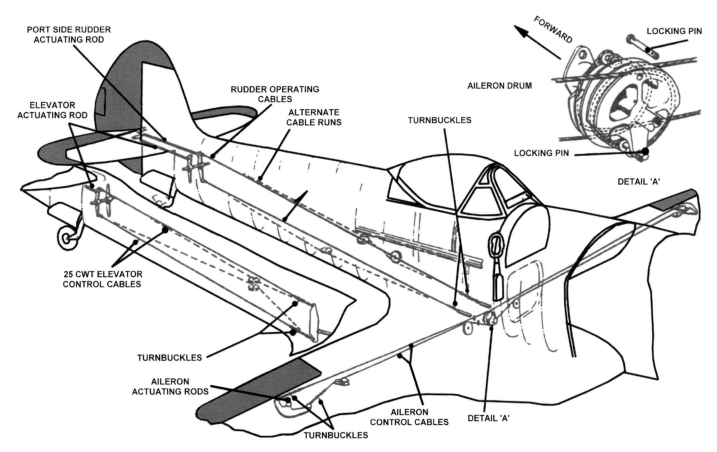

Later-build Seafires featured alternate control runs for the elevator system, as shown here. BBA Collection

down so that at normal service loading the limit was 72kt (81mph or130km/h) and 76kt (86mph or 137km/h). Stall warning was first noted at approximately 10kt (11mph or 18km/h) above the given speed, the obvious signs being buffeting and aileron snatch. Once the stall had been entered, either a wing or the nose dropped. Recovery required the pilot to centralize the controls. The signs of a stall became more pronounced at speed and the aircraft was inclined to flick left or right. Recovery was straight-forward, requiring the pilot to do no more than relax the controls until the aircraft had recovered.

Deliberate spinning was forbidden. If it happened inadvertently immediate recovery action was necessary. Pilots were also warned about handling in a dive, particularly as speed increased. As a result, the aircraft needed trimming into the dive to counteract a tendency to become tail-heavy. Although use of the elevator trim tab was the recommended method of balancing the aircraft, pilots were warned to take care as incorrect use could have a powerful effect. As the Seafire 45 was fitted with a single-plane propeller unit, care was also needed to counter the aircraft's tendency to yaw. This was achieved through accurate use of the rudder trim tab. As they were equipped with contra-rotating propeller units, such action was not required with Mk 46 and Mk 47 aircraft.

Aerobatics required certain entry speeds to be observed. For a roll it was between 180 and 220kt (200 and 250mph or 325 and 360km/h), while a loop required an entry speed of between 320 to 340kt (360 and 380mph or 650 and 685km/h). A roll off a loop could only be undertaken between 330 and 350kt (370 and 415mph or 595 and 665km/h), while an upward roll required a range between 360 and 400kt (405 and 450mph or 648 and 720km/h). Flick manoeuvres were strictly prohibited. Inverted flight was permitted but only for the execution of other manoeuvres, because prolonged inversion caused a rapid oil pressure drop.

Preparing to Land

Having put the Seafire through its paces the pilot then had to prepare the aircraft for landing. The first action was to reduce the speed to below 140kt (157mph/252km/h) after which the canopy was opened and the access door set to its intermediate position.

With the flaps fully down, this Seafire XV has drifted upwards after catching the wire. Note the flap split under the centreline. FAAM Yeovilton

Should the aircraft be about to land on a carrier deck, the arrester hook had to be lowered and the indicator light checked, although it would not illuminate until speed had fallen below 110kt (124mph or 200km/h). At this point the pneumatic pressure had to be confirmed at 300psi (21bar), while the brake indicator pressure was supposed to read 140psi (9.7bar) or 80psi (95.5bar) on pre-Modification 489 aircraft. The fuel system had to be checked for contents and the booster pump switched on in the selected tank.

Once the supercharger, air intake filter control and radiator flaps had been selected to the correct positions, the undercarriage could be lowered. Should the aircraft be post-Modifications 498 and 519, this could be accomplished at a speed of 170kt (190mph or 305km/h) instead of 110kt (124mph or 198km/h). The undercarriage indicator lights were then checked and the rpm lever set to 2,600, after which the flaps could be placed in the down position and the pneumatic system re-checked.

With the aircraft under power and at maximum weight, approach speeds were 85kt (95mph or 150km/h) with flaps down and 90kt (100mph or 160km/h) with them up. Should the aircraft be landing without engine power, the recommended glide speed was 100kt (115mph or 180km/h) with flaps up or down. Less experienced pilots were required to add 10 to 15kt (11 to 17mph

or 18 to 27km/h) to the recommended speeds. The only other variation to final approach speeds was a reduction by 5kt (6mph or 9km/h) when much of the fuel and ammunition had been expended. It was possible to undertake flapless landings but pilots had to note that a longer landing run would be required and operation of the brakes would require care to avoid the aircraft nosing over. Recommended approach speed to a carrier deck was 75kt (85mph or 135km/h).

After a missed landing the aircraft would climb away quite easily with undercarriage and flaps lowered. At such times, full take-off power was not recommended with the Seafire 45 as this would cause major changes in directional trim. In contrast, only a slight trim change would be experienced with the Seafire 46 and 47. When recovering from a missed landing the throttle had to be opened to plus-9psi (0.6bar) boost, the undercarriage had to be raised and the aircraft re-trimmed for normal flight. Climb-away speed was increased to 115kt (130mph or 207km/h) with flaps down. At an altitude of 300ft (90m) the flaps were to be raised and the aircraft re-trimmed to compensate.

The Seafire 46 and 47 would put up with a sudden application of power but the Mk 45 was not so forgiving. Near the stall and with the application of power there was a tendency to roll strongly to starboard followed by a strong inclination to turn to

Having become misaligned with the deck centreline, the pilot of this Seafire XV aborts his landing, although everything is still out and down. FAAM Yeovilton

starboard. Under most circumstances control could be re-established using opposite rudder and aileron. Should the aircraft not respond, however, a crash could follow, especially at low altitude.

With the aircraft on the deck the flaps were raised, the propeller speed control lever was pushed fully forward and the fuel booster pump switched off. Before taxiing to dispersal the brake pressure had to be checked. When the aircraft had reached its parking position the engine had to be idled at 1,200rpm for a short period to check for possible magneto problems. When satisfied, the pilot could shut the engine down by moving the fuel cut-off control fully back. Once the engine had stopped the ignition switches were moved to 'off', the radiator shutters closed, the electrical switches set at 'off' and the fuel cocks closed.

Should the undercarriage lever jam and be impossible to move to the fully down position after moving from the gate, pilots were recommended to return it to the fully

Unhappily for the deck party, the starboard undercarriage unit on this Seafire has collapsed under the aircraft's fuselage after a misaligned landing had strained the undercarriage leg mountings. Will Blunt Collection

forward position for a few seconds to take the weight off the undercarriage locking pins. This allowed them to move freely, after which the lever could be moved to the down position. An alternative procedure was to put the nose down sharply or to invert the aircraft. Even after lowering the undercarriage the indicator would not always show the gear as locked down fully. The recommended remedial action was to retract the undercarriage and lower it again. Should this fail to produce the desired effect, the emergency lever was pushed forward and rotated through 110 degrees to release the contents of a CO_2 cylinder. This blew the gear down. Once it had been used the undercarriage could not be raised again until the gas had been bled from the system, the emergency lever reset and the cylinder replaced.

Should the tail wheel not lower, pilots needed to be aware that the tail hook fairing might be forced upwards, jamming the rudder and preventing the aircraft from going around again. Should the emergency lowering system be activated with the undercarriage lever in the 'up' position the gear would not lower unless the CO_2 pipeline was first broken and the gas allowed to escape. Later build aircraft were fitted with an emergency flap-lowering system, while earlier variants had this system fitted by Modification 600 action. Should the flaps fail to lower to the down position, or a pneumatic system leak occur, the flap lever had to be placed in the 'up' position before the emergency CO_2 lever was operated to blow the flaps down. As with the undercarriage system, the flaps were not to be operated until the CO_2 had been bled from the system and any defects rectified.

If a pilot had to abandon the aircraft it was possible to jettison the canopy by pulling a rubber knob inside the top of the canopy forward and downward and pushing the lower edges of the canopy outwards with his elbows. As this was to be done before ditching, the airframe had to be cleaned up to facilitate a safe landing on water. To clear the combat tanks from their position beneath the wings on the Seafire 46 and 47, the release levers on the left-hand side of the pilot's seat had to be pulled as far back as they would go. The centreline external tank could also be jettisoned but the drop tank cock had to be in the 'off' position before the release handle was pulled.

Emergency Action

Abandoning by parachute was preferred to a landing on water since the aircraft's ditching characteristics were considered to be poor. It such a landing was unavoidable, the external fuel tanks and canopy had to be jettisoned. The undercarriage then had to be confirmed as retracted, the pilot's safety harness tightened as much as possible and the R/T plug disconnected. If the engine was still running, it was recommended to use its power to keep the tail down before landing along the swell. In a gentle swell the aircraft could come down into the wind. Pilots were warned that the Seafire had a tendency to sink quickly due to the weight of the engine.

Before making a forced landing after engine failure, the first action was to drop external fuel tanks, after which the fuel cut-off control had to pulled fully back and the booster pump switched off. With the fuel system set to 'off' the canopy either had to be jettisoned or fully opened and the access door catch set to the intermediate position. The flaps were to remain retracted until the pilot was sure the selected landing area was capable of accommodating the aircraft and was within gliding range. Once it had been selected, the undercarriage and flaps could be lowered with the approach speed maintained at 95kt (107mph or 170km/h). If there was still some oil pressure left in the system the glide length could be lengthened considerably by setting the rpm control lever fully back past the stop on its quadrant.

Inspection and Repair

Keeping the Seafire flying required the attentions of the ground crew, who also had pre-flight routines to perform. Any hoar frost deposits had to be removed, the tail oleo checked for correct extension, the arrester hook latched up and a general check made of the airframe for damage. The de-icing fluid reservoir had to be topped up and the jets examined. Other items to be checked at this stage included the wing locks and indicators, pneumatic system pressure, that the flaps were set to the take-off position and that external covers and locks had been removed. The ground crew could then report the aircraft as ready for flight.

Following on from the daily pre-flight routine, the lubricant reservoir had to be topped up as required. In-depth inspections included checking the hydraulic system contents and filter, the CO_2 bottle and flap operating system. Flight control runs – including the cables, pulleys, chains, hinges, torque tubes, locking plates and screw jacks – also required detailed inspection. While the aircraft was in the hangar to enable these checks to be made, the rest of the airframe was given a thorough going-over for such things as damage, loose fasteners and, the bane of all sea-going operations, corrosion, which could affect magnesium alloy even more than aluminium.

Given the wear and tear suffered during carrier operations by the undercarriage and arrestor hook, both were subjected to extensive scrutiny. The undercarriage legs, both main and tail, required inspection for corrosion, damage and excessive play in their mountings. The arrester hook's mountings and structure were also checked for defects. Should the assembly be pre-Modification 351, the actual hook was to have its retaining nuts and bolts removed to enable the bolt holes to be checked for wear and elongation. Any defective items had to be replaced.

The propeller assembly could only be inspected with the spinner removed; this also had to be checked. The unit could then be generally inspected for damage, wear and leaks. Special attention was paid to the thrust race and bearing for tightness and freedom of movement. A general engine inspection covered tappet clearances and cylinder rockers and springs for compression and damage. Should the Merlin be a pre-Modification 297 unit, the auxiliary drive locking nuts had to be checked for tightness. In addition to a general inspection of the ignition system, the spark plugs had to be replaced at regular intervals, the contact-breaker points had to be cleaned should any roughness be discovered and the gaps reset.

With the starting system the key area of concern was that the cartridge safety indicators were intact. Being liquid cooled engines, both the Merlin and Griffon required regular coolant system flushing to maintain efficiency and remove any foreign objects. With the fuel system the most important check was for water contamination, this being accomplished by draining off some of the fuel. If it was found to be

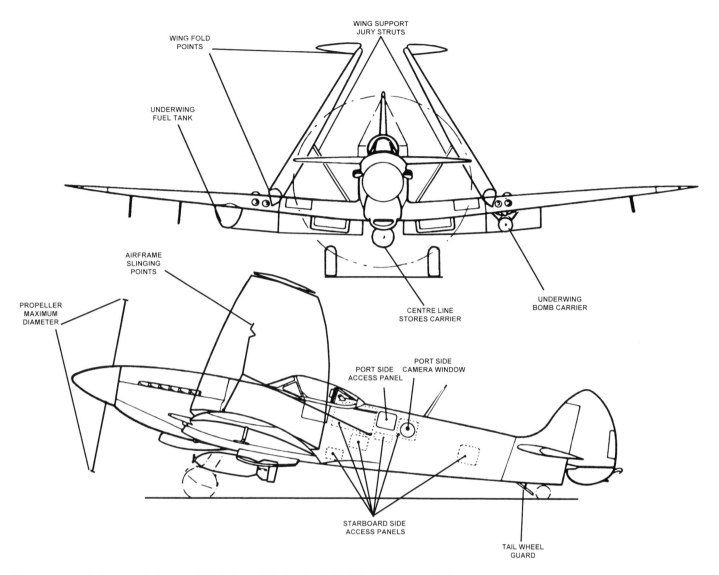

WING FOLD
POINTS

WING SUPPORT
JURY STRUTS

UNDERWING
FUEL TANK

AIRFRAME
SLINGING
POINTS

PROPELLER
MAXIMUM
DIAMETER

CENTRE LINE
STORES CARRIER

UNDERWING
BOMB CARRIER

PORT SIDE
ACCESS PANEL

PORT SIDE
CAMERA WINDOW

STARBOARD SIDE
ACCESS PANELS

TAIL WHEEL
GUARD

Shown here are the locations for the wing fold struts, as utilized by the Seafire XV and XVII. BBA Collection

At the end of their lives many Seafires ended up as instructional airframes, which is why one of this example's wingtips is drooping and the engine cowlings have been removed. CP Russell Smith

WRENS, members of the Women's Royal Naval Service, carry out aircraft maintenance. BBA Collection

contaminated the system had to be flushed and, if necessary, stripped for cleaning.

Slightly easier but no less messy was attending to the engine's lubrication system. It was recommended that servicing be carried out before the engine was fully cooled as it was easier to drain the oil when it was hot. The old oil and the filters were inspected for debris. Inspection of engine operating controls concentrated on checking for play in each linkage run, defective components being replaced as necessary.

Electrical System Maintenance

Before any electrical components were changed the entire system was subjected to an insulation test, followed by closer inspections of the fuel tank potentiometer, starter breech circuit, oil dilution valve, undercarriage indicator switches and pressure head. External and internal lights were then tested for serviceability and power supplies checked for correct operation together with the security of battery mounting. Special attention was paid to electrical connections that could be damaged by exposure to a salty atmosphere.

Gauges on the main cockpit panel were inspected for cleanliness, damage, legibility and security of mounting. Many were connected to items outside the cockpit, such as the pitot head, fuel pressure warning unit, vacuum pump and boost gauge. Only one other system required inspection, this being the oxygen system, which included the cylinder, the pipework and the gauges. These checks were followed by a test to ensure correct operation.

The final ground inspections concerned the aircraft's armament and included replenishing the ammunition as required,

The FAA policy of employing WRENS to service aircraft did not extend to working on aircraft carriers. These artificers are carrying out maintenance on the engine and propeller of a Seafire. BBA Collection

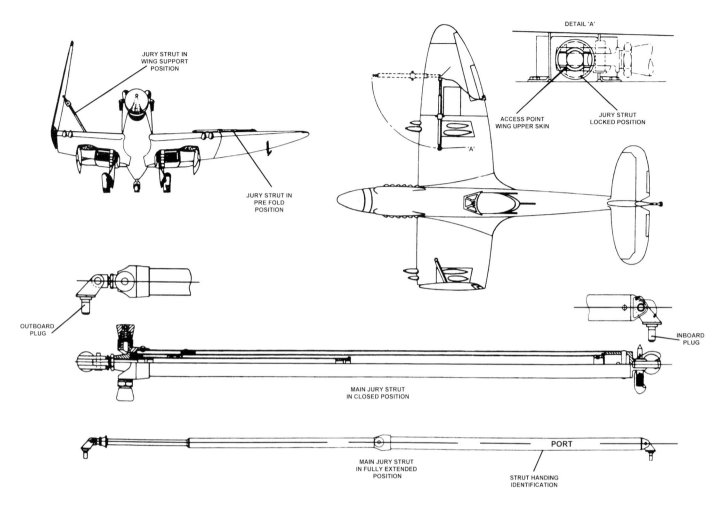

This diagram illustrates the wing support struts and their method of operation. BBA Collection

checking access panels and the cleanliness of the gun barrels. The external bomb carriers, rocket mountings and fuel tank mounts had to be inspected together with the appropriate connections and the fire control mechanisms. There were also checks to be made of the gun sight and its screen, the signal pistol, pneumatic operating gear, the cine camera and its mountings, plus the RATOG jettison control.

With the aircraft inspected, replenished and repaired as necessary, and the pilot fully trained, both were ready for combat.

Ground crew members work on a Seafire XV's engine. When they have finished, the wingtips will be locked in place and the aircraft cleared for flight. FAAM Yeovilton

CHAPTER SEVEN

Griffon Power

With the Merlin-powered Seafires entering service, the Admiralty turned its attention to the next stage of the type's development. Initial approaches were made to the Air Ministry to supply conversions of the Spitfire VIII, which was intended for service in the Far East, or the variant preferred for European operations, the Mk IX.

The Air Ministry handed over eight Mk VIIIs for trials on 9 January 1944. They included JG661, JG662 and JG663, although the first differed in featuring a sting-type arrester hook in place of the earlier 'A'-frame hook. After modifications at Chalgrove, the fighters were flown to Crail in April where they were assigned to No. 778 Squadron commanded by Lt Cdr P.B. Schonfield RN. Over the next few months the modified Spitfires underwent a full range of performance and handling trials together with extensive deck landing trials.

Naval Interest Grows

Although the Fleet Air Arm had no real interest in adapting the Mk VIII for naval use, it was interested in the type's performance as it featured a retractable tail wheel, which increased speed. In fact, the Admiralty was sufficiently impressed by the type's behaviour to issue Specification 471 covering a naval version of the Griffon-powered Spitfire XII, although the resulting aircraft was a mixture of Spitfire and Seafire variants already in service.

But this method of development allowed Supermarine, and to a lesser degree Westland, to speed up creation and construction of the next version. The engine and its mountings were to be based on the Spitfire XII, which retained the original Mk V-based cooling system, while the oil cooling system was borrowed from the Mk IX. This meant that the larger square-shaped fairing was fitted under the other wing, this being required to enable the aircraft to operate in any theatre.

The airframe was based upon the Seafire

III's, while the wing was borrowed from the Spitfire VC, complete with universal weapons fitments, although the structure would be modified for folding wing operation. The rear fuselage section was based upon that of the Mk VIII, with a broader chord rudder to help counter the torque of the more powerful engine. Also borrowed from the Mk VIII were the rear spar attachments, the retractable tail wheel and the main undercarriage units, which had to be strengthened for carrier operations.

The specified powerplant was the Rolls Royce Griffon VI, also known as the RG 14SM. Rated at 1,750hp, the engine drove a 10ft 5in (3.2m) four-bladed Rotol R22/4F5/8 propeller unit. This combination endowed the new variant with a maximum speed of 383mph (240km/h) at 13,000ft (4,000m). An altitude of 10,000ft (3,000m) could be reached in approximately two minutes. A total of 100gal (455ltr) of fuel could be contained internally in Mareng-type tanks. A further 60gal (270ltr) could

be carried in external wing tanks for which a complex but workable system was installed. Proposed armament was two 20mm cannon augmented by four .303in Browning machine-guns. Structural modifications enabled external weapons carriers to be mounted. A 500lb bombs could be loaded on to the centreline point, while 250lb bombs or rocket projectiles could be carried beneath the wings.

Prototypes Ordered

As the Admiralty was still not fully in control of ordering its own aircraft, the Air Ministry issued Specification N.4/43 to cover the six prototypes of what was now designated the Supermarine Type 377. Serial numbers for these machines were NS487, NS490, NS491, PK240, PK243 and PK245. Initially they were to be called Seafire XIIs, but as this would have caused

NS490 was a prototype Seafire XV and was dedicated to testing both the 'A'-Frame and sting-type arrester hooks. FAAM Yeovilton

confusion with the RAF's Spitfire XII the revised designation of Seafire XV became official from 15 July.

The first prototype, NS487, was rolled out in late November 1943 and, having successfully completed initial test flights, moved to the experimental hangar at Hursley Park. There it was found to weigh 6,013lb (2,733kg) tare, with an all-up weight of 7,861lb (3,573kg). Catapult spools had not yet been fitted. Although the prototypes had been built by Supermarine, orders for 503 production aircraft were placed with Westland Aircraft and Cunliffe Owen. These production machines differed from the prototypes in having slightly larger oil cooler housings under the port wing, larger spinners and longer engine cowlings.

Enthusiasm for the new variant was not universal within the Fleet Air Arm. At least one senior officer was so unimpressed by it that he composed a passionate and strongly worded objection in which he compared the Seafire XV unfavourably with the Chance Vought F4U Corsair and the Grumman F6F Hellcat. Obviously such views could not be allowed to pass unchallenged. The Directorate of Air Warfare and Flying Training explained in the strongest possible terms that in the Seafire XV the FAA would have the best possible interceptor. It was not only faster than the two US types but its deployment would also be invaluable in the forthcoming invasion of Europe and operations in the Far East.

Sting-Type Arrester Hook

Construction of the Seafire XV began in late 1944 with first deliveries beginning the following March. Some 384 airframes, the bulk of the production run, were equipped with 'A'-frame arrester hooks stressed for a loading of 10,500lb (4,800kg) rather than the 7,000lb (3,100kg) of the Merlin variants. The final batch of Mk XVs was fitted with the sting-type arrester hook, located in the lower part of the rudder. When released, the lower rudder section dropped down and the spring retainer was released, allowing the hook to extend to a length of 18in (44cm). Unlike the 'A'-frame hook, the sting-type had a built-in lateral movement of 30 degrees either side of the centreline. As before, there was an oleo pneumatic damper to stop rebounding after hard contact with the carrier deck. Once the landing was completed the hook

was released from the wire, the extender retracted and the whole assembly relocated manually.

Trials of the sting-type hook were undertaken during October 1944 at Boscombe Down using the prototype, NS487, after which the Seafire was sent to Farnborough for pre-service release trials. One of the first modifications to follow was the installation of a tail-wheel guard, as the hook's relocation to the rear left the wheel vulnerable to tangling with the arrester cables. While the trials organizations passed the sting hook for service use, they commented that the 'A'-frame assembly was better for stopping the aircraft. Moving the hook aft did, however, improve the centre of gravity. The cable guard was incorporated in production aircraft and retrofitted to earlier machines as they entered the servicing cycle.

Although the Seafire XV was capable of catapult or rocket-assisted take-offs, the Fleet Air Arm sought a way of launching more aircraft more quickly. The answer was tail-down acceleration, which preceded introduction of the steam catapult. The aircraft was fitted with reinforced pick-up points each side of the fuselage to which cables were attached. These cables were connected to a central launch shoe mounted on the catapult. The aircraft was held in place by a cable that was released when the catapult launch was initiated. Trials were undertaken at Boscombe Down with NS490 in September 1943 but they were considered unsuccessful because the undercarriage legs were unable to take the stresses involved.

Pre-Service Trials

The aircraft was sent on 14 January 1944 to Farnborough. There the undercarriage legs were replaced by link-type units but the launch loading had to be held at 2.75g to prevent leg failure. In June RAE was able to report favourably on tail-down acceleration and this prompted Supermarine to send a technical team to observe the trials. A total of twenty-two launches was made, during which the Seafire was loaded to an all-up weight of 7,850lb (3,568kg). At this weight there was some compression of the main-wheel tyres, although there was no evidence of damage with acceleration loads varying between 2.8 and 3.1g. As both parties were satisfied with the trials it was agreed that NS490 should be flown to

RNAS Arbroath for further test flying. These flights were, however, curtailed when the rear fuselage and tail unit were damaged on landing. Flying resumed on 19 July after a complete new tail unit had been fitted.

Westland's first production aircraft, SR446, was delivered to High Post on 2 October 1944 for weighing and centre of gravity determination. Basic weight was 6,274lb (2,852kg), while the all-up weight was 8,021lb (3,646kg). Cunliffe Owen's first production aircraft arrived on 23 March 1945, where it was found to weigh 6,245lb (2,839kg) basic and 8,018lb (3,645kg) at maximum load. Although both were from different manufacturers, the weight variation was reassuringly small. This indicated that the rigorous quality control procedure instituted early in the Seafire build programme was working correctly.

Carrier operating trials were carried out using the prototype, PK245, the chosen vessel being the trials and training carrier HMS *Pretoria Castle*. Flight trials began in July 1945. Conventional techniques were used at first, being followed by a series of tail-down launches. During the first sequence of nine departures the aircraft was launched at an all-up weight of 7,980lb (3,627kg), while for later accelerated launches the aircraft was fitted with a 50gal (223ltr) fuel tank and supplied with water ballast. After this PK245 was returned to Supermarine for the repair of structural damage sustained during use of the hold-back gear. Trials aboard *Pretoria Castle* resumed on 30 July. Out of a total of fifty-nine launches, fourteen were undertaken in the tail-down attitude. All were considered satisfactory. In between the assisted launches, forty-five unassisted ones were undertaken with the aircraft carrying a variety of under-wing and fuselage loads.

The first load carried was the 50gal external tank, which resulted in a maximum weight of 8,380lb (3,810kg) and a C of G point aft of 8.1in (20.6cm). With two empty 22.5gal (100ltr) tanks added, weight increased to 8,565lb (3,893kg) and trim moved to 8.15in (20.7cm) aft. When these tanks were removed and replaced by a pair of empty external 22.5gal (102ltr) tanks, plus a 500lb bomb and its carrier, the total launch weight rose to 8,530lb (3,877kg), while trim returned to 8.1in. All-up weight increased to 8,890lb (4,041kg) and the trim point shifted to the optimum 8in (20cm) point with full tanks. With the 45gal (200ltr) under-fuselage blister tank, all up-weight was 8,380lb

(3,810kg) and the trim point moved to 8.05in (20.4cm). The final trials configuration involved the addition of a pair of 22.5gal combat fuel tanks added to the normal loading. This produced a maximum weight of 8,340lb (3,791kg) with a trim position of 7.75in (19.7cm). The only deficiency noted during these trials was the aircraft's inability to be flown with rocket projectiles and external combat fuel tanks together.

The first production Seafire XV, SR446, was delivered in August 1944, being accepted for service trials the following month. Pre-service trials were undertaken at Boscombe Down in November and were followed in February by tests of the Identification Friend or Foe system and aircraft handling. Later tests of the different fine pitch settings required for deck landings were undertaken as it was felt that the original settings were not inducing enough drag during landing. It was eventually concluded the proposed changes did not warrant application throughout the fleet.

Together with the prototype, NS490, the third Seafire XV, SR448, was involved in trials of a new propeller assembly, C of G aft datum settings, carbon monoxide leak checks and use of metal-covered elevators. Both machines were then allocated to dropping trials involving the Mk XI depth charge as well as investigation of oil cooler and radiator system improvements. Smoke floats were also tested, as were the radios and the IFF system. SR448 was then sent to Boscombe Down for spinning trials, during which a Spitfire XII fin and rudder were fitted.

Severe Buffeting

The first main batch of production aircraft was delivered to No. 802 Squadron in May 1945, but the last Seafire IIIs were not withdrawn from service until June 1946. Five months after the type had entered service, the pilot of Mk XV SR483 encountered buffeting so severe that he lost control and became unconscious. He had taken the aircraft up to 35,000ft (4,500m), at which point he made a slow peel-off with the engine rpm setting at low and the supercharger gear changed to 'MS' when the buffeting started. By the time the pilot regained consciousness, the aircraft had dropped to 6,000ft (1,850m). After landing, some clever mathematics revealed that the aircraft had reached a speed of 310kt

This three-quarter rear view of SR449 clearly shows that the external strengthening of earlier aircraft had been incorporated internally. FAAM Yeovilton

Seafire XV SR449 was utilized by Rolls-Royce at Hucknall for engine trials, after which it went to Rotol for propeller trials. It was withdrawn in December 1951. FAAM Yeovilton

(350mph or 560km/h), equivalent to a true airspeed of 472kt (531 mph, Mach 0.80 or 850km/h) and been subjected to a maximum of 11g.

Structural investigation of the airframe revealed that the lower wing-fold locking pins were showing signs of shearing, while the lower skin plating aft of the main wing spar had been distorted to such an extent that it had buckled and some of the rivets

had failed. Other damage included the shearing of the elevator horns, while the complete rear fuselage was showing signs of distress. At the other end of the airframe, the propeller blades had been pushed to their stress limits with the wooden laminations forced apart. It was only the Seafire's automatic recovery behaviour that had prevented it from plunging into the ground at high speed.

A pair of No. 803 Squadron Seafire XVs pose for the camera. Eventually their Royal Navy titles would be replaced by those of the Royal Canadian Navy. FAAM Yeovilton

Development work of the type continued with the prototypes. NS487 was used for work on the long-chord sting hook as well as the interconnected throttle and propeller linkage, although test pilots recommended against this system's adoption on production aircraft. NS490 was also employed on sting-type arrester-hook tests. These tests confirmed the results obtained with NS487, although the addition of a protective tail-wheel guard was recommended. The broader chord rudder was also found to be beneficial to longitudinal stability, this being confirmed by spin tests at Boscombe Down at altitudes up to 29,000ft (8,900m). The aircraft was also used to test the metal elevators. It was after these flights that the pilots recommended the elevator range to be interlocked with the sting hook when extended. The premise behind this was that combining these components would limit elevator movement during deck approaches and prevent pilots from over-controlling the aircraft.

Equipped with a smaller rudder, NS490 was subjected to a full range of spinning trials. These involved taking the aircraft to 20,000ft (6,150m) and pushing the control column forwards, at which point the Seafire entered a flat spin. Various recovery methods were tried, including opening the throttle wide, but the spin continued until the tail-mounted anti-spin parachute was deployed. This stopped the spin and put the aircraft into a steep dive from which recovery was effected by use of ailerons and engine power. Such was the stress, however, that the built-in weak link had failed to trigger automatic release of the parachute. The aircraft's wide-chord rudder and sting hook were then replaced and the aircraft flown again. With the larger rudder it behaved as expected, being completely stable about all axes and throughout the flight envelope.

The prototype was also employed to test the automatic deck landing system. But Supermarine's chief test pilot, Jeffery Quill, declared it unfit for service use and it was therefore recommended that the propeller pitch angles be altered to increase drag. Although this was not adopted, Quill continued to complain about propeller pitch. He considered it too coarse, meaning that in its current form the Seafire XV, unlike the Mk III, would be difficult to land on a carrier deck. A new windscreen, however, improved pilot vision.

In March 1945 PK240 was at Aldermaston for undercarriage trials. The test units featured improved rebound-type legs, which it was hoped would improve landing characteristics. Landings with the new units were made at Aldermaston, Gosport and High Post and passed as satisfactory. The aircraft was next fitted with Westland-built metal elevators, which had been found to cause instability. As in many of these cases, the cure was fairly simple: fitting a strip of beading to the trailing edge of each surface. This brought a marked improvement in stability throughout the flight envelope but did not stop the search for further ways of improving in-flight behaviour. Tests were, for example, conducted to investigate behaviour with a flap stuck in the down position. These determined that although the aircraft had an obvious tendency to pull in the direction of the affected flap, it remained flyable throughout the take-off and landing sequence.

Once problems involving its ailerons and gyro had been corrected and the throttle-propeller linkage adjusted, PK243 was flown to Arbroath for deck landing trials. A five-

A Seafire XV reveals its four-bladed propeller unit and IFF aerials under the starboard wing. BBA Collection

bladed propeller unit was fitted in an attempt to increase drag and facilitate controlled deck landings but tests revealed no obvious gains. PK243 then began to misbehave. The starboard aileron drifted upwards by 2in (5cm) in a dive of 380kt (430mph or 608km/h), causing a reversal of trim from right to left. This airframe was also fitted with the original type of Westland metal ailerons and displayed a complete lack of stability throughout the flight envelope. To correct the aileron float, the starboard wing incidence was decreased by 15min of angle, but this did not improve lateral control. In fact, it exacerbated the problem. The port aileron drooped by 0.25in (6.3mm), while the starboard one floated upwards by 2in at 400kt (450mph or 640km/h). This made the aircraft almost uncontrollable in straight and level flight as the left wing exhibited a tendency to drop and it took all the pilot's strength to maintain control.

Further pilot observations revealed that the starboard wing's upper surface was panting at high speeds. This, coupled with the aileron drift problem, meant that the aircraft was becoming dangerous to fly and PK243 was unable to undertake type flight trials until these problems were corrected. The port wing incidence was increased, while that of the starboard one was decreased. While this produced some improvement, the starboard aileron still floated excessively. As a last resort, the trim tab was fixed 0.125in (3.2mm) above the datum. This resulted in an improvement that was considered sufficient to allow the aircraft to undertake its share of the trials work.

First flown on 22 February 1945, PK245 was used for evaluation of the Mk XV's engine and fuel systems with Rolls-Royce before it was returned to Supermarine for general handling trials with wing combat fuel tanks. These tests were completed successfully, after which the aircraft was fitted with hinged ailerons. Trials with the ailerons in various drooped positions revealed that during flight testing there was no appreciable deterioration in handling up to 360kt (405mph or 648km/h). It was a different story at 370kt (415mph or 666km/h) when control reversal occurred, inducing a left wing low attitude and a yaw to the left. At the same time, the propeller began to vibrate beyond acceptable limits, although full control was regained when speed was reduced. At the conclusion of the handling trials, PK245 resumed flight tests

with the combat fuel tanks in May 1945. Throughout these trials the tanks were released at various angles of attack; in each case the tanks cleared the airframe without interference.

Aileron Problems

Cunliff Owen's first production Seafire XV, PR338, was also allocated to flight-testing, which concentrated on the Westland-manufactured metal elevators. Supermarine's Deputy Chief Test Pilot, Patrick Shea-Simmonds, reported that although these ailerons behaved well, they were unsatisfactory as lateral trim reversed with an increase in speed. At the same time, the starboard aileron showed an excessive tendency to float upwards when the Seafire was put into a dive. After these faults had been rectified, PR338 was retained for general flight trials before being retired in April 1945.

Aileron problems continued to plague the Seafire XV, as SR446 exhibited the same instability when test-flown during October 1944. Modifications to the wings were made to improve lateral control, while a bigger rudder brought longitudinal handling within acceptable limits. Flight trials of SR446 in this condition were undertaken and indicated that handling was much better. Further improvements resulted from fitting stiffer ailerons and Castle Bromwich-made elevators. Better controlled landings were a bonus.

In June 1945, SR459 was prepared for despatch to the USA and a series of flight trials at the Naval Air Station, Patuxent River, Maryland. But its departure was delayed by the discovery of several defects. The major one was the tendency of the doors covering the port wing joints to remain stuck in the up position during flight. Stronger springs and a beading strip fitted to the trailing edge of each elevator corrected this problem. This enabled the aircraft to remain in the USA for several years for comparison trials. NS487 and NS490 were both employed on sting-type arrester hook trials. In June, NS490's tail wheel and rear fuselage were damaged while it was at Arbroath. After repairs, which involved a modified tail-wheel guard, the aircraft was sent in August 1944 to Farnborough where it was found to weigh 7,850lb (3,568kg) before flight trials. Successful carrier clearance trials aboard HMS *Illustrious* followed.

Meanwhile, NS487 was fitted with a modified welded-type sting arrester hook, together with experimental launch hooks. Trials aboard the *Pretoria Castle* during October 1944 were considered successful even though the deck barrier was engaged at least once and on one occasion both main-wheel tyres burst on touchdown. NS487 was then returned to High Post for modification work, which included a stronger 'A'-frame stressed to 2g, altered undercarriage fairings, a finer-pitched propeller and different radiator flaps. Both the sting and arrester hooks were tested successfully aboard HMS *Implacable*.

Tail-Down Launching

Although most shipboard take-offs were accomplished using the Seafire's own power, it had been realized that as the aircraft's weight increased a launch system was required which would avoid the use of a special cradle. The Rocket-Assisted Take-Off Gear (RATOG) system offered an alternative, albeit one that was complicated and which would reduce take-off rates. A more workable method was, however, under development. This was the tail-down launching system allied to trials already in progress of the steam catapult. Seafire XV PK245 was, therefore, allocated to another round of trials aboard the *Pretoria Castle* during July and August 1945. The Seafire had already been fitted with prototype catapult hooks tested at Farnborough using the establishment's cartridge-powered catapult.

It was during these launches that certain not-too-exceed parameters were laid down for the carrier trials. These included a normal service weight of 7,985lb (3,630kg) and a launch loading of 2.9g. With a 30gal (134ltr) fuel tank installed, all-up weight rose to 8,258lb (3,754kg) at 2.75g, values which changed to 8,347lb (3,794kg) and 2.7g with a pair of 22.5gal (100ltr) combat fuel tanks. A similar loading restriction applied when 45gal (200ltr) and 50gal (223ltr) tanks were fitted, weights rising to 8,389lb (3,813kg) and 8,400lb (3,818kg) respectively. A further decrease to 2.6g came when a 500lb bomb was mounted, accompanied by a rise in weight to 8,540lb (3,841kg). The loading dropped to 2.45g when a pair of combat tanks and 500lb bombs were mounted under the wings and centre fuselage. Weight rose to 8,902lb (4,046kg). The only restriction placed upon landing was that the maximum weight should not exceed 8,073lb (3,670kg).

Aboard the *Pretoria Castle* the only major problem encountered during the first series of launches was that the launch bridle became caught up on the centreline fuel tank. At the conclusion, the rear tie-down was attached to the sting hook and the centreline fuel tank filled with water. To ensure that there was no adverse effect on landing, rip patches attached by cords to the undercarriage released the water as the gear retracted. In later launches a 500lb trials bomb was mounted on the centreline, while a pair of combat tanks, this time filled with fuel, were mounted beneath the wings. Before landing the bomb was dropped and the fuel transferred to the main system. At the conclusion of these trials, the Seafire XV was cleared for tail-down launches, which was a bonus as the aircraft was now compatible with the catapults fitted to American-built escort carriers.

Other trials were conducted by the manufacturers and the RAE to test the Mk XV's ability to carry the range of external tanks available. A contemporary weapons report warned that rockets should not be carried together with under-wing combat tanks. It added that, although launching with tanks and bombs had not been tested, there was no reason to prohibit such a combination in service. But some restrictions involving the carriage of external stores were introduced. No tanks or weapons were to be attached to centreline mounts during a four-point catapult launch as the store would obstruct the fuel-tank venting system. Also banned under the same conditions was the carriage of bombs. While manoeuvring was unrestricted up to 8,500lb (3,860kg), it was recommended that all external tanks be jettisoned before combat or dive bombing.

Although first production Mk XVs started to come off the assembly line in September 1944 the type was not released for service until the following April. Deliveries to front-line units began in August, the first to receive the type being No. 802 Squadron at Abbotsinch, No. 803 Squadron at Arbroath and No. 805 at Machrihanish. No. 802 Squadron, commanded by Lt Cdr R. E. Hargreaves DSC RN, was the first to take the variant to sea when it spent six days aboard HMS *Premier* for deck landing training from 23 October. Both No. 802 and No. 803 had been intended to join the British Pacific Fleet but the war against Japan ended first.

In August 1946 a fault with the supercharger clutch led to the Seafire XV being confined to operations from land bases. The clutch had shown a tendency to slip when high power and boost settings were applied for take-off, which was considered dangerous in carrier operations. Rolls-Royce undertook remedial work and carrier operations resumed in 1947.

Cold Weather Testing

That year two Seafire XVs, PR494 and PR499, were involved in cold weather trials. The aircraft were sent to Fort Nelson near Edmonton, Canada in January for intensive winter trials. They were not uneventful. PR494 sustained undercarriage leg and propeller damage when landing on rough terrain. Initially, some problems were experienced with engine starts caused by under-priming and then over-priming after firing-up. Adjustments to the throttle controls improved starting. Ground handling was possible in winter conditions, although more manpower was required to move the aircraft. Wing folding was considered satisfactory but there were warnings about undertaking this operation in high winds. Pilots also stressed the need for cockpit heating during operations in cold conditions.

The Mk XVII Appears

The development of what was to emerge as the next Seafire variant, the Mk XVII, began when the sixth prototype Mk XV, NS493, was delivered to Westland Aircraft for a programme of alteration. This involved the installation of a bubble canopy with a cut-down rear fuselage. It was then discovered that, as with similarly-modified RAF machines, this new version of the Seafire was also unstable when the rear fuselage fuel tanks were full. The improved vision was much appreciated by the pilots, however. Despite this instability the aircraft was passed fit for service during flight trials at Boscombe Down. To speed introduction of this new version, the final batch of thirty Seafire XVs under construction by Westland were diverted to cover the start of the new contract.

During re-manufacture of the first aircraft, a stronger main spar was incorporated. An improved and strengthened undercarriage increased its stroke from 4.9in (12.5cm) to 8in (20cm), which helped keep the propeller clear of the ground during hard landings. These changes enabled the Seafire XVII to carry a heavier weapons load, while stability was improved with a larger fin and rudder. The type was also capable of mounting two F.24 cameras, and later models had a 33gal (147ltr) rear fuselage fuel tank. The variant's overall fuel capacity was 145gal (646ltr), carried in two fuselage tanks ahead of the pilot, with the remainder in bag tanks in the wing forward sections. The fuel system had to be managed carefully throughout the flight envelope to maintain stability. This meant that the contents of the rear fuselage tank had to be used first.

Westland's first aircraft, SW987, was delivered to High Post on 16 May 1945 for weighing and C of G determination. Fitted with a Griffon VI engine and a four-bladed Rotol wooden propeller, the aircraft's basic weight was found to be 6,243lb (2,837kg) and the maximum all-up weight 8,017lb (3,644kg). The first Supermarine-built machine, SX232, which had arrived at High Post on 3 April with the same engine and propeller combination, weighed in at 6,385lb (2,906kg) and 8,148 lb (3,704kg). While both aircraft performed as expected, the test pilots did complain about glare reflected around the cockpit from the bubble canopy. As a result, the surrounding area was painted black.

Deck landing trials were undertaken using SX311 and SX314 aboard HMS *Triumph* starting in late 1945. Over 100 landings and eight assisted take-offs were made. SX311 undertook the first seven take-offs and nineteen landings, which confirmed that the longer-stroke undercarriage legs not only better absorbed landing shocks but also eliminated the previous tendency of rebounding on touchdown. This good behaviour was not to last. On one occasion, the aircraft approached the carrier at too low an angle, its port main wheel and hook hitting the round-down. The resulting landing saw the Seafire hooking the fifth wire and slewing across the deck to end up in the port catwalk. Inspection revealed that the rudder, arrester hook, port wing skins, radiator and propeller were damaged. The undercarriage, however, was completely undamaged.

The next Seafire XVII to arrive at High Post for weighing and trim checks was SX334, which, unlike earlier machines, had already undergone many modifications. The most obvious was installation of a curved windscreen assembly. Together with other

NS493 was originally built as a Seafire XV, although, as seen here, it was rebuilt as a Seafire XVII prototype. FAAM Yeovilton

This side-on view of Seafire XVII SX334 shows off the type's sleek lines and the location of the reconnaissance camera windows. The aircraft spent some time as a general trials machine before joining No. 1832 Squadron at Culham. BBA Collection

SX334 seen from the other side, showing the camera window, the under-wing pitot head, tail-wheel guard and sting-type arrester hook.
BBA Collection

internal modifications, this resulted in a tare weight of 6,420lb (2,836kg), while the maximum weight was 8,245lb (3,748kg). This aircraft was one of the first Mk XVIIs to be fitted with the reconnaissance package from the start, resulting in a change of designation to FR XVII. It was also one of the few to be fitted with a vibrograph unit – installed in the port side of the cockpit – to measure engine vibrations and record their effects on the airframe and the gun camera.

While most Seafire XVIIs were passed as fit for flight, SW987 was reported to be unstable around the pitch axis, but handing improved markedly after beading had been applied to the elevator trailing edges. The starboard aileron also exhibited a tendency to float upwards outside limits but the aircraft was eventually re-trimmed successfully. SX297 went to Boscombe Down in July 1946 for trials involving the Type 3A rocket projectile, but it was replaced on 13 November by SX360 after sustaining damage during high-speed firings. During these tests, rockets were launched with the aircraft carrying several different combinations of external stores. On some flights centreline tanks were fitted. As sighting

for rocket launching required a different aiming point to the wing guns, sights with switchable graticules were tried. A total of 104 rockets with 60lb warheads was also fired.

Like the Mk XV, the Seafire XVII entered Fleet Air Arm service after the war had ended. The first recipient of the variant was No. 883 Squadron. Front-line service was brief, the majority of aircraft being relegated to reserve or training units until retirement in late 1954. It had been intended that the Mk XVII would be followed in production by the Mk XVIII. Designated by Supermarine as the Type 395, this was planned as a reconnaissance version of the Mk XVII, powered by the Griffon 36, an example of which was sent to the manufacturer for installation in the first airframe. Wing armament was to have comprised four Browning 0.303in machine-guns and the airframe was to have plumbing for under-wing combat fuel tanks. But even as this specification was being developed, the Fleet Air Arm decided to combine all the fighter reconnaissance roles, which it believed would increase the flexibility of its air wings.

Towards the F.20 Series

In the event, therefore, the next stage of Seafire development was rather more radical because it involved a change in wing planform. The first aircraft to receive the modified wing was Spitfire Mk VIII, JF319, which was also fitted with the Griffon 60 engine. This fighter was to enter RAF service as the Spitfire F.21, the use of Roman numerals in aircraft designations having ended. Although interested, the Admiralty decided to await flight trial results before placing an order. Meantime, two versions were initially schemed, a high-speed interceptor able to meet land-based counterparts on equal terms, and a fighter able to accompany a carrier-launched strike force to its target, deal with any airborne opposition and escort its charges.

To get the aircraft into service the Admiralty was prepared to accept Spitfire F.21s with the minimum amount of modification necessary for naval operations: an arrester hook, catapult launch gear and a some localized strengthening to cope with the altered stress paths. Supermarine's response was designated Type 474. It was to be powered by a two-stage supercharged

Seafire XVII SX156 displays its re-painted fin and rudder after transfer from No. 767 Squadron at Milltown to Yeovilton. Although the aircraft was refurbished in February 1951, it went straight into storage and was scrapped in 1956. Ray Sturtivant

Seafire XVII SX345 of No. 800 Squadron is pictured here with under-fuselage fuel tanks. Its service life was short as it entered service in May 1946 and was written-off in a crash aboard HMS *Triumph* in January 1949. FAAM Yeovilton

Seafire XVII SX358 of No. 800 Squadron pictured on the ground at Hal Far, Malta, while its parent carrier HMS *Triumph* is in Valetta harbour. Prominent in this view are the under-wing combat tanks. Ray Sturtivant

Griffon engine driving a contra-rotating propeller assembly and mounted in a Seafire XV/ XVIII fuselage. It was also to have the laminar-flow wings developed for the Spitfire F 21 with a fold just outboard of the undercarriage bays. The undercarriage itself had the much-requested wider track, which, it was hoped, would improve stability on a pitching carrier deck. Great effort was also made to improve the view over the nose, especially during ground mano-euvring.

A bubble cockpit canopy was featured with a cut-down rear fuselage. Armament was to be four 20mm cannon with 150 rounds per gun. From the outset the aircraft was to be capable of accelerated launching and arrested stops. Internal fuel capacity was set at 116gal (517ltr) with a further 45gal (200ltr) available in external tanks. The aircraft had a span of 35ft (11.8m) with wings spread and 17ft (5.2m) with them folded. Fuselage length was 32ft 3in (9.9m) and propeller diameter would be 11ft (3.4m). Basic weight was estimated to be 6,560lb (2,981kg) to which would be added 200lb (90kg) of armour and 395lb (180kg) of military equipment. Other unspeci-fied items lifted tare weight to 7,155lb (3,252kg). Total operating weight was esti-mated at 9,060lb (4,118kg), the difference being made up of 960lb (436kg) of other consumables, 835lb (380kg) of fuel and 80lb (36kg) of engine oil. With a Griffin 61 engine, top speed was 424mph (678km/h) at 26,000ft (8,000m), with a

stalling speed with a full military load of 88kt (99mph or 158km/h). Initial rate of climb was estimated to be 4,900ft (1,500m) per minute. Service ceiling was set at 41,750ft (12,850m).

To cover this proposal the Admiralty issued Specification N7/44 for what was basically a navalized Spitfire F 21. The task of adapting the drawings to meet the new specification was allocated to Cunliffe Owen. This version of the Seafire would be designated Mk 45. From the outset it was regarded as being an interim phase-one design; phase two would be the Mk 46 and phase three the Mk 47. The programme started on 15 August 1944 when the Ministry of Aircraft Production directed Vickers to remove two Spitfire F 21s from the production line and send them to Hursley Park for conversion to Seafire Mk 45 prototypes under Contract Acft/4425/C.23c.

Three machines had originally been ordered for conversion but one was later cancelled, leaving the first converted aircraft, serial TM379, to shoulder the deve-lopment burden, together with TM383. TM379 was delivered to High Post for weighing and C of G checking on 24 October 1944. Although not fully con-verted to naval standard, it featured a sting hook installation, which increased its length to 33ft 4in (10.2m). It also featured slinging points, main undercarriage leg doors modified to clear arrester wires and re-profiled outboard doors. TM379 was powered by a Griffon 61 engine rated at 2,035hp and driving a five-bladed Rotol propeller with laminated wooden blades. Tare weight was 7,121lb (3,237kg).

A few days later, TM379 was at Boscombe Down for flight, handling and deck suitability trials. It was during this period that its maximum weight was determined to be 9,410lb (4,277kg), while the C of G aft datum point was given as 4.9in (12.5cm) aft. From the outset the Seafire 45 was fitted with a larger fin and rudder, but even then the power of the Griffon engine meant that full left rudder was required on take-off to compensate for the torque. Once airborne the Seafire exhibited a tendency to slight starboard wing drop, which was easily correctable. During the glide approach phase of the flight trials, speed was held at 90kt (101mph or 162km/h) with flaps and undercarriage down. Stability and control response during this phase was reported to be excellent.

Seafire XVII SX277 of No. 741 Squadron is pictured in the hangar at St Merryn. In April 1950 the aircraft was transferred to No. 1831 Squadron at Bramcote and written-off in a crash on *Illustrious* in September 1950. FAAM Yeovilton

TM379 was the first Seafire F.45 prototype, having been ordered as a Spitfire F.21. Originally fitted with a standard engine and propeller, as shown, the aircraft was later fitted with a Griffon 85 and contra-rotating propeller. BBA Collection

There was some cause for concern, however. At 25,000ft (7,700m), to which altitude the aircraft was limited, longitudinal stability at maximum speed was marginal. The Admiralty was less willing than the RAF to accept this limitation in the short term. Supermarine proposed various rudder and trim-tab modifications but there was also concern that installation of a contra-rotating propeller might also induce instability. Should correction prove necessary a fin extension was proposed. TM379 returned to the manufacturer for an extension to the leading edge of its fin. After the usual post-manufacturer's checks at High Post the aircraft was flown by Supermarine test pilots Quill and Shea-Simmonds.

Testing Starts

Quill was the first to fly the aircraft in its modified form during October 1944 when he found that it showed a tendency for the left wing to drop in a dive. Although overall directional stability was assessed as poor, Quill considered that the rudder with the sting hook fitted provided adequate control for carrier operations. Further flights reinforced Quill's initial thoughts. He also commented that without protective armour, the C of G was further forward than preferred. Work continued on finding an answer to the lack of stability. Eventually, in late January 1946, the Rotol contra-rotating propeller was replaced by a de Havilland unit. Quill reported that this made stability fore and aft far more positive but still not good enough for service use. He also commented on the unit's vibration, which became noticeably worse as speed increased.

Shea-Simmonds got his hands on TM379 in April 1946 and his first comment concerned a restrictor wire across the throttle, which restricted boost to plus-12psi (0.8bar); this was a temporary measure. On completion of the test flights it was intended to remove the wire to allow the throttle to deliver maximum boost of plus-18psi (1.24bar). He also commented on the directional instability, which was especially noticeable around the pitch and yaw axes above 360kt (405mph or 648km/h). As the Spitfire F 21 and Seafire Mk 45 were similarly afflicted, this behaviour was considered unacceptable for general service use. Temporary fixes were proposed but the only real cure was to fit

larger control surfaces to the rear of the aircraft. Beading applied to the rudder's trailing edge and a bigger balance horn produced improvements considered just acceptable for service use, but a split trim tab had no significant effect.

With the stability problems now under control, and TM379 cleared by RAE Farnborough for arrested landings up to 3g, it was time for deck landing trials aboard the *Pretoria Castle*. These began in November 1945. The aircraft had also been fitted with an S.32 forged steel hook instead of the previous welded assembly. The primary purpose of these trials was to examine handling up to a maximum weight of 9,400lb (4,273kg) at deck wind speeds of 20, 25 and 30kt (36, 45 and 54km/h). Approach speed was between 85 and 90 kt (153 and 162km/h) with touch-down and wire engagement speeds averaging 60kt (108km/h). For the tests, wind speeds varied between 27 and 35kt (49 and 63km/h). A total of four arrested landings was made, the sequence being terminated when the aircraft was damaged on landing. This followed a stall that caused the wing to drop, resulting in damage to the wing and propeller tips.

Contract Placed

Regrettable though this incident was it did not prevent the Ministry of Aircraft Production from issuing on 26 February 1945 Contract B.981687/39/c.23(c) to cover the manufacture of 600 Seafire 45/46/47s to Specification N7/44. This stipulated that delivery was to start in early August. Initially, five Mk 45s were to be produced each month until a total of twenty had been manufactured, after which 200 Mk 46 aircraft were to be delivered. The programme was scheduled to end in June 1946. Seafire 47 production was to start in September 1945 and be completed in December 1946.

Seafire Mk 45 LA436 undertook manufacturer's flight trials on 10 and 11 May 1945, before being flown to High Post a week later for the obligatory weight and C of G testing. Tare weight was determined to be 7,050lb (3,205kg) with maximum weight at 9,358lb (4,254kg). Further carrier trials covering the behaviour of the Seafire Mk 45 continued with LA440 and LA441 operating together with Seafire XV PK245, the latter being configured for tail-down launches. It also had under-wing combat

fuel tanks for comparison trials with the Mk 45s.

The Seafire XV made nine launches, operating at weights of between 7,980lb (3,627kg) and 8,336lb (3,789kg). Both the Mk 45s undertook a similar series of launches, but LA440 dropped out following an impact with the protective barrier rigged across the deck. On its eighth landing the overstressed arrester hook was pulled from its mountings. The impact was such that the front section of the fuselage forward of the firewall was totally wrecked, although the cockpit remained intact. The remains were later returned to High Post for inspection, leaving LA441 to complete the programme without further incident. A further two Mk 45s, LA454 and LA480, were allocated for deck landing trials aboard the *Pretoria Castle* during October 1945. Together the pair made 200 deck landings which helped clear the type for service use.

The Seafire 45 production run began with LA428 and ended with LA499, a total of fifty being delivered to the Fleet Air Arm. This variant's time in the front-line was short-lived, however, as it was soon replaced by the Seafire 46 and 47. But this was not the end of its usefulness. In late 1951 three aircraft, LA439, LA442 and LA445, fitted with contra-rotating propellers, were handed over to RAE Meadow Gate for crash-barrier testing. The purpose was to clear the Westland Wyvern – also featuring a contra-rotating propeller unit – for safe barrier entry. In the first trial LA439's engine was set to run at 800rpm with its tail raised. Additional propulsive power from sixteen 3in rocket bodies pushed the speed up to 60kt (108km/h). With the airframe accelerated to flight speed, the Seafire flew on its own until it engaged the barrier. LA442, however, suffered some propeller damage, as did LA450 on its first trial launch. The second series of launches and short flights saw LA439 overturning after engaging the barrier, while LA450 was badly damaged beyond economic repair after its final launch.

The facility at Meadow Gate was also used for testing the proposed Seafang contra-rotating propellers to see how they stood up to a crash landing. Mounted tail-up on the launch cradle, and with its undercarriage in the up position, LA448 was launched at 56kt (63mph or 100km/h). The pilotless Seafire travelled no more than 90ft (28m) before hitting the concrete. It skidded off the runway and ploughed across

Seafire F.45 LA543 was used for type trials from January 1946 to September 1949, when the aircraft was transferred to No. 1832 Squadron at Culham. It remained there until its withdrawal from service in January 1950. FAAM Yeovilton

the grass at the side. Further destructive trials involved this small batch of aircraft in testing the steam catapults that were to soon to enter service with the Royal Navy's aircraft carriers. The outer wing panels were removed, the reasoning being that with reduced wing area the aircraft would plough into the sea soon after launch. But this did not happen. After launch the aircraft not only continued to fly but also orbited the carrier in ever-decreasing circuits, eventually crashing into the sea.

There were several significant differences between the Seafire 46 and its predecessor. It featured a contra-rotating propeller assembly and the original Spitfire/Seafire tail unit was replaced by that developed for the forthcoming Spiteful. Missing from this version was the wing-folding capability, which limited carrier deployment. As a result, only twenty-four of the 200 aircraft originally ordered were delivered. Before its diversion to Cunliffe-Owen for conversion, the prototype Mk 46, TM383, had originally been intended to be the third Mk 45. In its new guise, TM383 made its first flight on 8 September 1944 and the flight test programme began in earnest by the end of the year.

Although the aircraft was reported to be more stable in flight, early tests revealed that the flaps had a tendency to drop down during a dive. Indicators and a camera were

Side-on view of Seafire F.46, LA541. The differences between this variant and the later F.47 were few, the main one being the lack of folding wings. LA541 was employed on trials work, which ended in 1950 when the aircraft was sold. FAAM Yeovilton

fitted for subsequent flights, but despite strenuous efforts this tendency was never fully cured. TM383 was also used to test a modified sting hook and metal elevators, both of which introduced directional instability. During subsequent spinning trials it was discovered that in right-hand spins, the aircraft recovered without any pilot input. At the completion of these

flights, TM383 was reconfigured to represent production airframes and it was considered to be even better than the Seafire XV. Deliveries of the Mk 46 had been completed by March 1947. But because there were so few, and with the Mk 47 about to emerge, most of the airframes were utilized in the later variant's test and trials programme.

Seafire F.46 LA550 was originally delivered to No. 778 Squadron in July 1946. The aircraft remained in service until it was withdrawn in March 1949. FAAM Yeovilton

Final Variant: the F.47

As the final variant to enter service, the Mk 47 showed how far the Seafire had come since the original Mk IB, which had joined the Fleet Air Arm just a few years earlier. The only feature the two had in common besides the name was outward retracting undercarriage, although that on the Mk 47 operated at a different angle and was capable of bearing greater weights. There were some differences between the Mk 47 and its immediate predecessor; some were more obvious than others. As standard, the Mk 47 featured the larger Spiteful tail, an extended ram air supercharger intake under the engine and fittings for tail-down launches, plus manual and power-operated wing-folding.

Because so much useful data had been garnered from the Mks 45 and 46, there was no prototype for the Mk 47. The first two production aircraft, PS944 and PS945, were used for type clearance. Constructed at South Marston, the first made its maiden flight on 25 April 1946 with the other following on 12 October. Both were powered by the Griffon 87 driving a six-bladed contra-rotating propeller unit, as were the following twelve aircraft. The final seventy-three aircraft from serial VP428

were fitted with the Griffon 88, which featured a Mk II combined injector and fuel pump. This unit improved the aircraft's 'g' performance but at the cost of an additional 70lb (32kg) weight. Only the first four aircraft featured manual wing folding, which required struts to support them in the position. The other machines all had power folding using a dedicated hydraulic system. In both cases the fold point was just outboard of the cannon bays.

PS944 was delivered to Boscombe Down in November 1946 for handling trials. In an effort to improve stability, the Mk 47s were fitted with spring tab elevators, a large inertia weight mounted in the elevator control run and beading strip on the elevator trailing edges. With these features the limiting Mach number rose from 0.77 to 0.82 at which point pitching became obvious. Internal fuel tankage was 287gal (1,279ltr). Range could be extended to 1,250miles (2,000km) with a 170gal (758ltr) ferry tank. Although these trials were considered successful, the test pilots did comment on the effort needed to put the aircraft into a sideslip and to centralize the rudder in the climb. None of the initial remedial attempts was fully effective and the eventual consensus of opinion favoured a short dorsal. In the event, the difficulty

of introducing such a modification into a production run meant that the Seafire Mk 47 entered service almost unchanged.

Performance trials were undertaken using PS945, the results being compared with those from the earlier Mk 46. These comparisons revealed that the Mk 47 was some 15mph (24km/h) slower, the difference being traced to the carburettor intake, that on the later aircraft being longer because it ended just behind the spinner base. The third production aircraft, PS946, had been completed as an FR.47 and it was used to prove the variant's range and endurance.

Air-Sea Rescue?

Air-sea rescue duties would not normally have been performed by a high-performance fighter, but Seafire 47 VP463 was used to test the Type G ASR container mounted on a bomb carrier under the port wing. Dropping it required the Seafire to fly level at an altitude of 4,000ft (1,200m) at 150mph (240km/h). Initially, the container hit the wing when it was released as the airflow pulled the front section down. A minor alteration to its shape improved its aerodynamic performance and cured the problem.

Contrasting beautifully with the lighter countryside below is this Seafire F.47, which reveals the clean lines of this variant. FAAM Yeovilton

PS944 was the first folding-wing Seafire F.47. It was fitted with a Griffon 87 engine and contra-rotating propeller, being used mainly for clearing the type for flight. FAAM Yeovilton

This three-quarter rear view of a Seafire FR.47 clearly shows the Spiteful tail unit fitted to this variant. The larger tail improved the type's longitudinal stability. BBA Collection

The same aircraft was then employed on drop trials involving the 90gal (401ltr) overload tank. Incorporating lessons learned from the ASR container release and clearance difficulties, the tank was configured to release from the rear mounting, after which it fell away cleanly. Further trials revealed that the tank had an occasional tendency to hit the aircraft's fuselage. A camera was installed to provide evidence that separation was not always clean. A papier mache rear section designed to crumple on release was later fitted. While the 90gal tank was being modified, VP463 was used for tests of the 50gal (223ltr) tank. This required the crutch mountings to be altered to permit a trouble-free release.

Accelerated launch trials were held at RAE Farnborough during July 1949 using VP437. These tests involved catapult launches and arrested landings. RATOG units were also used. During these flights the Seafire carried various combinations of rocket carriers, combat tanks, overload tanks and bombs. Maximum all-up launch weight was set at 12,900lb (5,864kg). Maximum speed with two empty combat tanks was 450mph (720km/h). Carrier trials were undertaken aboard HMS *Illustrious* during May 1947 using aircraft PS945, PS948 and PS949. The pilots involved were content with their aircrafts' behaviour and particularly praised the larger flaps, which made the Seafire easier to control during carrier landings.

Like most of the late-build Seafires, the Mk 47 had a short career. It was no longer used for front-line operations after completing its Korean War service in 1950. Reserve use ended some two years later. Supermarine made one last attempt to maintain the Spitfire/Seafire line through the development of the Spiteful and Seafang. Designated the Type 382 by the manufacturers, the naval version of the Spiteful, the Seafang, was first mentioned in the Spiteful specification, released in February 1943. This was followed in October 1943 by that for the Seafang. It envisaged an aircraft that was essentially a carrier-based fighter based on the Seafire XV, powered by a Griffon 61 engine and featuring laminar flow wings. Contra-rotating propellers were also specified and armament was to comprise a pair of 20mm cannon in each wing with 150 rounds per gun. Internal fuel capacity was to be 116gal (517kg) with a further 45gal (200ltr) in external tanks. Initially, the Royal Navy showed little interest in the specification; getting the Seafire into front-line service took priority. It was not until 21 April 1945 that the Air Ministry issued on the navy's behalf Specification N.5/45 for a single-seat naval fighter. Two prototypes were ordered and were allocated the serials VB893 and VB895.

Even though the Seafang was on order for the Admiralty, their Lordships' enthusiasm for the type was beginning to cool as the Sea Fury and Sea Hornet were coming into service. In any case, there was no chance of the Seafang entering service before 1947. Their conclusion was that a handful might be useful for training pending the arrival of the proposed Jet Spiteful/

Seafire FR47 VP482 banks towards the camera. After serving with No. 800 Squadron aboard HMS *Triumph*, the aircraft was transferred to No. 1833 Squadron at Bramcote, being withdrawn in September 1953. FAAM Yeovilton

PS944, the Seafire F.47 development prototype, shows its wings in the folded position. Of note is the changed wing planform featured by this variant. BBA Collection

Seafang. The Jet Seafang did appear, but by then its name had been changed to Attacker; from it would evolve the Swift and Scimitar. Meanwhile, the navy order was finally settled at 150 aircraft and this was confirmed by letter on 7 May 1945. A Spiteful F XV, RB520, was fitted with a sting-type arrester hook for tests. It remained at High Post for two years before being accepted on behalf of the Royal Navy, which then scrapped it.

The programme eventually got back on schedule. The Griffon 89 engine delivered to Hursley Park in October 1945 was installed in VB895 to drive a contra-rotating propeller unit and enable it to make its maiden flight at the beginning of 1946. It was then called Seafang XXXII and equipped with power-operated folding wings. After an extensive manufacturer's test-flying programme, the aircraft was delivered to RAE Farnborough for pre-service trials. During these flights the rudder horn balance kept failing when stressed by the deceleration of arrested landings. The original aluminium balance was later replaced by a high tensile unit but this did not provide a remedy. The rudder assembly had to be removed and completely re-skinned and strengthened.

Landing trials followed at Chilbolton and Ford during June 1947. During these flights the flap setting for landings was determined to be 76 degrees, while the take off-setting was optimised at 30 degrees. The best landing speed with flaps at 76 degrees was found to be 95kt (107mph or 170km/h). In his report on the trials, Supermarine test pilot Mike Lithgow praised the Seafang for its good landing behaviour. He noted that the forward view was better than the Seafire's and also that there was no tendency to float when the throttle was cut just before touch-down. This programme represented a follow-up to flights already undertaken aboard HMS *Illustrious* in May 1946.

Such was the report's enthusiasm that the pilots at the Service Trials Unit, formed at RNAS Ford, were anxious to get their hands on the aircraft. The Royal Navy would have to wait, however, as VB895 was lent to the manufacturers to enable it to be demonstrated to the Dutch Air Force at Valkenburg on 19 August 1946. The same week it was also shown to representatives of the US, French and Netherlands navies.

On return to Britain the Seafang became involved in the development of external fuel tanks. These were new items although

the release sequence was similar to the Seafire's. There were two versions – containing 90 and 170 gal (400 and 760 ltr) respectively – which were released at speeds up to 255kt (287mph or 460km/h) and few problems were encountered. The sixth production Seafang F 32, VG741, actually made its first flight before the prototype aircraft and was accordingly downgraded to Mk 31 standard. This meant that it lacked folding wings and featured a standard five-bladed Rotol propeller in place of a contra-rotating unit. The aircraft joined VB895 in the development programme alongside VG474 whose task was to investigate lateral control behaviour. The Seafang was initially fitted with standard slotted tab-balanced

ailerons which gave it a rate of roll of 270ft (83m) per second at 500mph (800km/h). In November 1947 VG747 was equipped with a Lockheed Servodyne power-operated control unit and one of its fuselage fuel tanks had to be removed to make room for it. While pilots appreciated the power assistance, the lack of feel and fine sensitivity meant that the aircraft needed careful handling.

Seafang VG475 was used to determine the wing's drag coefficient, for which purpose a pitot comb was fitted to the trailing edge to measure the wake turbulence bleeding from it. John Derry, later to become a de Havilland test pilot, was assigned to these flights, which were

RB520 was originally built as a Spiteful before being transformed into the prototype Seafang, although its naval features were limited to an arrester hook.
BBA Collection

The work on the Spiteful/Seafang was not completely wasted as their laminar-flow wings were later used on the jet-powered Attacker. BBA Collection

undertaken on 23 June 1947. During the first flight, the aircraft reached Mach 0.69 in a dive from 24,000ft (7,385m) without incident. In the second dive, during which Mach 0.77 was achieved, Derry encountered severe pitching. This continued to 6,000ft (1,800m) even though the engine had been throttled back. The cause was suspected to be disturbed airflow over the wing's trailing edge generated by the test equipment and interfering with elevator operation. Although a fairing was fitted over the pitot comb to smooth out the airflow, the programme was abandoned after a few further flights.

The hardest worked Seafang, VB895, was returned to the manufacturers in June 1948 for the installation of improved gun bay ventilation following an explosion during acceptance trials of the Hispano Mk.5* 20mm cannon at Boscombe Down in April 1947. This installation comprised two small scoops per bay, with a pair of vents in the wing's upper surface. This avoided the build-up of dangerous gasses and allowed the trials to be completed successfully.

Eventually, only nine Seafangs, VG741 to VG479, were delivered from the ordered total of 150 aircraft, although seven more were delivered in kit form. One last attempt was made to maintain Supermarine's production of propeller-driven aircraft.

Designated the Type 391 by the manufacturer, this design was intended to be powered by the Rolls-Royce 46H Eagle driving contra-rotating propellers. There were to be radiator cooling intakes in the wing leading edges and, as with the Seafang, the undercarriage units would retract inwardly with the wheels rotating for vertical stowage in the fuselage. Proposed armament was four 20mm cannon with 150 rounds per gun and top speed was estimated at 500mph (800km/h). Although this design never got off the drawing board, many of its main features found their way into the Attacker. R.J. Mitchell's immortal design had moved into the jet age.

The Griffon Seafire Specification

When Specification No.7/44/P1/SU was issued on 1 October 1944 it covered production of the navalized version of the Spitfire F.21, later to be known as the Seafire F 45. It covered the production aircraft but not the first two prototypes. The basis of the new variant was its Spitfire equivalent, except where changes were required for naval operations. While most of the specifications in the Naval Operational Requirements schedule had to be adhered to, for some unstated reason the pilot's headrest was not required to be moved.

As this was a new Seafire variant, the third aircraft would be regarded as the first production machine, all of which were to be fitted with the Rolls-Royce Griffon RG4SM series engine. If available, a contra-rotating propeller unit was to be installed. Although not intended as a reconnaissance aircraft, the Seafire F.45 was to incorporate mountings for one oblique and one vertical camera to be fitted at a later date in early-build machines. Production machines would feature them as soon as possible.

The Admiralty requirement for the Seafire F.45 was covered by Specification N7/44. This called for the aircraft to operate world-wide from the decks of the Royal Navy's aircraft carriers. It demanded that the aircraft be capable of remaining under full control during deck landing approaches at a speed of approximately 85kt (96mph or 153km/h) without the application of more than two-thirds engine power. Other required qualities included good fore and aft stability, good longitudinal, lateral and directional control and ease of throttle operation. Also required was adequate drag to ensure rapid deceleration after throttle closure to prevent unnecessary float.

When making take-offs without catapult assistance into a 27kt (49km/h) head wind, the Seafire F.45 was required use no more than 500ft (154m) of the deck. In flight excellent rolling characteristics were expected, together with the smallest possible turning circle. The arrester hook was to be of the sting type and the aircraft had to be capable of tail-down take-offs using Rocket-Assisted Take-Off Gear (RATOG). The Seafire had to capable of being winched aboard ship with wings folded or spread. Unlike its land-based counterpart, it had to incorporate extra lashing-down points for bad weather securing on deck or below in the hangar.

Although the Admiralty accepted the standard fuel tank capacity as adequate, the specification called for the capability to carry 50gal (223ltr) or 90gal (400ltr) external fuel tanks. Provision also had to be made for two semi-permanent under-wing tanks able to hold 25gal (111ltr) each. They had to be jettisonable or capable of being quickly removed on the ground. Provision for an external ferry tank capable of being jettisoned was also required.

Although the Admiralty was prepared to accept the standard armour plate fitting, a special request was made for additional protection for the Type 2BX beacon if possible. A variety of radio fits was also specified, including the SCR 522, although the TR 1196 was acceptable. Also required was a Beacon Receiver Type ZBX, an IFF Mk 3 or 3GR, plus a tail warning radar Type AN/APS 13. Although this equipment would not necessarily be available at the time of manufacture, cabling was required to be planned into the production run.

Flight testing required the aircraft to be fully equipped to military delivery standards, but as the first examples were to be also test flown at the Aircraft and Armament Experimental Establishment (A&AEE), a full set of distant reading oil thermometers had to be installed, plus gauges to measure the scavenge oil pressure at the cooler inlets. Another provision for the A&AEE test flights was a tail parachute for spin testing.

During the experimental test flights the aircraft had to be capable of inverted flight up to a maximum of minus-2.75g. In high-speed flight, wing lift reversal without reference to any compressibility effects had to exceed 625mph (1,000km/h). The ailerons and wing structure had to be of a strength and stiffness that allowed maximum rolling performance to be safely utilized. Spinning was to be limited to two turns, at which point the aircraft should automatically recover. As the arrester hook was to be of the sting type, the specification called for a maximum deceleration loading of 2g. The undercarriage was to be capable of withstanding a vertical velocity of 11.5ft (3.5m) per second. When fitted with wing folding systems, the wing mountings had to be capable of remaining undamaged in the face of a 35kt (63km/h) wind, whether the wings were folded or spread.

Before delivery to A&AEE a contractor's flight trial had to be undertaken, which was then certified for the DTD. During these flights the Seafire was to be spun both left and right and all details noted.

CHAPTER EIGHT

Against the Rising Sun

When the escort carrier HMS *Atheling* embarked No. 889 Squadron in April 1944 this marked the first deployment outside the UK for the Supermarine Seafire III. The aircraft, from the first production batch, were joined by No. 890's Wildcats and by pilots from No. 834 Fighter Flight who had flown Mk IICs from HMS *Battler* during its foray into the Indian Ocean earlier in the year.

After a period of working up, *Atheling* joined the fleet carrier HMS *Illustrious*, now with Corsairs and Fairey Barracudas aboard, for Operation *Councillor*, which was intended to provide a distraction while US forces attacked Japanese positions in the Marianas. The British vessels formed a twenty-four-ship task force together with the US carrier *Saratoga*, whose objective

was Sabang, Sumatra. The Japanese were not fooled and the British ships were ignored.

On 23 June, *Atheling*'s aircraft provided air cover for *Illustrious*, which had just refuelled, before fifty-one aircraft were launched for attacks on Port Blair in the Andaman Islands. It was during this operation that tragedy struck. The Seafire squadron's CO, Lt Cdr F.A.J. Pennington RNZVNR, collided with his wingman and both were killed. There was a further accident six days later when a landing Seafire completely missed the arrester wires and ploughed into another aircraft. Two pilots and three deck party members were killed. No. 889 was now down to six pilots and five aircraft and, as *Atheling* had been too slow to keep up with the main fleet, it

was decided that the ship and her air group should be re-assigned. Both *Atheling* and No. 889 had seen the last of the Seafire: the ship was to act as a ferry carrier supporting the British element of the US-led Task Force 57, while No. 889 was to be re-equipped with Hellcats.

Atheling's replacement was the fleet carrier HMS *Indefatigable*. Having been assigned to the British Pacific Fleet, she left Portsmouth on 19 November for the Far East. On board was No. 24 Fighter Wing, comprising Nos 887 and 894 Squadrons equipped with Seafires together with a strike element provided by No. 1770 Squadron's Fireflies and No. 820's Grumman Avengers. The carrier arrived at Colombo on 10 December to form part of No. 1 Aircraft Carrier Squadron (1 ACS), British Pacific

Escorted by Chance Vought F4U Cosairs, this Barracuda heads for its next target. While the Fairey type was not particularly popular it did fulfil its intended role, although it was replaced in the BPF by the Grumman Avenger. FAAM Yeovilton

Flying them aboard was the quickest way of transferring replacement aircraft, but the preferred method was to ferry them to the carrier in a lighter and then winch them up to the deck. Both these machines are destined for HMS *Atheling*. Rick Harding Collection

Fleet (BPF). After acclimatization training, the carrier was declared fit for service and ready for Operation *Lentil*, together with HMS *Victorious*. Accordingly, the air wings mounted strikes on oil refineries at Pangkalan, Brandan and Sumatra. During this operation the Seafire IIIs not only mounted combat air patrols but were also required to fly early morning reconnaissance flights and fleet anti-submarine patrols.

This latter role was one previously undertaken by multi-seat aircraft, but these were now required for strike duties. On the face of it, the Seafires' lack of anti-sub-marine armament might seem to render them unfit for anti-submarine work, but the mere presence of cannon-armed fighters was considered sufficient to deter any Japanese submarine and force it to submerge. No submarines were spotted during these sorties and no submarine attacks were ever made on British aircraft carriers by the Imperial Japanese Navy.

Attacks on Oil Refineries

Although cutting supply lines and choking off fuel supplies might have been less headline-grabbing than assaults on Japanese military forces, such attacks were identified by the strategic planners as crucial to the enemy's defeat. This was the role assigned to 1 ACS, which now comprised the fleet carriers *Illustrious*, *Indefatigable*, *Indomitable* and *Victorious*. It was commanded by Rear Admiral Sir Philip Vian flying his flag in *Indomitable*. The first sorties were launched on 24 January 1945 as part of Operation *Meridian*, a further attack on aviation fuel refineries and storage depots at Pladjoe, Sumatra. As these strikes were to be launched off the island's south-west coast, the time in transit was used for air defence exercises, during which Seafires played the roles of both defending and attacking fighters. Changeable weather, however, resulted in the inevitable landing accidents. There were three on the 17th as the ship was pitching in a heavy sea and rain was sweeping accross the decks. The heavy rain was also responsible for frequent cases of radio failure.

Indefatigable launched Seafires at 06.30hr on the 24th to provide cover and anti-submarine patrols over the fleet. The twenty-two Seafire IIIs and sixteen L.IIIs of No. 24 Naval Air Wing were employed on providing seven hours of patrols. Despite the sea state remaining rough, with carrier decks pitching quite violently at times, Seafire losses in landing accidents were minimized. One Seafire L.III, though, had to be abandoned by its pilot when the undercarriage failed to lower, but he was quickly rescued by the guard destroyer. Two of *Indefatigable*'s Seafires – one of each variant – were damaged beyond repair as the No. 7 wire was malfunctioning, presenting a bottomed wire to arrester hooks and leading to overstressed rear fuselages. Another pair of Seafires suffered buckling and a fifth aircraft was overstressed when a tyre burst on landing.

Pitching combined with a slight corkscrewing effect caused the deck landing control officer (the 'batsman') to wave-off many approaching aircraft. The resulting delay in the landing rate caused some concern among command staff. Many had made no secret of their distrust of the Seafire nor their preference for its American counterparts. The attack, however, was a success. The strike destroyed the refinery at Pladjoe and depleted Japanese fuel supplies. Five days later the carrier group's aircraft were in action again. This time the target was the refinery at Soengi Gerong, which formed the second refinery complex

The sea is calm, the weather is bright as a Seafire II roars off the deck of an escort carrier complete with a 250lb bomb on the centreline. In the background ground crew swarm like bees around further aircraft all carrying bombs. Once the strike has been completed the Seafires will start looking for other business. Rick Harding Collection

With wheels and debris scattered everywhere, a Seafire III heads for HMS *Indefatigable*'s barrier. Rick Harding Collection

Surrounded by crew members and the rescue party, and covered in fire suppressant foam, this Seafire has just crash-landed aboard HMS *Indefatigable*. Rick Harding Collection

Draped unceremoniously over *Indefatigable*'s side is this Seafire III of No. 894 Squadron. Such was the force of the impact that the starboard wing has been torn off and fuel and oil dribbles down the other. Rick Harding Collection

in the Palembang group. It had been intended to follow up the first strike against Pladjoe but the weather was unfavourable. Heavy swells, sweeping rain and problems with replenishment equipment meant that the fleet was unable to launch attacks as soon as planned. Even so, *Indefatigable's* fighter pilots were in the air at first-light for their normal patrolling duties, thirty-three Seafires being available.

With a refinery and storage complex now destroyed the Japanese counterattack came as no surprise, and the British carrier force was shadowed by the Japanese. Ship-borne radar detected an incoming aircraft at 07.40hr and, although Seafires were vectored towards it, they failed to engage. Having completed their patrol, this group of Seafires landed at 08.25hr having been replaced by a similar number of aircraft. At 09.13hr a fast-moving incoming contact was reported. A section led by Sub Lt J.H. Kernahan RN of No. 887 Squadron was directed to the area but failed to make contact. Thirty minutes later, Kernahan's section spotted a Mitsubishi Ki 46 recon-

naissance aircraft (Allied reporting name 'Dinah') travelling fast 15,000ft (4,600m) above the fleet.

Seafires Against 'Dinah'

Under normal circumstances the Seafire would struggle to catch an aircraft as fast as the Ki 46. But in this case the 'Dinah's pilot made an error of judgement by making a shallow turn just as the Seafires reached his altitude. Kernahan fired a long burst, sending the 'Dinah' spiralling down in flames. It was the wing's first aerial 'kill'. As an additional precaution, it had been intended to increase the number of aircraft in the day's third patrol to twelve but two suffered defects just before launch. These fighters spent much of their time during their patrol chasing targets that turned out to be strike force aircraft returning to their carriers. These fruitless diversions meant the need to conserve fuel towards the end of the patrol. Four more Seafires were launched to provide a reinforcement.

Although they increased the aerial strength to seventeen, six fighters were desperately short of fuel while two others were experiencing radio faults. Into this situation at 11.47hr flew a mixed force of Mitsubishi Ki 21 'Sally' and Kawasaki Ki 48 'Lily' bombers on their way to attack the fleet.

A flight of No. 887 Squadron Seafires led by Lt J.W. Hayes RNVR was the first to attack the intruders. A Ki 21 was shot down but the bomber's defensive fire severely damaged the attacking fighter's engine, leaving its pilot with no option but to bale out. By the time the rest of the flight had joined in, the Japanese force had entered the fleet's defence zone, which meant that the fighter pilots were chasing them through a hail of anti-aircraft fire. Despite this, another bomber was shot down by a Hellcat. The next Seafire pilot to achieve a success was Lt Cdr J. Crossman RNVR, CO of No. 894 Squadron, who shared his first kill with a Corsair pilot. His second was a solo achievement when he downed a Ki 48 close to *Indefatigable*. Two Ki 21s were shot down by Sub Lt K. Ward RNVR.

With bombs already exploding in the background, this BPF Avenger turns toward its target. The Avenger was a popular aircraft as it was a typical solidly built Grumman product. FAAM Yeovilton

Pictured just as it hits the barrier, this Seafire III of the Third Naval Fighter Wing has started to shred its propeller. The landing has obviously been a hard one as the tail wheel has been sheared off and the hook forced back into its recess. Ray Sturtivant

British losses were one Seafire after engine failure, the pilot being rescued, while Crossman's radiator was hit, which meant a hasty return to his carrier. A Hellcat was damaged by anti-aircraft fire from the battleship HMS *King George V*. Defensive gunfire caused further damage when *Illustrious* suffered casualties and the loss of two parked aircraft. A Seafire suffered tyre failure while landing on *Indefatigable*. Overall it had been a successful day for No. 24 NAW as everything had gone according to plan. Two attacks on other targets in the Netherlands East Indies had been planned but, due to the shortage of fuel combined with a lack of fleet oilers, the oil refineries were left alone for the time being. The fleet therefore headed for Fremantle, Western Australia, for replenishment before continuing to Sydney to prepare for operations with Task Force 57 in the Pacific.

While the fleet carriers were in Australian waters to make ready for strikes against Japan, another carrier force was preparing for war in the Indian Ocean. The vessels chosen to form this task force were HMS *Attacker*, *Emperor*, *Empress*, *Hunter*, *Khedive* and *Stalker*, which were assigned No. 21 Aircraft Carrier Squadron of the East Indian Fleet, commanded by Commodore G.N. Oliver. *Attacker* had completed a refit at Taranto in December 1944 before leaving for Trincomalee on 1 April 1945

with No. 879 Squadron and its Seafires. But now, like four of the six carriers, she was a Hellcat operator. Only *Hunter*, with No. 807 Squadron, and *Stalker*, with No. 809 Squadron, had the Supermarine fighters aboard.

Operations in Burma

After a photo-reconnaissance mission to Port Swettenham and a strike on Emmahaven by Hellcats and Avengers, Seafires participated in Operation *Dracula* – strikes on Rangoon and the Tenasserim coast – during May. The force, now commanded by Rear Admiral A.W. le T. Bisset, flying his flag in the cruiser *Royalist*, had a total fighter strength of forty-four Hellcats and fifty-four Seafire L.IIIs and LR.IIIs. Spare aircraft were carried aboard *Stalker*. Further replacements were held by the Ruler class carrier *Shah*, which was operating with HMS *Ameer* to provide a backup covering force between Rangoon and Sumatra.

During the approach to Burma, the Seafires undertook thirty-six combat air patrols during which there was only one minor incident. On 1 May, just as the sun was setting, a flight of Lockheed P-38 Lightnings was spotted heading towards the task force at low level by the final Seafire

patrol of the day. As the operation was being carried out under a total radio black-out, it was not possible to contact the US aircraft by radio, nor was the flight leader confident the American pilots would be able to read light signals. The only alternative was to fire a warning burst across the nose of the leading P-38, action which succeeded in diverting the American fighters away from the ships. The same day a Seafire of No. 809 Squadron, returning to *Stalker*, missed the arrester wire, bounced over the fore-deck barrier and ploughed into two parked aircraft. Such was the force of the impact that one aircraft was pushed over the side and the second was wrecked. Nobody was injured. It was the only deck landing accident of the voyage.

Operation *Dracula* was launched in the early hours of the following morning. Poised to strike a decisive blow against the Japanese, the pilots were disappointed to encounter negligible resistance around Rangoon as the Japanese were in the process of pulling out. For the Seafire pilots this meant unopposed bomb runs against the remaining anti-aircraft guns and coastal defence batteries near Thakutpin. All eight bombs dropped hit their targets. Supporting the four fighter-bomber attacks were thirty-six air patrols and tactical reconnaissance sorties. These drew no enemy fighters and reconnaissance failed to reveal anything of

With the debris from its recent dramatic landing scattered around, a Seafire III of No. 807 Sqn settles in the classic nose-over pose seen aboard many an escort carrier. Wisely the crew of HMS *Hunter* are staying clear until the drama is completed Rick Harding Collection

interest. As the Seafires recovered from their sorties, a heavy swell and persistent drizzle following a monsoon storm meant several deck landing accidents aboard *Hunter*. Only two aircraft were written-off but three others had to be struck down below to await repair in port.

The monsoon conditions returned to keep all aircraft on their carriers. A short break in the weather allowed a few missions to be flown the following day, but the monsoon returned and an adverse forecast prompted the force's withdrawal. In any case, the carrier group had completed its tasks on the first day. The carriers were redeployed off the coast of Tenasserim to search for better weather and for targets. Arriving during the morning of 5 May, the

carriers soon had combat air patrols in the air and an additional flight of six Seafire L.IIIs was launched from *Stalker* to seek inshore shipping targets. On their way back they passed a dozen of *Hunter*'s Seafires engaged on the same task but carrying centreline-mounted bombs.

Having swept the area and found no targets, the Seafires had to jettison their bombs. There was one sign of resistance, however, as a No. 807 Squadron Seafire sustained slight damage from anti-aircraft fire while passing the coast. The only other incidents were a barrier engagement, resulting in minor damage, while an aircraft from No. 809 Squadron landed too fast, bounced into the barrier and ripped off its undercarriage. There were no casualties and

once the wreckage had been cleared a pair of Seafires was placed on immediate readiness. They were scrambled late in the afternoon when an incoming aircraft was detected, but the target turned out to be a Consolidated B-24 Liberator whose Identification Friend or Foe (IFF) equipment had been incorrectly set.

On 6 May the carrier group launched another strike of bomb-carrying Hellcats escorted by Seafires. Their target was Port Victoria. While the Hellcats dropped their bombs on the port facilities and sank a barge, the Seafire pilots strafed targets in the area. The afternoon's sorties were performed by No. 809 Squadron, the pilots' mission being to attack enemy shipping. But the monsoon had followed the carrier force and the accompanying thunderstorms were more violent than before. As the Seafires were incapable of flying over the thunderclouds, it was decided to rejoin the main fleet.

Sink the *Haguro*!

While *Stalker*'s aircraft were busy with the roving strike, *Hunter*'s were providing a combat air patrol over the carriers. But they were diverted later in the day to search for the Japanese cruiser *Haguro*, which was reported to be en route to the Andaman Islands to assist in evacuating the garrison there. The search was fruitless as the Japanese had got wind of the search and ordered the cruiser back to port. By the time the two searching Seafires returned to their carrier the light had almost gone and they had to land in near-darkness. The flight leader touched down on *Hunter* and promptly wrote off his Seafire, while his No. 2 headed for *Stalker*. The landing was successful even though the aircraft snagged the last arrester wire and hit the barriers. As its engine had been throttled back the damage to the propeller tips was minimal. While *Stalker* ploughed through the rough sea, her ground crew carefully trimmed the damaged blades, enabling the aircraft to return to *Hunter* the following day as the fleet headed for Trincomalee. The ships arrived on 9 May for repair and revictualling.

The post-operation report from the flying squadrons made for mixed reading. The Seafire unit commanders complained that their roles during *Dracula* had been far less interesting than those of their Hellcat counterparts. The flying commanders agreed that little of value had been achieved, mainly due to bad weather. Another cause for concern was the rise in landing accidents, although it was pointed out that many pilots were inexperienced in operating from escort carriers. Against this, 146 sorties had been flown over the five days.

With Rangoon now in Allied hands, the Japanese High Command decided to withdraw from the Andaman Islands. Most of the long-range flying boats that had operated reconnaissance missions from there had either been destroyed or damaged beyond repair. As the garrison would be much better employed in defending other parts of the Empire, further efforts would be made to evacuate it. On 9 May 1945 the

Royal Navy launched Operation *Dukedom* in response to a sighting of the *Haguro*, which had left Singapore in company with the destroyer *Kamikaze* bound for Port Blair. They were spotted by reconnaissance submarines in the Malacca Strait on 10 May and a British force under the command of Vice Admiral Sir Arthur Power was assembled to hunt them down. This included the carriers *Hunter*, *Khedive*, *Emperor* and *Shah*. Aboard *Hunter* was the Seafire-equipped No. 807 Squadron with No. 809 aboard *Shah*.

Designated Task Force 61, this fleet had put to sea as soon as the *Haguro* had been sighted. The Japanese detected the British ship the following day and *Haguro* and her consort promptly reversed course and headed back to Singapore. On the 14th, *Haguro*, now flying the flag of Vice Admiral Hashimoto, again departed for Port Blair. Task Force 61 had remained in the area and *Shah* launched reconnaissance Seafires of No. 809 at first light. By mid-morning these aircraft had spotted the Japanese ships and a strike package of Avengers was assembled with Seafires flying combat air patrol over the fleet. The Avengers' attack was unsuccessful, and an unserviceable catapult on board *Shah* meant that they were unable to return for another attempt. *Haguro* remained under surveillance and by midnight on 16 May the heavy cruiser was within torpedo range of the 26th Destroyer Flotilla. Although the smaller ships were outgunned by the heavy cruiser's ten 8in weapons, they did get close enough to launch torpedoes. Mortally damaged, *Haguro* started a 30-degree list and sank by the bow in the early hours of 17 May. *Kamikaze* escaped but returned to rescue 320 of the cruiser's crew.

The Japanese reacted to the loss of the *Haguro* immediately by despatching reconnaissance aircraft to shadow the British fleet, but low cloud prevented the combat air patrol aircraft from intercepting them. Despite cloud reaching up to 20,000ft (6,150m), a combat patrol from No. 807 Squadron was vectored towards a large radar blip which turned out to be four Nakajima Ki 43 'Oscars' travelling at high speed towards the fleet some 500ft (1,500m) below. In the event the Seafire pilots' eagerness prompted them to open fire too early, although they did manage to damage two and drive the rest away.

A further pair of 'Oscars' was spotted by the next patrol and all four Seafires dived to the attack. One of the Japanese aircraft was damaged but both escaped after violent

manoeuvres. These encounters represented the only two aerial engagements between the fighters of No. 4 Naval Fighter Wing and the Japanese Army Air Force in the Bay of Bengal region. The post-operation debrief focused on the Seafire pilots' lack of air combat experience. En route to Trincomalee, the fleet maintained anti-shipping patrols. Although no enemy vessels were spotted, one air interception was made: a Consolidated PBY Catalina not transmitting an IFF signal. On 19 May *Khedive* and *Shah* arrived in port followed two days later by *Hunter* and *Emperor*.

While the carriers headed for harbour, No. 4 Fighter Wing's aircraft flew ashore to Trincomalee. The Seafire squadrons remained there because sufficient Hellcats were available to provide fighter cover for continuing carrier operations, although No. 809 Squadron was aboard HMS *Stalker* on 18 June for Operation *Balsam*. The objective was a photographic reconnaissance of the airfields in southern Malaya, followed by an attack on those on Sumatra. *Shah* sailed in company with *Ameer* and *Khedive*. The reconnaissance sorties were completed on 20 June and, while bomb-carrying Hellcats attacked Medan and Bindjai airfields, the Seafire L.IIIs of No. 809 Squadron strafed Lhokseumawe airfield. During the attack a Ki 43 was destroyed and a Ki 21 damaged, while airfield buildings were damaged. During the return trip at least one train was destroyed and a second severely damaged. This was one of the Seafires' most successful sorties as no aircraft were lost during the attack and all would return to *Stalker* without incident.

Japanese Surrender Malaya

On her returning to Ceylon *Stalker* joined *Emperor*, *Hunter* and *Khedive* in exercises to prepare for Operation *Zipper*, the reoccupation of Malaya and Singapore. It began on 10 September but without RAF air cover and bombardment support from the Royal Navy. The targets were Port Dickson and Port Swettenham and the four carriers formed part of a much larger force, along with *Archer*, *Pursuer* and *Trumpeter*. No. 807 Squadron flew four sorties on 8 September and another twenty-nine the following day. But further offensive action was cancelled at lunchtime as the Japanese had surrendered. Over 100,000 British troops were landed at various points along the coast to be met with light resistance.

At the completion of *Zipper* the fleet entered Singapore harbour in triumph on 11 September to accept the official Japanese surrender.

Meanwhile, HMS *Attacker* became involved in plans for landings at Penang code-named Operation *Jurist*, for which purpose No. 879 Squadron's Seafires had been embarked. On 17 August 1945 *Attacker* and *Hunter* sailed for Penang where they arrived on 28 August. Both ships remained offshore until 3 September, although calls for their services were limited. Royal Marines landed without opposition. *Hunter* sailed to join Operation *Zipper*, while *Attacker* joined the rest of the fleet in Singapore Roads on 11 September. After the Japanese surrender the operational service of No. 21 Aircraft Carrier Squadron as well as that of No. 4 Naval Air Wing had been completed. By the end of 1945 all the escort carriers had returned to Britain for return to the US Navy.

When the BPF was assembled for the assault on Japan it represented the largest gathering of British warships since the Grand Fleet sailed to fight the High Seas Fleet at what became known as the Battle of Jutland. Operations in the Atlantic and the Mediterranean had kept the Royal Navy fully occupied and it would be much later in the war before Britain could turn its attentions to recapturing territory lost to the Japanese in 1942. The first operations had been undertaken in the Indian Ocean before the fleet carriers split off and headed for Australia. Some US commanders had opposed the British participation in their operations against Japan. But Winston Churchill's pressure on President Roosevelt obliged them to accept the Royal Navy's contribution to the Pacific war.

The Fleet Train

The next task was to arrange for the fleet's logistical support. In two years of fighting the Japanese in the Pacific, the US Navy had brought its operations there to an unmatched level of efficiency. A key development had been a highly sophisticated organization called the fleet train to keep the fighting ships fuelled and supplied. The US Navy was concerned that the Royal Navy might be obliged to depend on this logistical organization at some point. The British, however, were determined to remain independent. To learn from US experience, a British mission headed by Rear Admiral C.S. Daniel went to the USA and visited the Pacific theatre. But although great efforts were made there were never enough oilers, ferry carriers or supply ships.

Operating bases represented a further headache: they would have to be created virtually from scratch. The chosen location for the main base was Sydney, although the necessary work took longer than expected. Plans were also laid to create intermediate bases along the projected attack route but in the event these were not needed as the Americans allowed the Royal Navy to share their base at Manus. This was fortunate because, lacking an organization like the US Navy's Seabee construction units to develop bases in a short time, a British intermediate base would not have been ready before October 1945. Meanwhile, the Torres Strait between the northern Australian coast and New Guinea was deepened to allow the passage of large warships and facilitate their transit to and from the Indian Ocean.

The BPF's actual deployment in the Pacific was strongly influenced by the Battle of the Philippine Sea in June 1944. Although the Japanese committed much of their remaining ships and aircraft to this confrontation, overwhelming American strength obliged them to pull back their forces to protect bases in Malaya and the home islands and protect vital oil supplies. Initially the Americans had planned to work their way up the chain of Japanese-held islands to the Philippines, but Admiral William F. Halsey Jr, commander of the US Third Fleet, changed the plans at the last moment. Massive air strikes were therefore undertaken against air bases on Formosa and Okinawa in the Ryuku Islands as well as minor ones in between.

Not only was massive damage done to these facilities but 50,000 tons of enemy shipping was sunk. Allied losses were minimal. The twelve-strong carrier force was surrounded by battleships and cruisers, all of which formed a highly-effective anti-aircraft umbrella that attacking aircraft found almost impossible to penetrate. During mid-October the strikes continued, culminating in a heavy attack on Japanese bases at Luzon in the Philippines. This was the moment the Americans had been waiting for. A massive assault was launched on the Philippines as land, sea and air forces piled into the attack.

Action in the Philippines

The Japanese forces were caught off guard. The lack of effective air power meant that the American fleet was virtually untouchable. On 20 October General Douglas MacArthur, the US Commander, South-West Pacific, waded ashore at Luzon to keep a promise he made two years earlier to return to the Philippines. Meanwhile, between the 23rd and 26th a series of naval battles was fought in the seas around the Philippines, which have come to be known collectively as the Battle of Leyte. MacArthur declared that Japan had suffered its most crushing defeat of the war. Indeed, it had been the biggest naval battle in history. In response the Japanese turned to a weapon of desperation, the 'Kamikaze' or 'Divine Wind' suicide missions, the tempo of which would increase as the Allied fleets drew closer to the home islands.

The British Pacific Fleet comprised the most modern ships available to the East Indies Fleet in 1944. It was commanded by Admiral Sir James Somerville. Its first operation in concert with US forces had come early in 1944, with the fleet carrier *Illustrious*, together with the battleships *Queen Elizabeth* and *Valiant*, plus screening cruisers and destroyers under the command of Admiral Sir Arthur Power, the BPF's second-in-command, flying his flag in the battlecruiser *Renown*. Aboard *Illustrious* were Corsairs and Barracudas. The fleet carriers *Formidable*, *Indefatigable*, *Indomitable* and *Victorious* were scheduled to join the fleet within weeks. The repair carrier *Unicorn*, plus the escort carriers *Begum* and *Shah*, formed part of the supply train to ferry replacement aircraft to the bigger carriers and provide emergency flight decks.

The first attack was mounted on 16 April 1944 in company with the US Navy carrier USS *Saratoga* against targets at Sabang, Sumatra. The fleet numbered twenty-six vessels, which included the French battleship *Richelieu* and the Dutch cruiser *Tromp*. The first sorties were flown off in the early hours of 19 April, when the fleet was 100 miles (160km) south-west of Sabang. The strike force comprised forty bombers, mainly Avengers, and forty US-made escort fighters. The refinery suffered extensive damage. Two merchantmen were sunk and the harbour and airfield facilities were damaged. One US Navy fighter was lost, although the pilot was rescued by a submarine.

With the Barracudas now replaced by Avengers, another attack was undertaken on 17 May against oil refineries at Soerabaya, Java. Again the *Saratoga* was involved in the operation, which improved its chances of success. One of the attacking aircraft was lost to anti-aircraft fire. After this strike the *Saratoga* returned to US Navy control. Even though the force was now smaller, Somerville's operations staff were planning another raid. The chosen target was Port Blair in the Andaman Islands. As it was intended to launch the strike closer to the target, the Barracudas replaced the Avengers. Of *Illustrious'* complement of fifty-seven aircraft all but six were launched for the operation. While little damage was achieved due to the lack of suitable targets to attack, it was now clear to Japanese commanders that they now had to contend not only with the American advance through the chains of Pacific islands but also with British attacks on their fuel supplies.

At the end of this mission the carrier group withdrew to Ceylon for rest and replenishment. *Indomitable* and *Victorious* arrived at the beginning of July, and as both ships were new to tropical waters, both vessels undertook an extensive work-up. *Victorious'* first strike, made in company with *Illustrious*, was undertaken on 25 July in an Operation code-named *Crimson*. Their role was to provide air cover for battleships bombarding Sabang as part of the process of softening up Japanese forces in the area.

The air strike, launched as usual in the early morning, comprised eighty Corsairs and nine Barracudas. Eight of the fighters were to spot for the guns of the fleet, a dozen were to form a combat air patrol role while the remainder were briefed to attack the airfield at Koetaradja. The weather was not entirely favourable but there were enough clear patches to allow the airfield attack to proceed, keeping the Japanese fighters on

the ground. The heavy ships duly carried out their bombardment and the only loss was a single aircraft whose pilot was picked up by the cruiser *Nigeria*. At the completion of Operation *Crimson*, *Illustrious* was detached for a much-needed refit in Durban, South Africa. Somerville also left to take up a post in the USA, being succeeded by Admiral Sir Bruce Fraser, who had commanded the Royal Navy force that sank the German battle-cruiser *Scharnhorst* in December 1943.

In the absence of *Illustrious* it would fall to the other two fleet carriers to carry the fight to the enemy. On 29 August their aircraft struck targets in the vicinity of Emmehaven and Indaroeng. Operation *Light* – a series of attacks on the Nicobar Islands – followed on 18 October. With Fraser's second-in-command, Admiral Power, in charge, the fleet left Ceylon on 15 October to provide a diversion for American attacks elsewhere in the region.

Seafire FR.47 VP455 was assigned to No. 804 Squadron in December 1948. It was badly damaged in this accident, which resulted in it being written off. FAAM Yeovilton

By comparison, the British attacks represented little more than an annoyance to the Japanese, whose main attention was focused on the activities of the US task force.

Command Changes

The operation would, however, mark a parting of the ways for Fraser and Powers, who had been appointed to command the East Indies Fleet. Fraser was joined by Admiral Sir Phillip Vian who took over the 1st Aircraft Carrier Squadron, with Vice-Admiral Sir Charles Daniel in charge of administration. Actually, Daniel's role was a highly important one, which entailed more than mere paper shuffling, for it included the provision of logistic support and planning as well as the allocation of manpower. But while Fraser was in command of the BPF, its subordination to the US Navy meant that to avoid possible embarrassment Vice-Admiral Sir Bernard Rawlings assumed command of the fleet at sea. This arrangement meant that Fraser was based initially in Australia, moving his headquarters northwards towards Japan as the war progressed.

Before joining the rest of the BPF, the carrier force under Vian's command was ordered to undertake Operation *Outflank*. In company with *Illustrious* and *Indefatigable* were three anti-aircraft cruisers plus five screening destroyers. Having left port on 17 December, the fleet arrived at its launch point in the Malacca Strait on the 20th. The original target was Pangkalan Brandon, but as it was completely obscured by bad weather the secondary one at Belewan Deli was attacked instead. Oil refineries and port installations were badly damaged. No aerial resistance was encountered and no aircraft were lost to the light anti-aircraft fire encountered.

On 1 January 1945 the carriers were officially assigned to the BPF's 1st Aircraft Carrier Squadron. The same day, Fraser flew to Pearl Harbor for a meeting with the commander-in-chief of the US Pacific Fleet, Admiral Chester W. Nimitz. Together with his senior subordinate commanders, Nimitz expressed his satisfaction at being able to count the BPF as part of the total strength. Meanwhile, the fleet under Vian sailed on 4 January to attack the oil production facilities at Pangkalan Brandon under the code-name of Operation *Lentil*. Such was the accuracy and power of this assault that the refinery and associated storage facilities were completely wrecked, resulting in a massive and permanent reduction in Japanese oil supplies, sapping their ability to fight. On 16 January, the squadron sailed for Australia to prepare for their participation in the final assault on Japan.

Sailing as Task Force 63 on 24 January, all four available carriers, *Indomitable*, *Illustrious*, *Indefatigable* and *Victorious* were deployed to attack the Pladjoe refinery. *Indefatigable* was the only carrier equipped with Seafires. Assigned to the strike were forty-three Avengers carrying a total of 172 500lb bombs, twelve Fireflies and fifty fighters drawn from all four carriers. While the American-supplied fighters provided an escort for the Avengers and Fireflies, the Seafires from *Indefatigable* performed air patrol duties over the fleet. The mission was highly successful and five days later the group struck the Soengi Gerong refinery. This time, however, sixteen aircraft were shot down, but the defenders paid a high price: thirty Japanese fighters were shot down while a further thirty-eight were destroyed on the ground. This group of refineries had originally been operated by Standard Oil and Royal Dutch Shell. It processed at least 50 per cent of all the oil used by Japan and, even more importantly, 75 per cent of its total aviation fuel. The attacks again caused massive amounts of damage to add to the steady toll of oil tankers being taken by Allied submarines.

Having withdrawn from the area, the British vessels refuelled en route to Fremantle, where they arrived on 4 February. Six days later the Fleet arrived at Woolloomooloo near Sydney, this being the BPF's permanent base in Australia. *Illustrious* had to go into dock for attention to her centre propeller shaft, which had been thrown out of alignment during a bomb attack in January 1941. As neither the facilitates nor the time were available for such a major repair, the only answer was to remove the shaft. Although this reduced the carrier's top speed to 24kt (43km/h), it did mean that the carrier was still available to the squadron.

Organizational Changes

As it was clearly impractical for a naval strike force to withdraw to its main base after every attack, the BPF was able to use the facilities at the US Navy base at Manus. Other important decisions were made to ensure that the all-important logistical arrangements were in place. Forward of this base an area of ocean was designated the Operating Area, which was to be close to the targets but far enough away to keep the vulnerable tankers and stores vessels safe from attack. The fleet train, comprising oilers, supply and ammunition ships, plus escort vessels, were to operate between

Seafire F.45 LA488 displays the codes of No. 771 Squadron based at Lee-on-Solent. After later service with No. 773 Squadron, the aircraft was damaged in a crash-landing in May 1950. FAAM Yeovilton

With its chocks lying on the leading edge of the wing, this Fairey Firefly is moved to another part of the deck by _Indefatigable_'s handling party. Rick Harding Collection

these areas. Within the Operating Area, refuelling operations were to take place at dawn and it was planned that the ships of the task force would arrive in the Operating Area to find their respective oiler steaming in the same direction. Each combat ship would come alongside its designated oiler, refuel and then make way for another.

After refuelling, ships requiring stores or ammunition were to go alongside the relevant supply vessel. As the BPF fleet train had been assembled in a hurry, some of its arrangements were not as sophisticated as those of the US Navy whose fleet train consisted of specially-designed ships outfitted with the best handling equipment available. Also included were the escort carriers, whose role was to supply replacement aircraft and ferry repairable machines to the BPF's repair facilities. Initially, refuelling and replenishment after each strike took at least three days. Slicker handling procedures and the use of battleships and fleet carriers to refuel smaller ships reduced this to two days. The entire force and the fleet train remained at sea for up to four weeks unless there were cases of damage or major mechanical defects.

Task Force 57

While the US Navy maintained four large task forces and supporting fleet trains, the BPF's periodic withdrawal meant no British in-theatre presence for days at a time. Rear Admiral Fisher managed to keep the BPF supplied with its needs at all times. He was, however, helped considerably by the establishment of forward bases at Ulithi and Leyte. While the Allies had either driven the Japanese out of many captured territories or else neutralized them, it was quickly realized that a decisive attack on a key base could shorten the war. Planning therefore began for a massive assault on Okinawa code-named Operation _Iceberg_. The BPF's task was to control the area round the Sakishima Gunto Islands and block the flow of aircraft and supplies from either the Japanese home islands or Formosa.

Now designated Task Force 57, the British fleet operated in conjunction with the US Navy's Task Force 58 to form a 1,200-strong armada converging on Okinawa. The American fleet began its operations on 14 March by striking airfields in the south of the islands. A Japanese counterattack four days later resulted in

damage to the carriers USS _Intrepid_ and _Enterprise_, but given the size of the force, its striking power was barely dented. Five days later the Americans again struck Okinawa. The surrounding sea was swept clear of mines to enable the battleships to close in and deliver the heaviest-ever naval bombardment. This commenced on 24 March and two days later the neighbouring island of Kerama Retto was captured, enabling the Americans to establish a base and repair facility.

Task Force 57 had sailed from Manus on 14 March. It comprised the 1st Battle Squadron, the 1st ACS, the 4th Cruiser Squadron plus three flotillas of destroyers. By the following day the fleet train, designated Task Force 112, was also on the move. Task Force 57 was divided into task units, 112/2/1 formed around the escort carrier _Stalker_, TU 112/2/5 consisted of three oilers with air defence provided by the ferry carrier _Speaker_. Task Force 57 comprised: the battleships _King George V_ and _Howe_; the fleet carriers _Indomitable_, flying Vian's flag and carrying twenty-nine Hellcats and fifteen Avengers; _Illustrious_ (thirty-six Corsairs and sixteen Avengers); _Indefatigable_ (forty Seafires and twenty Avengers); and _Victorious_ with thirty-seven

Slow and ungainly it might have been, but the Supermarine Walrus was a welcome sight to ditched airmen when the alternative was sharks or the Japanese. Ray Thomas Collection

Corsairs, fourteen Avengers and two Supermarine Walrus for air-sea rescue duties. This fleet was screened by five light cruisers and eleven destroyers.

The intention was for the force's American-built aircraft to form the strike component while the Seafires with their limited range would provide combat air patrols above the fleet. During the voyage to the combat zone all the vessels were refuelled, after which there were anti-aircraft exercises with a Martin B-26 Marauder unit providing towed target drogues. In the early hours of 26 March, command of the fleet passed to Admiral Vian in line with the policy of the aircraft carriers and their operations being the controlling influence during combat.

The first fighter sweeps were launched when the carriers were 100 miles (160km) due south of Miyako Jima, their targets being the airfields at Ishigaki and Miyako, which were heavily defended by anti-aircraft batteries. Only one aircraft was lost during the first sweep, the pilot being rescued by one of the Walrus amphibians. For the second attack a full strike package was launched from all four carriers with a large fighter escort. The result was heavily cratered runways – soon repaired – and several aircraft destroyed on the ground.

An American technique adopted for this operation was for air group commanders to fly over the target zone, select the best targets and pass the information to the strike force while it was en route. The air commanders then co-ordinated the strikes, switching targets as needed. At the completion of the first attacks, the fleet withdrew as a 'Dinah' reconnaissance aircraft had been spotted. It continued to shadow the fleet, despite fire from one of the escorting anti-aircraft cruisers and a near-interception by a Hellcat. On 27 March, the BPF returned to within 100 miles of Ishigaki to launch a fighter sweep in an attempt to draw up defending fighters. As before, this was followed by a strike. Avengers attacked targets missed the previous day, while others were diverted to attack coastal shipping. Two were lost although both crews were rescued.

The next phase of the attack was to have been a bombardment, but as some ships were running low on fuel and a typhoon was menacing the refuelling area, the operation was cancelled. As the assault on Okinawa was scheduled to begin on 31 March it was more important that all vessels were ready for air strikes on the BPF's designated targets during the next three days. In the early hours of 31 March, Task Force 57 was in position. Its first aerial reconnaissance missions were launched soon afterwards. Again, the airfields on Ishigaki and Miyako were the targets and

again, losses were light, being confined to a single Avenger whose crew was rescued by a US submarine.

Invasion of Okinawa

At 06.00hr on 1 April American forces stormed ashore and quickly established a wide bridge-head. But the Japanese defenders were well prepared, having survived a massive bombardment. Kamikazes were also up in force. BPF fighter patrols were flown off as usual, being quickly diverted to intercept any unidentified incoming aircraft. On one occasion they were reinforced by further fighters but a handful of Japanese aircraft managed to break through even after four of their number had been shot down.

They strafed *Indomitable* and *King George V* to provide a diversion for a Kamikaze aircraft to hit *Indefatigable* at the base of the island. Fourteen men were killed and sixteen injured but this toll would have been greater had not avoiding action been taken. The suicide attacker was engaged by Bofors gun crews and the resulting hail of shells hit one of *Indefatigable*'s Seafires, killing the pilot. Unlike their American counterparts with their wooden flight decks, the British carriers had armoured decks, enabling them to be ready for action after an attack in the minimum amount of time. This factor was much-appreciated by a Seafire pilot whose engine was malfunctioning and threatening to fail.

The same day, US Task Force 58 was attacked by 700 aircraft of which 50 per cent were deemed to be Kamikazes. Although over 300 were destroyed, some picket ships were lost and other vessels damaged. Meanwhile, on 7 March the US Navy avenged the Pearl Harbor attack by sinking the Japanese super-battleship *Yamato* despite its 18in guns. The huge warship had been heading for the transport fleet off Okinawa when she was overwhelmed by 380 torpedo and dive bombers.

Zero Shot Down

On 8 April the Americans requested the BPF to turn its attention to the airfields on Formosa as it was considered that the British crews were now sufficiently experienced to take on the battle-hardened Japanese based there. Accordingly, two days later the BPF altered course towards Sakishima, reaching a position some 30 miles (48km) off Yonakumi Shima on 10 April to begin a sequence of strikes on Matsuyama airfield. As usual, the first launches were scheduled for dawn, but they were hurriedly brought forward as incoming aircraft were detected by the radar pickets. The Seafires on patrol quickly dived into the fray, shooting down one out of four Mitsubishi A6M 'Zekes' and damaging another.

Meanwhile, the strike aircraft and their escorting fighters were heading for Shinchiku and Matsuyama airfields. But bad weather over the latter meant that this element of the attacking force was diverted to attack Kiiran harbour, an adjacent chemical plant, shipping, a railway station, a factory and a bridge. Enemy aircraft were intercepted by a pair of Fairey Fireflies over Yonakumi Shima. As they had dropped their bombs they were able to become long-range fighters and shoot down four Mitsubishi Ki-51 'Sonias' and damage a fifth. By mid-afternoon the attacking aircraft had returned to their carriers, refuelled and re-armed and were able to intercept a large formation of Japanese aircraft. All four carriers launched their on-guard fighters, while others were quickly brought to readiness and launched. The BPF pilots tore into the attackers, downing eight before the attack fizzled out. The BPF suffered a single loss when a Hellcat crashed on landing, killing the pilot.

The next day began with further dawn attacks on the fleet. Fighters rose to attack while the strike aircraft left to hit the airfields again. This time the weather was clear and both airfields were attacked with vigour, the bombers hitting its infra-structure while the escorting fighters strafed aircraft on the ground. All aircraft returned safely to their carriers, which then withdrew to the south to take up their night positions. They withdrew to the operations area for refuelling on 14 April. There *Formidable* was waiting to replace *Illustrious*, which sailed for Sydney for repairs.

Two days later the BPF was back on station to resume operations. Strike packages plus escorting fighters were launched against the airfields at Ishigaki and Miyako as well as the radar station at the latter location. All the attacking aircraft returned safely, although *Indefatigable* lost three in a deck accident. A Seafire making a fast landing bounced over the barrier and ploughed into an Avenger and a Firefly. Two crewmen were knocked into the sea,

A Seafire III of No. 894 Squadron shudders to a halt aboard *Indefatigable*. The aircraft has been stopped by the barrier, although this was not purely the result of a landing accident, as the hole in the wing caused by anti-aircraft fire indicates. Rick Harding Collection

Circling its carrier, this Firefly prepares to enter the landing pattern. Although not as speedy as the Seafire, the Firefly combined reasonable load-carrying capacity with better range, which gave it an edge over the Seafire. FAAM Yeovilton

one being killed. By this time the carriers were running short of fighters, not only for escort duties but also for combat air patrols. Vian advised Rawlings to withdraw, but the US commander requested one more attack.

On the morning of 17 April a strike force was despatched to attack Miyako, which left the airfield devastated. One Avenger was forced to ditch off the coast and the crew of a Walrus rescue aircraft undertook a daring rescue to pick up the crew. At the close of the day's operations the fleet withdrew to Operation Area Mosquito for refuelling and replenishing, returning for further strikes on the airfields on Ishigaki and Myako Islands the following day. The Task Force then left the area, arriving in San Pedro Roads, Leyte, on 23 April.

While the British fleet was away the tempo of Japanese attacks on US ships increased and many vessels were damaged. But the war on land had stalled and it was not until 11 May that US forces pushed forward in strength to fight from bunker to bunker in an effort to clear the enemy out. The Japanese showed no inclination to surrender and Kamikaze raids increased in violence and strength. Even at this stage in the assault on Okinawa, the American High Command wanted the BPF diverted to attack Borneo, but Admiral Nimitz persuaded them otherwise.

Sakishima Gunto

So it was that on 1 May Task Force 57 sailed to begin attacks on Sakishima Gunto. This time the fleet comprised the battleships *King George V* and *Howe*, the carriers *Formidable*, *Indefatigable*, *Indomitable* and *Victorious*, plus four cruisers and fourteen destroyers. After further refuelling the fleet arrived at its attack station on the 4th. Drawing on previous experience, the defensive fighter patrols were launched just before dawn, being quickly called into action to intercept a small incoming raid. The fighters shot down one aircraft and dispersed the others. While the fighters were covering the fleet the strike packages had departed to attack the airfields at Ishigaki and Miyako, where, it was noted, the intensity of anti-aircraft fire had increased.

The Japanese use of high-flying reconnaissance aircraft was a continual worry to the BPF as its patrolling fighters were unable to reach their altitudes. Even the heavy guns of the battleships failed to deter the shadowers and Rawlings detached the battleships to bombard their bases. As the smaller ships gathered around the carriers to make up for the loss of the bigger vessel's defensive power, incoming raids were reported. It was clear that the battleships' departure had been reported by the shadowing aircraft. One group angled south of the carriers to draw the defending fighters away, while the others dropped low to avoid radar detection, popping up to catch the fleet unawares. When they were spotted the Japanese aircraft began to dive-bomb the carriers.

Kamikaze Attacks

Formidable was singled out and she twisted and turned in an attempt to throw off the attackers' aim. But one managed to drop a bomb close to the ship before crashing on to the flight deck. The resultant conflagration set fire to many aircraft in the deck park. It also tore a large hole in the armoured deck, killed eight crew, wounded forty-seven others and rendered most of the radar equipment useless. As *Formidable's* damage control parties struggled to bring the fires under control, *Indomitable* was selected as the next target for a pair of attackers. One was chopped out of the sky

just short of the ship, while the other aimed for the starboard bow. But the ship was turning away and the attacker, riddled with shell hits, slammed into the flight deck at a shallow angle, skidded across the deck and plunged into the sea. Other attackers were shot down by the air patrols before they even reached the fleet. Eventually, the fires aboard *Formidable* were quenched, the deck was repaired and carrier declared ready for operations.

The battleships, meanwhile, were in position to begin their bombardment of the airfields and other installations, spotting being undertaken by escorting fighters. The bombardment lasted nearly an hour and

HMS *Implacable* seen from above. Note the extensive anti-aircraft armament installed in Illustrious-class carriers. BBA Collection

proved highly effective. Shells from the battleships' big turrets marched up and down the runways and other areas of the airfields, causing great damage. At the completion of the shelling, the battleships and their escorts hurried back to the carriers to reinforce their defences – just in time to repel the latest round of attacks. Most of the attacking aircraft were shot down by *Indefatigable*'s Seafires and fighters from other carriers. The BPF then withdrew to Operating Area Cootie for refuelling and to enable replacement aircraft to be transhipped. While there the fleet heard that the war in Europe had ended with Germany's surrender.

The fleet returned to the combat area on 8 May but increasingly bad weather resulted in all attacks being delayed for a day. The chosen target was Hirara airfield, which the reconnaissance aircraft had reported as being fully usable. But that was changed by the four strike packages launched to attack it. The Avengers and their escorts suffered no casualties. On their way back they passed the Seafires, which had spent much of the day chasing Japanese reconnaissance aircraft away. By late afternoon the enemy retaliated. The attackers came in fast and low. Stand-by fighters were launched, while those already airborne were vectored to the attack. Seafires intercepted them 15 miles (24km) out. They shot down at least one, although the others were able to evade the fighters. They also evaded the second group of defenders and lined up on the carriers, now twisting and turning below. Even so, at least one attacker, burning and slowly disintegrating, hit *Victorious*' flight deck and exploded. Damage control parties quickly brought the fires under control but a second aircraft hit the deck, destroying four fighters in the deck park before sliding off into the sea.

Formidable was the next carrier to receive the attention of a Kamikaze. The carrier and escorting warships put up a hail of steel but the battered attacker continued towards the carrier to plough into a crowded deck park. The resulting explosion destroyed seven aircraft but the armoured deck was not penetrated. To assist the fire crews in fighting the conflagration, the carrier was slowed down. As they continued to fight the fires, fuel leaking from the damaged aircraft seeped into the hanger below to start a second fire. The ship's fire suppression system and dividing doors kept the consequent loss down to eighteen aircraft. *Formidable* was soon able to resume limited

operations but the task force left for Operating Area Cootie for replenishment and damage repair at night-fall.

During this lull both the damaged carriers were inspected and cleared for further service, although one of *Victorious*' aircraft lifts was still causing concern. Despite this, the BPF was back on station by 12 May ready to resume operations against Ishigaki and Miyako. Casualties were light and no Kamikazes approached the fleet. Operations continued over the next few days, finally ending on 25 May when the fleet withdrew. After sixty-two days at sea on Operation *Iceberg*, the BPF staged via Manus to Australia to prepare for the next series of operations.

Of the four carriers *Indomitable* was found to be in a far worse condition than previously thought and her place in the task force was taken by *Implacable*. While she had used the transit time to train her aircraft crews, they had no recent combat experience and the ship was tasked with an attack on Truk. Once the main Japanese base in the area, it had been subjected to a massive US strike in 1943, which rendered it virtually useless especially as most of its remaining aircraft and ships had been dispersed to the Philippines and Malaya. The BPF ships selected for this attack were designated Task Force 111/2 and placed under the command of Rear Admiral E.J.P. Baird. The nucleus of his force comprised *Implacable*, with the forty-eight Seafires of No. 38 Naval Fighter Wing and twenty-one Avengers of No. 828 Squadron, and the escort carrier *Ruler* with No. 885 Squadron, a composite unit equipped with Avengers and Hellcats. Avengers and Seafires duly savaged Truk on 16 June, after which the fleet returned to Manus unscathed.

On 16 July the BPF, now designated Task Force 37, joined the US naval force. The British ships were the carriers *Formidable* – Admiral Vian's flagship – *Implacable* and *Victorious*, together with *King George V*, six cruisers and fifteen destroyers. *Howe* was still being re-fitted at Durban, while *Indefatigable* was at Manus to repair defective air compressors. Command ship of the US Third Fleet was the USS *Missouri*, flying the flag of Admiral Halsey, and it was there that Rawlings consulted the US admiral about his fleet's future role. From these discussions it emerged that one option was for TF37 to become part of the Third Fleet and become fully integrated in future US operations. It could also operate semi-independently and

work on its own against softer Japanese targets. Rawlings decided that the first option was best for TF37, his decision being much welcomed by Halsey.

Target: Tokyo

On 17 July 1945 the final assault on the Japanese home islands began. As the country was being heavily pounded by USAAF Boeing B-29 Superfortresses, it was clear to the Japanese that an Allied invasion was only a matter of time. As part of the softening-up process, TF37 was assigned targets in the Tokyo Plain. All three carriers launched strike aircraft and fighters to attack airfields, factories and other worthwhile targets. But bad weather meant that only eight days of flying were possible in the first twenty-five days of operations, during which 1,000 sorties were flown.

Operations in the Hiroshima area scheduled for 3 August were abruptly cancelled by signal the previous evening and the fleet was ordered to withdraw from Japanese coastal areas. The reason became clear later. That day a B-29 Superfortress of the USAAF's 509th Composite Group piloted by Col Paul Tibbets had dropped the first atomic bomb on the city. Operations by the British force resumed on 9 August when shipping anchored in Onagawa Wan were attacked. It was during this attack that Lt R.H. Gray DSC RNVR of No. 1841 Squadron was awarded a posthumous Victoria Cross for attacking a Japanese destroyer whose anti-aircraft fire was threatening his comrades. The same day TF37 attacked airfields and other targets in the Honshu area. Much damage was done and 250 aircraft were destroyed on the ground without loss to the attackers.

That day, too, a further atomic bomb was dropped, this time on Nagasaki. Peace negotiations started the following day, and the aggressive Halsey proposed to encourage them with further heavy attacks on the remaining military and industrial targets. By this time TF37 was running short of almost everything, exposing the inadequacy of its fleet train. To retain a British naval presence in the area, TF38/5 was formed around *Indefatigable* and *King George V*, plus two cruisers and nine destroyers. The remainder of the fleet returned to Manus for refuelling and much-needed repairs.

Despite the two atomic bombs, the Japanese fought on pending the outcome of

S-114 is the clearest visible aircraft in this line-up of Seafires aboard HMS *Indefatigable* as the ship enters Wellington Harbour. Rick Harding Collection

With the escort carrier HMS *Stalker* in the background, HMS *Hunter* prepares to anchor off Singapore. The leading aircraft, NN300, D5-dash zero, is that of Lt Cdr Baldwin. Its camouflage paint had been removed and the aircraft now has silver finish with black SEAC recognition bands and anti-dazzle panel. FAAM Yeovilton

HMS *Indomitable* served in both the Atlantic and the Pacific theatres. She was sold for scrap in 1955. BBA Collection

The hills of Hong Kong form the background to this view of a Seafire XV in BPF markings as its engine is run-up before it takes off on its next sortie. This aircraft was operated by No. 806 Squadron aboard HMS *Glory*. CP Russell Smith Collection

surrender negotiations. By this time Kamikaze attacks represented their major weapon against the Allied fleets. But few penetrated the ships' defensive fire. The final mission for *Indefatigable* was undertaken on 15 August when a force of Avengers and Seafires were attacked by a dozen Zeros. During the ensuing melee eight Japanese fighters were shot down for the loss of one Seafire.

At 07.00 hours the following day Nimitz signalled that all offensive operations were to be placed on hold until further notice. It would appear that the Japanese had not read this order, however, as at least one aircraft managed to get close enough to *Indefatigable* to drop two bombs alongside the carrier before being shot down by the orbiting Seafires. This action brought

to an end the series of actions fought by what had now become the most modern element of the Royal Navy. Yet despite fighting its way across two oceans, facing great dangers and being in at the end, the exploits of this force are still largely ignored. No wonder the survivors refer to themselves as the Forgotten Fleet.

Not the normal backdrop for a portrait, but the ground crew of Squadron Seafire XV SW786 seem quite happy with it. FAAM Yeovilton

HMS *Indefatigable* enters Portsmouth in 1946 after war service. The carrier entered long-term reserve before being scrapped. BBA Collection

HMS *Indefatigable* manoeuvres carefully into New Zealand's Wellington Harbour with her crew lining the sides and Seafires along the deck. Note the array of anti-aircraft weapons. Rick Harding Collection

A Seafire III is lowered to the deck of the escort carrier HMS *Atheling* in 1945. Rick Harding Collection

CHAPTER NINE

One More War

In the early hours of 25 June 1950 North Korean troops crossed the 38th parallel of latitude to begin an invasion of South Korea, which would touch off a war lasting three years. British forces joined the Americans to fight under United Nations auspices in an attempt to eject the invaders. Extensive naval operations involved Royal Navy aircraft carriers joining their US Navy counterparts in strikes on North Korean positions. The Seafire was at war again.

The end of the war against Japan resulted in the dispersal of the British Pacific Fleet, which had been built up into one of the biggest RN fleets seen since the end of World War I. Most of the ships were returned to home waters to await further orders, although many were to be de-commissioned. The first to go were the escort carriers, which had to be returned to the USA under the terms of the Lend-Lease agreement. Of the fleet carriers, HMS *Formidable* spent the final months of 1945 and the early part of 1946 ferrying released Allied prisoners from Japan to Australia, the ship having disembarked her air wing. Following two round trips to the UK, the carrier paid off at Portsmouth in November 1946 and was placed in reserve. She was sent for scrapping in 1953.

Having disembarked her air wing at Leyte in the Philippines in May 1945, HMS *Illustrious* sailed to Sydney for repairs. She arrived at Rosyth the following month for a complete refit. The end of the war meant that a refit that had been planned to last four months stretched to twelve. During this period the flight deck was improved, together with the radar and communications installations. Over the following ten years the carrier was employed on a variety of tasks before being sold for scrap in November 1956. Other members of her class, *Implacable*, *Indefatigable* and *Indomitable*, were also the subject of post-war refits. They were eventually laid-up in 1955 and scrapped. HMS *Victorious*, however, would have a longer career, retiring in 1967.

New Carriers

New vessels replaced these wartime stalwarts. Seven Colossus-class light fleet carriers were built to operate aircraft, an eighth being delivered as a maintenance vessel. The name ship was commissioned in December 1944, being followed into service by *Venerable* and *Vengeance* in January 1945, *Glory* in April, *Ocean* in November, *Theseus* the following February and *Triumph* in May 1946. The first four ships formed No. 11 Aircraft Carrier Squadron under the command of Rear Admiral C.H.J. Harcourt. Departing home waters in May 1945 with units operating Corsairs and Barracudas, the squadron arrived off Ceylon in July. Of the Colossus class only *Glory*, *Theseus* and *Triumph* were to operate Seafires.

Glory was commissioned in August 1945 and after modification work the ship was allocated to Rosyth Command for flying trials involving the Sea Hornet and a modified Vampire. At the beginning of December *Glory* was re-assigned to the Mediterranean Fleet, having embarked No.

805 Squadron's Seafire XVs. Also aboard were No. 816 Squadron, equipped with Fireflies, and a detachment of No. 784 Squadron with Hellcat night fighters, the latter being aboard for night flying trials. After working up, the air group participated in flying exercises before disembarking at RNAS, Hal Far, Malta, in June 1946 as the carrier was needed for trooping duties.

No. 805 was temporarily equipped with Fireflies but the Seafires returned in December. During this period the carrier's aircraft provided cover for the withdrawal of British forces from Palestine, the RAF having departed. In August 1948 the air group now comprised No. 804 Squadron with Seafire XVs and No. 812 with Fireflies. After four trooping assignments, which included two trips to ferry reinforcements and equipment for the United Nations forces operating in Korea, the air group re-embarked and stayed aboard until the carrier returned home for a refit. When she was re-commissioned, the ship's fighter component comprised Hawker Sea Furies in place of the Seafires.

At least one Seafire remained behind in New Zealand after the visit of *Indefatigable*. **As it was not repaired the RNZAF utilized the airframe for ground training purposes.** CP Russell Smith Collection

Seafire F.47 PS946 was used as a trials aircraft. In between tests, it was flown by No. 787 Squadron pilots for comparison purposes. FAAM Yeovilton

Theseus did not embark her air group until February 1947, when it comprised No. 804 Squadron with Seafire XVs and No. 812's Fireflies. As the situation in the Far East remained uneasy the ship was sent to join No. 1 Aircraft Carrier Squadron, returning at the end of the year. The aircraft were flown off to RNAS Ford while the carrier entered Rosyth for a refit. By the time the ship was re-commissioned early the following year the Sea Fury had started to replace the Seafire.

Triumph was the longest serving post-war Seafire operator. She was employed as a training and trials carrier before becoming the flagship of the Commander-in-Chief, Home Fleet, Lord Fraser. In May 1947 she formed part of the escort force for HMS *Vanguard*, which was conveying King George VI home after a visit to South Africa. The air group comprised No. 800 Squadron equipped with Seafire XVs and commanded by Lt Cdr D.G. Parker DSO DSC RN. The unit shared deck and hangar space with the Firefly-equipped No. 827 Squadron. By June the carrier had become the flagship of the Mediterranean Fleet and it was during this period of service that the vessel was visited by King Paul I of Greece, who watched the air group in action. Following a post-refit shakedown in early 1949, the carrier re-embarked the same units, which formed 13 Carrier Air Group, to join the Far East Fleet for strikes against Communist guerrillas in Malaya as part of Operation *Firedog*. By June 1950 the carrier, under the command of Captain A.D.

PS951 was built as a Seafire F.47 and features the early-type tail unit. FAAM Collection

Torlesse DSO RN, and her escorts were in Japanese waters for flying training exercises.

The Seafire 47 Arrives

By this time No. 800 Squadron had been re-equipped with the Seafire FR.47 and these exercises served to highlight one of the type's main weaknesses. At least four aircraft were damaged when they landed slightly off-centre, causing severe wrinkling and distortion at the point where the tail unit joined the fuselage. This was similar to the damage caused by the aircraft stalling on to the deck, placing such a load on the tail wheel and its mounting structure that the upper skin surface became wrinkled. Not so visible was the tensile separation of

VP436 is hauled out of the sea after going over the side of HMS *Ocean*. The Seafire had lost its canopy on take-off, causing the pilot to lose control. FAAM Yeovilton

Seafire FR.47 VP431 is pictured on HMS *Ocean*'s lift. The aircraft was later transferred to *Triumph* where it was damaged in a landing accident. After returning home aboard HMS *Unicorn*, it went to Eastleigh for repairs, but the aircraft never re-entered service, being scrapped in July 1951.
CP Russell Smith

Seafire FR.47 VP465 was assigned to No. 804 Squadron aboard HMS *Ocean*, although it is pictured here while ashore at Hal Far. The aircraft was struck off charge in November 1949. Will Blunt Collection

Having survived its service with No. 800 Squadron, VP455 was re-assigned to No. 1833 Squadron at Bramcote, remaining there until it was withdrawn from service in 1953. FAAM Yeovilton

the skin from the frames. This could only be detected by inserting a feeler gauge between frame and skin.

The damage caused by an off-centre landing, exacerbated by the deceleration loading, forced the rear fuselage to whip from side to side. The result was skin wrinkling on one side, while the frames on the other were separated from their skins.

Supermarine had recognized this defect and had prescribed a range of limits that would allow the Seafire to continue flying. Once they had been exceeded, the aircraft had to be grounded and returned to the manufacturer for repairs.

On 24 June *Triumph* departed Ominato, Japan, bound for Hong Kong. A warning about the imminence of Typhoon *Elsie*

prompted the double lashing of all aircraft in the hangar, but the storm blew itself out before hitting the ship. This allowed the carrier to reverse course the following day as Rear Admiral W.G. Andrewes, Second-in-Command Far Eastern Fleet, had ordered her to return to Japanese waters where news of North Korea's invasion of the south had been received.

War In Korea

The origins of the Korean war can be traced back to 1905 when the country became a Japanese colony. Under the Potsdam Declaration of 1945, however, Britain, China and the USA declared that Korea, once a Chinese province, should become an independent country at the end of hostilities. The USSR had declared war on Japan in the dying days and Soviet forces entered Korea, moving to the 38th Parallel to face US forces on the other side of this unofficial demarcation line. The Soviets established Kim Il Sung, a ruthless and unpredictable Communist functionary who had spent the war in Moscow, as president of what was proclaimed to be the Peoples' Republic of Korea. The Americans withdrew in 1948. Kim, who was dedicated to re-uniting the two halves under his control, bided his time.

In January 1950, US Secretary of State, Dean Acheson, made a speech in which he listed the countries America was prepared to defend against Communist aggression. South Korea was not on the list. Years later Acheson admitted that the omission had been an inadvertent one. But the damage was done. In Pyongyang it was treated as the green light for invasion. Accordingly, in the early hours of Sunday 25 June 1950, in darkness and driving rain, 90,000 North Korean troops, supported by hundreds of Russian-made T34 tanks, swarmed across the 38th Parallel in half a dozen places.

Initially, US concerns were mainly for American nationals in South Korea. This deepened after reports that North Korean aircraft had attacked Seoul's Kimpo airfield. On 26 June, President Truman offered military aid to South Korea and British Prime Minister Clement Atlee called the invasion 'naked aggression' which 'must be checked.' The United Nations passed a resolution calling on the North Koreans to withdraw their forces from the south. Only the Soviets abstained. A second resolution passed on the next day called on member

Seafire FR.47 VP458, complete with wing-root RATOG packs, roars down the flight deck of HMS *Triumph*. Having joined No. 800 Squadron in July 1949, the aircraft was lost in a crash in December after the engine failed. FAAM Yeovilton

countries to 'furnish such assistance to the Republic of Korea as may be necessary to meet the armed attacks.' Eventually sixteen nations, including the UK, sent forces to fight the Communist invaders under UN auspices with their operations placed under US control.

› Aboard *Triumph*, meanwhile, a flight of Seafires had been placed on deck-alert the day after the invasion. At Kure both *Triumph* and the destroyer *Cossack* were refuelled, after which the carrier was secured alongside the jetty to enable damaged Seafires to be off-loaded. By 29 June the Admiralty had placed all Royal Navy assets under US naval command. Vice Admiral C.T. Joy, the US Navy's commander of operations in Korean waters, decided that the British and Commonwealth ships should form the Western Korean Support Group, operating under the designation CTG 96.8, under the command of Rear Admiral W.G. Andrewes. Coverage of the east coast was the responsibility of the US Navy's CTG 96.5. Although Vice Admiral Joy issued orders to the flag officers commanding each task group, each was responsible for day-to-day operations, which included the inter-theatre ship transfers that were occasionally required to maintain the balance off each coast. This freedom of

Having proved itself in the Pacific War, the Fairey Firefly also undertook combat missions during the Korean conflict. Here the crew climb aboard their aircraft for another sortie. FAAM Yeovilton

movement was practised throughout the period of the Korean conflict.

In the early hours of 29 June *Triumph*, still with *Cossack* in attendance, left Kure to join Admiral Andrewes flying his flag aboard the cruiser HMS *Belfast*, which was steaming towards Okinawa in company

with the cruisers *Jamaica* and *Consort*. While it was not known if North Korea possessed submarines, no chances were taken and the Fireflies were sent on anti-submarine patrol. The force arrived at Okinawa on 1 July and refuelled soon afterwards. When they joined the US

Navy's Seventh Fleet, *Triumph* and her consorts were re-designated as Task Force 77.5. During the voyage the carrier flew off some Seafires and Fireflies to enable US personnel to become familiar with the appearance of the aircraft.

First Attack on Korea

On 3 July the ships arrived at their appointed station and prepared to launch aircraft. The strike group departed in the early hours of the morning and comprised twelve Seafires and nine Fireflies after a sterling effort by No. 800 Squadron. Their target was Kaishu, Haeju, airfield, 120 miles (192km) away. The Seafires were divided into three flights numbered 71, 72 and 73. The intention was for 71 Flight to approach from the west, closely followed by 73 Flight, then the Fireflies with 72 Flight bringing up the rear. As none of the aircraft forming the primary target were found, the attackers followed the usual practice of strafing, bombing and rocketing airfield facilities. Before launch the pilots had been warned not to fly below 600ft (185m) due to the possibility of debris being thrown up. But at least one Seafire pilot misjudged his height and suffered engine damage. The pilot managed to get his ailing aircraft back to the carrier where he made an emergency landing, the engine failing completely on touch-down. Once all the aircraft had returned those remaining serviceable were refuelled and re-armed to enable a series of combat air patrols to be mounted in the afternoon.

The following day's strike force comprised twelve Fireflies escorted by seven Seafires, an eighth having been forced to return to the carrier. Their brief was to attack targets of opportunity, which included army bases, strategic buildings railway facilities and military vehicles in the vicinity of Haeju, Ongkin and Yonan. Coastal anti-aircraft batteries also received attention. No aircraft were lost but a Firefly landed with one undercarriage leg retracted, while a Seafire arrived with fuel streaming from a damaged tank. With all aircraft safely recovered the fleet headed south, the cruisers and destroyers making for Sasebo, while *Triumph* was bound for Okinawa and refuelling. The carrier stayed in port for repairs and aircraft maintenance until 9 July. It was during this time that the Seafires and Fireflies received black and white stripes as the Americans had convinced themselves

that both types resembled the Russian-built Yak-9.

This was the last time that the British fleet used Okinawa, as the facilities at Sasebo were considered more suitable for the largest vessels. Although the repair carrier HMS *Unicorn* was in-theatre, it was decided that her facilities should be brought ashore to HMS *Simbang*, Sembawang, Singapore while the ship herself was to be used for replenishment duties to reduce the logistical strain on the front-line fleet.

On 13 July *Triumph* sailed from Okinawa for a training programme that concentrated on practising talk-down procedures so that aircraft returning from sorties as dusk fell would not have to rely on visual signals from the deck control officer. The carrier returned to harbour for a briefing on the proposed US landing at Pohang. It was intended that the Fireflies would carry out anti-submarine patrols with Seafires providing patrols over the fleet. But both types were excluded from the strikes as they suffered from a lack of range. The landings took place on 18 July. No. 800 Squadron's strength was reduced to ten aircraft when one of its Seafires sustained extensive accidental damage. Landing aboard *Triumph* late in the afternoon, the aircraft engaged the arrester wire off-centre. This caused the port wing to drop and resulted in the aircraft's transfer to *Unicorn* for repair.

There were more Seafire and Firefly sorties the following day when another Seafire was damaged. Its exhausted pilot caught the last arrester wire, which sent the aircraft drifting slowly into the barrier. As only its propeller assembly was damaged, the aircraft was available for flying the next day. *Triumph*, on the other hand, was forced to withdraw as the packing in her starboard propeller shaft gland had been causing trouble. The carrier left on 21 July having completed 140 hours of flying. Repairs were made at Sasebo where *Unicorn* transferred seven replacement Seafires and accepted two for repair. *Triumph* was ready three days later and departed with her escorts for a position north of Quelpart Island to form part of TF.77. As before, the Seafires and Fireflies undertook CAPs and anti-submarine patrols, although two Seafires were damaged during recovery. One landed off-centre, causing excessive skin wrinkling, while a second suffered damage when the deck handling party pushed the tail wheel over the edge of the flight deck.

On 26 July *Triumph*'s area of operations shifted to the east coast, although lack of flyable Seafires meant that No. 827 Squadron's Fireflies had to perform both tasks. After many hours of diligent work, the majority of Seafires were declared ready

Complete with Korean War stripes and RATOG units, this No. 800 Squadron Seafire FR.47, VP479, departs from HMS *Triumph*. The aircraft was badly damaged in a landing accident in April 1950. Although returned to the UK for repairs, it saw no further service and was scrapped in 1956 after a period in storage. FAAM Yeovilton

The classic landing pose: a Seafire FR.47 of No. 800 Squadron prepares to land on HMS *Triumph* with everything out and down. FAAM Yeovilton

for flight, although No. 800 lost another on the 28th. A CAP was vectored to investigate a radar trace, which turned out to be a flight of Boeing B-29 Superfortresses. Having confirmed that the aircraft were friendly, the Seafires passed to the rear of the formation only to be engaged by one of the bomber's gunners. One of the Seafires was hit in the rear fuel tank, which promptly burst into flames. The pilot rolled the aircraft on its back and bailed out, being rescued by the destroyer USS *Eversole*.

On 29 July, the carrier returned to Kure for aircraft maintenance and ship repair. The two damaged Seafires were off-loaded, but no replacements were forthcoming and the squadron's complement of aircraft was reduced to fourteen. *Triumph* departed for Sasebo on 9 August. During the voyage three Seafires were catapulted off the carrier, bound for the airfield at Iwakuni. There they underwent compass swinging, returning to the carrier later in the day. While they were away, the remaining aircraft practised

deck landing. This resulted in another Seafire being damaged in an off-centre landing. The following day *Triumph* embarked Admiral Andrewes and his staff and headed for the west coast of Korea to enforce a blockade of the inlets and islands that were unsuitable for warships.

When a Seafire flight was launched for a reconnaissance mission over Mokpo and Kunsan airfields on 13 August, the pilots found both deserted following air and sea bombardment. They took the opportunity to rake some small junks with 20mm cannon fire. That afternoon, the Seafires visited the port of Inchon, which was found to have been badly damaged by US forces. The following day, aircraft from *Triumph* attacked targets at the key North Korean naval base of Chinnampo, following an early-morning photo reconnaissance run by the ship's Seafires. The photographs had revealed little shipping in the harbour but the attacking aircraft still encountered heavy anti-aircraft fire. This did not prevent

six Seafires and six Fireflies from attacking shipping in the Taedong estuary. Three vessels were heavily damaged by 60lb rockets and cannon fire.

On 15 August, the normal A/S and CAP duties were resumed as well as an armed reconnaissance mission to Inchon and the surrounding coast. *Triumph* then left for Sasebo, returning to the Korean west coast after three days to concentrate on patrolling the Inchon-Kunsan area where they operated alongside units of the US Seventh Fleet. No. 800 Squadron sent a flight of Seafires up the coast towards the North Korean capital of Pyonyang. No targets were spotted, although the aircraft were subjected to heavy anti-aircraft fire. Seafire strength had now dropped to nine aircraft as a further three had suffered rear fuselage damage following off-centre landings.

On 23 August HMS *Triumph* arrived at Sasebo for rest and repair, leaving three days later for another four days of operations.

During the voyage there was deck landing training for three new Seafire pilots and three others returning to the type. Yet another Seafire was damaged on landing by one of the tyros, resulting in all the newcomers being sent for further training ashore. Once on station the Seafires were back on CAP duty to prevent a sneak attack by Korean torpedo boats, while the Fireflies undertook reconnaissance and attack missions over the harbour areas.

It was while the strike force was returning at the completion of a mission that a Firefly landed with a faulty arrester hook, which led to an impact with the crash barrier. This caused one of its propeller blades to break off and fly into the operations room, killing No. 800 Squadron's CO, Lt Cdr I.M. MacLachlan RN. He was buried at sea with full military honours that evening, being succeeded by Lt T.D. Handley RN. Back in Sasebo the following day Triumph was able to replenish her air group with six Seafires and eight Fireflies, transferred from Unicorn, which had arrived from Pusan a few hours earlier.

Another round of CAP and armed reconnaissance missions began on 3 September. Two armed junks were destroyed, but during the CAP's launch the belly fuel tank on one of the Seafires pulled free of its mounts, causing extensive lower fuselage damage. After launch the aircraft landed-on safely, although it was no longer fit for operations. On 5 September, Triumph sailed for the east coast to relieve US Seventh Fleet carriers that had been withdrawn for rest and refitting. Three days later the task force was 50 miles (80km) from the North Korean port of Wonsan. The first strike group of six Seafires and a similar number of Fireflies strafed and rocketed the port and its surrounding facilities, causing severe damage to rail facilities. Another six Seafires and four Fireflies attacked the marshalling yards at Kowon and Yonghung and destroyed numerous boxcars. One Seafire was badly damaged when its port undercarriage failed to lower on landing, while another had to be abandoned by its pilot when the arrester hook failed to lower. These losses reduced the squadron's strength to ten aircraft.

Bad weather on 9 September reduced the number of missions to one. A pair of Seafires and two Fireflies attacked Koryo airfield with rockets and cannon fire, causing considerable damage. During maintenance in preparation for the next day's flying, a further four Seafires were found to have been damaged beyond flyable limits. As this made No. 800 Squadron no longer viable, it was decided that Triumph should be withdrawn and she arrived at Sasebo the following day. The carrier remained in harbour for the next three days to enable the Seafires to be repaired in preparation for the vital US landings at Inchon.

Landings at Inchon

CTF91, still commanded by Admiral Andrewes, was assigned to maintain the west coast blockade, to carry out reconnaissance missions before the landings, provide air cover for units in transit to the Inchon area and to carry out interdiction missions during the operation. Operation Chromite began on 12/13 September with a bombardment of North Korean positions by US and British warships and massive air support from USN carriers. Triumph launched her first sortie on the morning of 13 September, the objective being Haeju. No worthwhile targets were found and the Seafires and Fireflies turned their attention to Chinnampo where junks and barges were strafed and attacked with rockets. An anti-aircraft position was also destroyed as the aircraft prepared to leave the area. Although returned safely to the carrier, a further Seafire was badly damaged after a heavy landing. Overall, the landings at Inchon were successful. The North Koreans were taken completely by surprise and subsequently driven back beyond the 38th Parallel. Over the following few days Triumph's aircraft flew armed reconnaissance sorties in the Haeju area during which gun positions and junks were destroyed.

In the early hours of 17 September a pair of North Korean aircraft attacked UN shipping off the coast at Wolmi-do. The cruiser USS Rochester was struck by a bomb and HMS Jamaica was hit by cannon fire, although the ship's anti-aircraft guns shot down one of the attackers. Triumph's standing flight was later scrambled twice but both alerts proved to be false alarms. Over the following two days the Seafires flew further armed reconnaissance sorties during which they attacked shipping. But it was not without cost. One aircraft required a new propeller unit despite a gentle impact with the safety barrier, while a second was badly damaged when it too hit the barrier. On 20 September two of the remaining operational Seafires undertook an armed reconnaissance mission over Chinnampo

The Supermarine Type 224 was to prove a blind alley in fighter development, but it was still a monoplane without external bracing, which was then quite a novelty. The Type 224 was let down by its inefficient engine, cooling system and fixed trousered undercarriage, which slowed the aircraft down considerably. Eric Morgan Collection

estuary, during which a barge was badly damaged.

As the carrier's aircraft complement had now fallen to eleven serviceable aircraft, Admiral Andrewes decided to withdraw as her replacement, HMS *Theseus*, was due within the week. *Triumph* therefore reached Sasebo on 21 September for temporary repairs before returning to Britain. She was employed on trooping duties from November 1952, a role she would retain until disposal in 1981. No. 800 Squadron was disbanded on 10 November 1950 and did not reform until August 1951, when it was re-equipped with another Supermarine product, the jet-powered Attacker.

Although the squadron had been the main front-line Seafire operator, there were other units still flying the type including Royal Navy Volunteer Reserve squadrons. The first was No. 1830 Squadron, which formed at Abbotsinch on 15 August 1947. Initially equipped with three Seafire XVIIs and three Firefly Is, it was assigned to undertake fighter and anti-submarine missions, although the Seafires were dispensed with in 1948. No. 1831 Squadron

Seafire XV SW847 displays the early post-war external finish as it awaits its pilot. The centreline fuel tank is worthy of note. FAAM Yeovilton

Displaying the markings of No. 1832 Squadron, a reserve unit, this Seafire XVII was based at St Merryn. After service with another reserve unit, No. 1833 Squadron at Bramcote, the aircraft was scrapped in 1956. FAAM Yeovilton

formed as an RNVR unit in June 1947. It had seen active service in World War II and in its new guise at Stretton it operated a mix of Seafire XVs and XVIIs, which were later replaced by Sea Furies and Attackers. Another wartime veteran was No. 1832 Squadron, which reformed at Culham in July 1947 with Seafire IIIs, although these were soon replaced by six Seafire F.46s, and six Seafire XVs with Mk XVIIs replacing the F.46s in 1950. Later came Sea Furies and Attackers. No. 1833 Squadron reformed at Bramcote in August 1947 with six Seafire XVIIs, these being supplemented by five Seafire XVs. The Seafires were replaced in turn by the Sea Fury and the Attacker. All RNVR units were disbanded on 10 March 1957 as part of that year's defence cuts, which also affected the RAF's auxiliary squadrons.

These aircraft of No. 807 Squadron await inspection. The leading Seafire XVII, SX200, later moved to No. 767 Squadron, in whose service it crashed on landing in March 1948. BBA Collection

Foreign Seafire Operators

The Fleet Air Arm was not the only Seafire operator, for many surplus airframes found their way to other air arms. Among them was France's L'Aeronautique Navale, which was in its infancy during November 1942. Having no aircraft carriers and little equipment, crews and aircraft were concentrated in Morocco. During the fight against Germany these units flew Spitfires alongside their air force counterparts. Experience of the Spitfire during the war led to the acquisition of Mk Vs immediately afterwards and a contract for the supply of Spitfire IXs was agreed in November 1945. These were seen as representing an interim move as the French Navy wanted an aircraft carrier and the aircraft to operate from it.

Seafire F.45 LA488 displays the codes of No. 771 Squadron based at Lee-on-Solent. After later service with No. 773 Squadron, the aircraft was damaged in a crash-landing in May 1950. FAAM Yeovilton

French Seafires Delivered

The former need would be satisfied by the arrival of HMS *Colossus*, which was transferred on a five-year loan to the French Navy as the *Arromanches* in August 1946. The aircraft came from Royal Navy stocks, the first batch of fifty Seafire IIIs being secured in February 1946, although forty-eight would actually be delivered. Groups of *Navale* pilots arrived at Lee-on-Solent to collect their aircraft in batches of six, although this number varied according to serviceability. The first batch departed on 15 March 1946 with the remainder following at five day intervals. Lt Cdr P.J. Hutton RN flew some of the aircraft to

Many post-war Seafires ended their lives in storage at Stretton, which is where this Seafire XVII, SX358, is pictured awaiting disposal. CP Russell Smith

Seafire XV PR497 is surrounded by rescuers after crash landing aboard HMS *Illustrious*. **The aircraft was on the strength of No. 767 Squadron, normally based at Milltown. It was withdrawn from service after this accident.** FAAM Yeovilton

Mureaux, which had been chosen as the reception point due to the location there of North American Aircraft workshops. The airframes were reconditioned, camera equipment mounts were installed and the aircraft test flown before the appropriate colour scheme was applied.

The aircraft were deployed to *Flotille* 1.F, No 4S, *Escadrilles de Servitude*, No 10S, the test centre at St Raphael, No 54S, the school of aircraft embarkation at Hyeres, together with the Naval School at Rochefort. Some Spitfires were retained for use as target tugs, being operated by Nos 1S and 3S. The French Navy collected *Arromanches* from Portsmouth in August 1946. The loan was subject to restrictions on the carrier's use in Indo-China where France was desperately trying to reclaim its colonial territories in what is now Vietnam. En route to France the carrier – now designated *Navale Aeronautique* Group No. 2 – and her escorts undertook a series of training exercises.

The French pilots encountered similar problems with the Seafire to those experienced by their Fleet Air Arm counterparts. Nose-overs were a continuous hazard after a hard and fast landing. Unlike the Royal Navy, which assigned aircraft to pilots on an availability basis, the French Navy preferred to allocate an aircraft to a specific pilot. But a surplus of pilots rendered this

option impossible and the air group proceeded to lose aircraft at a faster rate than expected. To make these losses good the French bought a further sixty-five Seafire IIIs at a knock-down price of £80 each. Thirty were to be delivered as complete aircraft with the others shipped as spares, being marked 'Usable by the French Navy Only'. The first batch came complete with documentation, while the remainder, being undocumented, were supposed to have been shipped in crates. But as the time and cost involved was considered too great the French decided to fly them home. Airframes and engines, which had been intended for spares only, were determined as being fully fit for further service.

Due to the number of Seafire accidents, Admiral Jozan appointed a committee of investigation. Starting work in January 1949, it determined that the airframes were basically tired, that the engines needed a full overhaul and that the systems should be replaced or overhauled. These were, however, aircraft that had been destined for wartime service and were expected to have a life of 240 flying hours. These aircraft had comfortably exceeded this. The admiral therefore called for each surviving airframe to be fully stripped down and rebuilt, incorporating repairs and strengthening as required. The engines were to be similarly overhauled to re-life them.

France Buys Griffon-Seafires

The loss of so many Seafires meant that *Arromanches* had no air wing. At the beginning of 1949, therefore, *L'Aeronautique Navale* purchased Seafire XVs to enable the carrier participate in a planned NATO exercise at the end of the year. As before, the aircraft were assembled at Lee-on-Solent and all were delivered during June. Being Griffon-powered, these replacement aircraft presented different problems to their pilots. The engine torque was in the opposite direction to that of the Merlin-powered Seafires and several were damaged during the first few weeks of operation. During the early months of 1950, France's other carrier, the *Dixmunde*, was despatched to the USA to collect Grumman Hellcats and Helldivers as part of a Mutual Assistance Package. Meanwhile, No 12F participated as planned in Exercise *Symphony*. This represented one of the last appearances of the Seafire under Western Union-NATO auspices as the number of accidents involving the type meant that the last flyable aircraft were withdrawn by the end of 1951.

While in French Navy service the Seafires equipped two main units, No 1F and No 12F. The former had been reformed in October 1945 at Cuers. Before receiving its aircraft, some of its pilots took part in a Fleet Air Arm-run experience programme, which enabled them to fly both the Seafire and the Firefly. The unit was initially equipped with NC.900s, French-built Focke-Wulf Fw 190s. A move to Hyeres in December 1945 was undertaken to prepare for the first batch of Spitfires, which were used for training purposes from the beginning of 1946. By April 1948 the *Flotille* received its complement of Seafires and was then able to begin deck landing training on the airfield. Some Spitfires were retained for general flying training and to act as adversaries in combat flight training. The use of Rocket-Assisted Take-Off Gear, which had also been practised, was quickly discontinued as the French regarded it as unreliable and hazardous. No 1F was declared ready for operations at the end of 1946, having completed a full range of flying training exercises, including 306 deck landings at Hyeres.

By 1947 the unit was operating twenty-four Seafires, the last remaining Spitfires having been retired. The squadron began operations aboard *Arromanches* in Spring 1948. While the ship was cruising in the

Atlantic and Mediterranean the Seafires undertook combat exercises against various French Air Force units. At least three aircraft were damaged in landing mishaps but then, on 28 June 1948, came a more serious accident when a Seafire and pilot were lost during a mock diving attack on a Sunderland flying boat of No 7F. The Seafire's engine failed and such was the speed of the dive that the pilot was unable to escape. *Arromanches* completed her first cruise in July 1948 when the Seafires returned to their land base of Hyeres.

As part of an expansion plan, No 1F was divided in two in August, with the second part becoming No 12F, also Seafire-equipped. During that month No 1F lost another three aircraft. In one accident, the pilot was lucky to escape after another engine failed in a dive. This time there was enough height available for the aircraft to pull out and enable the pilot to bail out. At the end of October *Arromanches* left Toulon for Indo-China, dropping anchor in the Saigon river on 29 November. Aboard were the Seafires of No 1F and Douglas Dauntless dive-bombers of No 4F.

Indo-China Operations

The air group undertook strike missions in the Tonkin area, but the number of aircraft available dropped steadily due to accidents and lack of spares. This forced the carrier to return home in January. By mid-June 1949, the Seafire III was considered no longer viable and the unit was re-equipped with Mk XVs. The older aircraft were relegated to training duties, initially in the air and later for ground use only. The arrival of the newer Seafires allowed *Arromanches* to take part in Exercise *Verity* in July. Further exercises in October and November 1949 (*Primagas*) and December (*Tertragas*) kept the carrier and crew fully occupied. But these exercises also marked the end of Seafire operations for the *Arromanches*. Many of pilots had gone to the USA for training on the Grumman Hellcat. No 1F began to run down its operations yet it still managed to lose a Seafire in a landing accident at Toulon on 2 March 1950.

Although No 12F had gained a cadre of experienced Seafire pilots on its creation in August 1948, four aircraft were lost during its first four months of operation, reducing its strength to twelve. The inventory changed in June 1949 when six Seafire XVs were added. This, however, did

not spell the end of the Seafire III as twelve were retained for conversion and training purposes. No 12F also served aboard *Arromanches*, gaining the dubious honour of suffering the last crash of the type aboard ship when a Seafire XV was written off on 8 March 1950. Given the overall losses suffered by *L'Aeronautique Navale*, it was hardly surprising that the Seafire was withdrawn from service to be replaced by surplus US Navy aircraft like the Hellcat and Corsair.

Burmese Seafires

Like many other countries in the region formerly occupied by the Japanese, Burma was beset by insurgents determined to undermine and topple the government. Ranged against the incumbent administration were groups from the Chinese Nationalists, the Burma Separatist Movement, various Russian-inspired Communist organizations, to say nothing of various bandit groups active in the hilly regions of the country. Desperate to acquire air power to support its frequently beleaguered ground forces, Burma looked to Britain. As the country's finances were under pressure, Burma could only afford refurbished second-hand aircraft. The first were Supermarine Spitfire XVIIIs, which were followed by a batch of twenty Seafire XVs. These machines, like the Spitfires before them, were refurbished by Airwork Ltd at Gatwick. As their naval features were not required, the arrester hooks, catapult spools and folding wings were removed, the latter being replaced by spare components from redundant Spitfire XVIIIs. Delivered via Malta in 1951, the Seafires were used extensively in the ground-attack role, operating with both rockets and bombs against targets often hidden by the jungle canopy. The Seafires remained in service until they withdrawn in 1954. They were replaced by Hawker Sea Furies.

Seafires for Canada

The Royal Canadian Navy's use of the Seafire came almost by default. On 15 June 1945 No. 803 Squadron formed at Arbroath with twenty-five Seafire IIIs, being intended for service as part of the 19th Carrier Air Group aboard an Implacable class aircraft carrier. The Japanese surrender curtailed these plans and the squadron remained at

Arbroath to exchange its Merlin-powered aircraft for Seafire XVs in August. Although still operating under RN auspices, the Royal Canadian Navy assumed control over the unit on 24 January 1946 when the Colossus class fleet carrier HMCS *Warrior* was commissioned. HMCS *Warrior* had been launched in May 1945, although completion was delayed by the war's end. Instead of being left with another carrier swinging at anchor the Admiralty approved the *Warrior*'s loan to the RCN. With No. 803 Squadron, together with the Firefly-equipped No. 825, aboard, the carrier left Portsmouth for Halifax on 23 March. Eight days later she arrived in Canadian waters, where the squadrons undertook an intensive work-up. The group reappeared in May 1947 when the *Warrior*'s air wing was re-designated, but this newly-renamed organization did not stay long as the carrier sailed for Belfast in January to deliver stores and manpower for HMCS *Magnificent*, which was soon to be commissioned. On 1 March 1948, *Warrior* arrived in Portsmouth to be formally returned to the Royal Navy three weeks later.

The Majestic class light fleet carrier *Magnificent* was based on the successful Colossus class but featured numerous improvements, the most significant of which was the ability of the lifts to accept heavier aircraft. As the ships were being completed just as the war was ending, the Admiralty had no use for them, preferring instead to lend or sell them to allied navies. HMCS *Magnificent* was launched in November 1944, although she was not commissioned until April 1948 when Commodore H.G. de Wolf CBE DSO DSC RCN transferred his broad pennant from *Warrior* to his new command. Sea-going acceptance trials were undertaken during May with aircraft loaned by the Fleet Air Arm to exercise the arresting and launching equipment and help train deck-handling personnel. At the completion of these trials the *Magnificent* tied up alongside the jetty at RNAS Sydenham where the aircraft of the 19th CAG were winched aboard, as were No. 806 Squadron's mixed complement of Sea Vampires, Sea Hornets and Sea Furies. They were bound for the USA where they were scheduled to take part in a series of air displays. The carrier sailed for Canada on 25 May.

A few days later the aircraft and excess stores were landed at Halifax before the carrier began a short shake-down cruise designed to reveal any outstanding defects.

Seafire XV SW909 was assigned to No. 1 Training Air Group. It was badly damaged in a landing accident in February 1948, although it was later repaired and re-assigned to No. 803 Squadron. CP Russell Smith

PR458 pictured while serving with No. 803 Squadron. After service with Nos 803 and 883 Squadrons, the Seafire was withdrawn in January 1950. CP Russell Smith

Seafire PR479 served with both Nos 803 and 883 Squadrons before being struck-off charge in June 1949. CP Russell Smith

Back at sea on 10 August, *Magnificent* re-embarked the 19th CAG for a period of intensive flying, during which 171 deck landings were made. Two aircraft were lost. *Magnificent* was then tasked with carrying out a series of simulated strikes on the Magdalan Islands at the beginning of September. By the middle of the month the aircraft had flown to RCNAS Shearwater while the vessel herself docked at St John, New Brunswick.

The aircraft returned at the end of the month, enabling the carrier to join the destroyers *Nootka*, *Haida* and *Swansea* to form Task Group 211.2 at the beginning of October. The subsequent cruise took the group to Quebec, Seven Islands, Charlottetown and Sydney, Australia for exercises with ships from other Commonwealth navies. Returning home in time for Christmas, the *Magnificent* was at sea again in early February 1949 to ferry RCN Firefly Mk 4 aircraft to Britain to be exchanged for a similar number of Mk 5s plus Seafires to replace losses. During the return voyage *Magnificent* ran into rough weather, which resulted in some damage requiring dockyard attention. After repairs at Halifax the carrier, accompanied by *Nootka* and *Haida*, sailed on 5 March as Task Group 215.8. Its mission was to carry out exercises in the Caribbean, the highlight being a simulated long-range attack on the cruiser HMS *Jamaica*. At the completion of these exercises, *Magnificent* returned to Canada and the air wing departed for Shearwater on 7 April, while the vessel docked at Halifax the next day.

Sea-going operations resumed at the beginning of May, the air wing rejoining the carrier soon after departure from Halifax. These manoeuvres came to an abrupt halt when *Magnificent* ran aground off Port Mouton, Nova Scotia, on 4 June. Aided by escorting destroyers, the carrier was pulled off and proceeded to St Johns for repairs. As they were quite extensive, a refit was also undertaken, keeping *Magnificent* in dock until October. Then, accompanied by *Haida* and *Swansea*, the carrier undertook a full work-up off Nova Scotia during which the fleet was diverted to help find the crew of a crashed USAF B-29. No trace was found despite an extensive search. During this time, the ships paid goodwill visits to Cuba and Puerto Rico before returning to Halifax in December. En route, the 19th CAG flew off to Shearwater.

HMCS *Magnificent* prepares to leave harbour. BBA Collection.

Another Canadian Seafire III operator was No. 883 Squadron, which received sixteen aircraft at Arbroath on 18 September 1945. This unit had previously been designated to join the 10th Carrier Air Group for operations with the British Pacific Fleet. With the surrender of Japan and the consequent difficulty of retaining sufficient Canadian personnel, it was disbanded at Machrihanish on 23 February 1946. A second attempt to activate the unit as part of the RCN was undertaken on 15 May 1947 at Dartmouth when it received twelve of the thirty-five Seafire XVs delivered to the service. No. 883 acted as the alternate operating unit aboard HMCS *Warrior*, while No. 803 Squadron was ashore. Assigned to the 18th CAG on its formation, the squadron retained its Seafires until September 1948 when Hawker Sea Furies arrived. The last Seafire XV was struck off charge in April 1954.

Considering its distinguished heritage, the Supermarine Seafire promised more than it actually delivered. But then it had never been designed to endure the rough and tumble of operations from aircraft carriers, and weaknesses that were never completely eliminated meant that more were lost to deck accidents than enemy action.

Even so, the aircraft had its moments of glory such as its participation in the Allied invasion of North Africa, the Salerno landings and providing combat air patrols for the British Pacific Fleet in its prosecution of the war against Japan. After the war, Seafires filled the gap between the departure of US aircraft supplied under the Lend-Lease arrangement and the arrival of the highly capable Hawker Sea Fury and the first of the jets. As this included supporting British naval operations in the opening months of the Korean war, the Seafire was able to go out in style. Indeed, the Mk 47 took the Spitfire family to its ultimate expression.

Two No. 803 Squadron Seafire XVs – PR470, nearest the camera, and PR461 – are captured on camera at Lee-on-Solent during the unit's working-up period. BBA Collection

As the original scheme applied to Royal Canadian Navy (RCN) aircraft was rather dark, the titling was not particularly visible, so the RCN applied a large maple leaf marking to the fin of PS470 to confirm its ownership. BBA Collection

VP464 displays the codes of Bramcote-based No. 1833 Squadron, having previously served with No. 800
Squadron. The aircraft was sold for scrap in August 1956. FAAM Yeovilton

Irish Air Corps Seafires

The order covering the delivery of twelve Seafire IIIs for the Irish Air Corps was confirmed on 31 August 1946. As the aircraft were
Intended for land operations, arrester hooks were removed together with other naval equipment. The aircraft were therefore similar to
Spitfire Mk Vs. Serialled 146 to 157, the first examples were accepted by an Irish Department of Defence official at South Marston on
24 January 1947. Delivery took place on 17 February. The final aircraft arrived at Baladonnel on 27 September. These machines,
together with a handful of Spitfire TR.9s, remained in Irish service until their withdrawal in 1955.

Enough to make a preservationist weep! Retired Irish Air
Corps (IAC) Seafire IIIs await scrapping after spares
recovery. CP Russell Smith

The IAC also purchased a handful of Spitfire TR.9s for
conversion and refresher purposes. Fortunately, at least
one of these machines has survived. CP Russell Smith

Seafire Production and Contracts

Spitfire I, Admiralty trainers, two aircraft
Spitfire I, two aircraft fitted with 'A'-frame
Spitfire II, two aircraft
Spitfire VB, forty-four aircraft
Spitfire IIB, three aircraft fitted with 'A'-frame
Spitfire VB, fifty-five aircraft fitted with 'A'-frame

Contract B981687/39, Type 340 Seafire IB:
SLMB328 to MB375, converted by Air Service Training
NX879 to NX989
PA100 to PA129

Contract B19713/39, total of 202 Type 357/375 Seafire IIC airframes to be built by Supermarine:
MA970 to MA999
MB113 to MB158
MB178 to MB222
MB235 to MB281
MB293 to MB326

Contract B124305/40 and Contract Acft/2605/C.23(c), ordered 25 November 1942, total of 110 Type 357/375/358 Seafire IIC/III airframes to be built by Westland Aircraft:
LR631 to LR667
LR680 to LR 712
LR725 to LR764

Contract Acft/2605/C.23(c), ordered 25 November 1942, total of 204 Type 358 Seafire III airframes to be built by Westland Aircraft:
NF514 to NF455
NF480 to NF526
NF531 to NF570
NF575 to NF607
NF624 to NF665

Contract B124305/40 and Contract Acft/2605/C.23(c), ordered 25 November 1942, total of 90 Type 358 Seafire III airframes to be built by Westland Aircraft:
LR765 to LR769
LR783 to LR820
LR835 to LR881

Contract B124305/40 and Contract Acft/2605/C.23(c), ordered 5 January 1943, total of 60 Type 357/375 Seafire Mk IIC airframes to be built by Supermarine:
NM910 to NM949
NM963 to NM982

Contract B124305/40 and Contract Acft/2605/C.23(c), ordered 5 January 1943, total of 200 Type 358 Seafire LIII airframes to be built Westland Aircraft:
NM984 to NM999
NN112 to NN157
NN169 to NN214
NN227 to NN270
NN283 to NN330

Contract Acft/2777/C.23(c), ordered 15 January 1943, 250 Type 358 Seafire III airframes to be built by Cunliffe-Owen:
NN333 to NN367
NN379 to NN418
NN431 to NN476
NN488 to NN528
NN542 to NN586
NN599 to NN641

Contract Acft/2901/C.23(c), ordered 8 March 1943, three Type 377 Seafire XV airframes to be built by Supermarine:
NS487
NS490
NS493

Contract Acft/2901/C.23(c), ordered 24 May 1943, three Type 377 Seafire XV airframes to be built by Supermarine:
PK240
PK243
PK245

Contract Acft/2605/C.23(c), ordered 17 July 1943, 250 Type 358 Seafire III/LIII airframes to be built by Westland Aircraft:
PP921 to PP957
PP969 to PP999
PR115 to PR156
PR170 to PR215
PR228 to PR271
PR285 to PR344

Contract Acft/2777/C.23(c), ordered 17 July 1943, 150 Type 377 Seafire XV airframes to be built by Cunliffe-Owen:
PR338 to PR379
PR391 to PR436
PR449 to PR479
PR492 to PR522

Contract Acft/2777/CB.23(c), ordered 14 August 1943, fifty Type 358 Seafire LIII airframes to be built by Cunliffe-Owen:
PX913 to PX 962

Contract Acft/2605/C.23(c), ordered 18 January 1944, 300 Type 358 Seafire III airframes to be built by Westland Aircraft:
RX156 to RX194
RX210 to RX256
RX268 to RX313
RX326 to RX358
RX373 to RX415
RX428 to RX469
RX481 to RX530

Contract Acft/2777/C.23(c), ordered 12 February 1944, 270 Type 358 Seafire III airframes to be built by Cunliffe-Owen:
SP116 to SP168
SP181 to SP223
SP236 to SP279
SP293 to SP327
SP341 to SP380
SP393 to SP438
SP453 to SP461; built as Mk XVII from SP323

Contract B124305/40 and Contract Acft/2605/C.23(c), ordered 23 February 1944, 202 Type 377 Seafire XV airframes to be built by Westland Aircraft:
SR446 to SR493
SR516 to SR547
SR568 to SR611
SR568 to SR645

Contract Acft/2605/C.23(c), ordered 3 April 1944, 500 Type 377 Seafire XV airframes to be built by Westland Aircraft:
SW781 to SW828
SW844 to SW879

SW896 to SW936
SW951 to SW993
SX111 to SX139
SX152 to SX201
SX220 to SX256
SX271 to SX316
SX332 to SX370
SX386 to SX432
SX451 to SX490
SX503 to SX546; aircraft completed as F.XVII from SW986 – see below for contract details

Contract Air/3853/C.23(c), ordered 3 April 1944, 213 Type 395 Seafire XVII airframes to be built by Westland Aircraft
Contract cancelled

Contract B981687/39, ordered 15 July 1944, three Type 388 Seafire F. 45 airframes to be built by Vickers Armstrong:
    TM379
    TM383
    TM389

Contract Acft/5176/C.23(c), ordered 12 March 1945, two Type 396 Seafang Mk 32 airframes to be built by Supermarine:
    VB893
    VB895

Contract Acft/5794/C.23(c) and Contract Acft/5794/CB.5(c), ordered 3 April 1946, sixty-four Type 388 Seafire FR. 47 airframes to be built by Supermarine:
    VP427 to VP465
    VP471 to VP495

Contract 6/Acft/636/CB.5(b), ordered 25 September 1946, ninety-two Type 388 Seafire F.47 airframes to be built by Supermarine
    VR961 to VR998
    VS107 to VS146
    VS152 to VS165; cancelled from VR973

Contract B981687/39 and Contract Acft/1951/C.23(c), total of seventy-five Type 388 Seafire F.45 airframes to be built by Vickers Armstrong:
    LA428 to LA457
    LA480 to LA519
    LA536 to LA540

Contract B981687/39 and Contract Acft/1951/C.23(c), total of twenty-four Type 388 Seafire F.46/FR. 46 airframes to be built by Vickers Armstrong:
    LA541 to LA564

Contract Acft/5794/C.23(c), total of fifty Type 388 Seafire F.47 airframes to be built by Vickers Armstrong:
    PS938 to PS987; only PS944 to PS957 built

Fleet Air Arm Seafire Units

Squadron	Variant	Code	Dates	Example	Remarks
700	Seafire IB		9/45	NX957	
	Seafire IIC		11/45–12/45	NM942	
	Seafire III		2/45–2/46	NN514	
	Seafire F.45		-/45–/45		
	Seafire XV	LOZ	3/46–7/46	SR458	
	Seafire XVII		9/45–11/45	SX125	
703	Seafire XVII	011/LP	8/47–8/49	SX360	Service trials unit
	Seafire F.45		12/45–46	LA496	
706	Seafire III		3/45–11/45	LR789	BPF conversion school
	Seafire XV		1/46–7/46		
708	Seafire 1B		5/45–6/45	MB357	Firebrand tactical trials unit
	Seafire IIC		5/45–6/45	MB264	
	Seafire III		5/45–8/45	NN575	
709	Seafire III	S5N	9/44–8/45	NF493	Ground attack school
	Seafire XV		11/45–1/46	SR604	
	Seafire F.45	S5A	-/45–1/46	LA449	
715	Seafire IB		8/44–/45	PA115	School of air combat
	Seafire III	S4B	8/44–12/45	NF551	
	Seafire XVII	S4H	8/44–12/45	SX125	
718	Seafire IIC	G3C	7/45–10/45	NM924	School of air reconnaissance
	Seafire III	G3R	6/44–10/45	NF634	
	Spitfire PR.XIII	G3K	6/44–10/45	R7333	
	Seafire III		8/46–9/46	RX300	Seafire conversion squadron
	Seafire XV		-/46–3/47	LR876	
719	Seafire IB		6/44–12/44	NX891	School of air combat
	Seafire IIC		-/44–12/44	NM918	
	Spitfire VB		6/44–8/44	BM371	
	Spitfire VB		6/44–12/44	BL628	Hooked
721	Seafire III		-/46–/47		General service unit
	Seafire XV		11/46–11/47	SW854	
727	Seafire XVII		12/46–2/47	SX365	Fleet requirements unit
728	Seafire L.IIC	M8A	1/45–1/46	MB281	Fleet requirements unit
	Seafire III	M8L	7/45–7/46	NF521	
	Seafire XV		9/46–9/48	PR495	
	Seafire XVII	504/HF	5/48–3/52	SP327	
731	Seafire IB	E3Y	5/44–2/45	MB335	Deck landing training school
	Seafire IIC		-/45–2/45	MB312	
733	Seafire III		10/46–12/46		Fleet requirements unit
	Seafire XV		1/47–12/47	SW878	
736	Seafire IB	AC-E	5/43–8/44	NX942	School of air combat
	Seafire III		8/44–2/46	NN511	
	Spitfire VA		3/44–8/44	R7202	
	Seafire XV	162/JB	4/46–6/48	SW852	
	Seafire XVII	197/JB	1/46–4/51	SX237	
	Seafire F.46	S5A	1/46–12/46	LA449	
	Seafire III	YOH	3/45–5/45	NF586	'B' Flight [bar the zero]
	Seafire XV		7/45–8/45		
737	Seafire XV		4/49–1/50	SR603	52nd training air group

No. 736 Squadron based at St Merryn was the operator of Seafire XVII SX311. The aircraft later served with Nos 799,1832 and 1833 Squadrons before its retirement in July 1952. FAAM Yeovilton

Under tow: Seafire XVII SX137 is currently preserved at the Fleet Air Arm Museum at Yeovilton. It served with Nos 1831, 759 and 764 Squadrons before retiring in 1959. FAAM Yeovilton

Squadron	Variant	Code	Dates	Example	Remarks
	Seafire XVII	112/GN	4/49–5/50	SX163	
738	Seafire XVII	164/CW	5/50–9/51	SP341	52nd training air group
	Seafire F.46		5/50–8/50	LA564	
741	Seafire III		2/47–11/47	NN241	Operational flying school
744	Seafire III		5/46–5/46	RX335	Joint A/S school
746	Seafire XVII		12/45–12/45	SX164	Night fighter dev Sqdn
748	Spitfire I		10/42–4/43	X4270	Fighter pool squadron
	Spitfire VA		2/43–7/44	R7305	
	Spitfire VB		3/45–2/46	P8708	Hooked
	Seafire IB		6/43–2/46	NX918	
	Seafire IIC	S1G	3/43–2/46	MA977	
	Seafire III	S7A	11/45–2/46	RX217	
751	Seafire XV		7/47–8/47	PR401	Radar trials unit
757	Seafire IIC		6/44–6/44	LR750	Operational training unit
	Seafire III	P40	5/45–1/46	NN200	
759	Spitfire I	J	6/40–8/44	X4337	No. 1 Naval Air Fighter School
	Spitfire II		8/43–10/43	P7786	
	Spitfire VA		5/43–10/44	X4987	
	Spitfire VB		5/43–10/44	AD536	
	Seafire IB		8/43–1/45	MB328	
	Seafire IIC		5/44–2/45	MB303	
	Seafire III	Y6F	12/45–2/46	PP999	
	Seafire XV		2/46–2/46		
	Seafire XVII	179/CW	8/51–7/54	SX250	
	Seafire F.47	162/CU	8/52–11/53	VP493	
760	Seafire III	S	10/45–1/46	PP929	No. 2 Naval Air Fighter School
761	Spitfire I	F	9/42–7/44	AR238	No. 2 Naval Air Fighter School
	Spitfire VA		4/43–1/45	N3281	
	Spitfire VB	G1U	4/43–1/45	AB201	
	Spitfire VB		11/43–2/45	AA904	Hooked
	Spitfire PR.XIII		3/44–6/44	W3831	
	Seafire IB	G1A	4/43–3/45	NX597	
	Seafire IIC		7/44–8/45	LR647	
	Seafire III	G3C	4/44–1/46	RX288	
	Seafire XV		7/45–1/46	PR339	
	Seafire XVII		11/45–1/46	SX125	
	Spitfire F.16		7/45–7/45	RW376	

Squadron	Variant	Code	Dates	Example	Remarks
762	Spitfire I		2/43–6/43	X4657	Advanced flying training school
764	Seafire XVII		-/45–8/45		User trials unit
766	Seafire III	I6J	8/46–9/47	NN497	Operational flying school
	Seafire XV	109/MV	6/47–11/51	PR497	
	Seafire XVII	122/LM	7/47–11/52	SW989	
767	Seafire III	IT3E	3/46–6/47	PR317	Deck landing training school
	Seafire XV	109/MV	5/46–2/52	PR497	
	Seafire F.46	129/VL	3/50–7/50	LA561	
768	Spitfire VA		7/43–2/44	X4846	Deck landing training school
	Spitfire VB		10/42–2/45	X4172	Hooked
	Seafire IB		7/43–2/45	PA124	
	Seafire IIC		1/44–4/46	LR647	
	Seafire III	L2T	6/44–4/46	NN172	
	Seafire XV		12/48–3/49	SW795	
770	Seafire IIC		9/43–9/43	LR692	Target tow unit
	Seafire IIC	D8R	5/45–10/45	MA970	
	Spitfire		5/45–7/45		
771	Seafire III	GP9L	3/46–1/47	NN545	Fighter direction school
	Seafire XV	GP9K	11/46–1/51	PR402	
	Seafire F.45	560/LP	12/47–9/50	LA438	
	Seafire F.46		5/47–12/47		
772	Seafire III	O9A	3/46–8/46	NF450	Fleet requirements unit
773	Seafire XV	510/LP	1/50–3/50	PR368	Fleet requirements unit
775	Spitfire I		6/43–6/43	P9311	Fleet requirements unit
	Spitfire VC		6/43–6/43	JK163	
	Seafire IIC		8/44–11/45	LR696	
776	Seafire IIC		5/45–10/45	NM973	Fleet requirements unit
777	Seafire XV		5/45–7/45	PK245	Fleet requirements unit
	Seafire XVII		12/45–3/46	SX161	
	Seafire F.45		5/45–6/45		
	Seafire F.46		5/45–6/45		
	Seafire F.47		5/45–6/45		
778	Spitfire VB		11/41–11/41	AB968	Service trials unit
	Spitfire IX		4/44–5/45	NH582	
	Spitfire XII		2/43–3/43	EN226	
	Seafire 1B		1/42–2/45	MB361	
	Seafire IIC		7/42–4/44	MA995	
	Seafire III	FD9R	6/43–3/47	RX173	
	Seafire XV	FD9M	3/44–8/46	SW862	
	Seafire XVII	016/LP	7/45–7/48	SX283	
	Seafire F.45	012/LP	6/45–10/47	LA450	
	Seafire F.46		7/46–1/48	LA550	
	Seafire F.47		12/46–3/47	PS947	
	Seafang F.32		5/47–5/47	VB895	
779	Seafire IB	Z	5/43–10/44	MB348	Fleet requirements unit
780	Seafire XV	U1E	7/46–10/46	SW902	Advanced flying training unit
	Seafire F.45		11/46–11/46	LA489	
781	Seafire IB		7/43–7/43	NX963	Fleet requirements unit
	Seafire III		8/44–8/44		
	Seafire XV		12/49–2/50	SW818	
	Seafire XVII	166/LP	5/49–10/49		
	Seafire F.46		3/47–12/47	LA560	
782	Seafire III		5/47–1/48	NN189	Flag Officer Flying Training HQ
	Seafire XVII		12/47–10/48	SX238	
787	Seafire IB		7/42–8/44	NX962	Air fighting development unit
	Seafire IIC		11/42–3/45	LR729	
	Seafire III		12/43–6/46	PR332	

No. 736 Squadron based at St Merryn was the operator of Seafire XVII SX311. The aircraft later served with Nos 799,1832 and 1833 Squadrons before its retirement in July 1952. FAAM Yeovilton

Under tow: Seafire XVII SX137 is currently preserved at the Fleet Air Arm Museum at Yeovilton. It served with Nos 1831, 759 and 764 Squadrons before retiring in 1959. FAAM Yeovilton

Squadron	Variant	Code	Dates	Example	Remarks
	Seafire XV		9/44–6/46	SR447	
	Seafire XVII		4/45–1/48	SP348	
	Seafire F.45		3/46–2/48	LA442	
	Seafire F.47		5/47–9/49	VP428	
	Seafire IB		6/44–10/44	NX885	'X' Flight
	Seafire IIC		6/44–10/44	LR651	
	Seafire III		6/44–2/45	NF601	
790	Spitfire VB		2/45–2/45	AD426	Fighter direction school
	Seafire IB		3/45–3/45	NX907	
	Seafire IIC		3/45–3/45	NM982	
	Seafire III		11/46–2/47	NN123	
	Seafire XV	152/CW	5/47–1/49	PR424	
791	Spitfire I		10/42–5/43	R7155	Fleet requirements unit
	Seafire XV		12/46–6/47	SR633	
794	Spitfire I		4/43–11/43	R6835	
	Spitfire VA		9/42–12/42	R6759	
	Spitfire VB		11/43–11/43	P8708	Hooked
	Seafire IIC		2/45–2/45	LR661	
	Spitfire VB		1/45–5/45	W3846	Hooked
	Seafire III	A5G	6/46–2/47	RX248	
798	Spitfire VB		4/45–6/45	W3370	Flying training unit
	Spitfire IX		12/44–2/45	BS390	
	Seafire IB		6/45–7/45	NX894	
	Seafire IIC		6/45–6/45	MB117	
799	Seafire IIC		8/45–8/45	MB299	50th Training Air Group
	Seafire III	769/LP	8/45–7/47	PP928	
	Seafire XV	772/LP	10/45–11/51	PR377	
	Seafire XVII	107/VL	12/47–6/52	SX134	
800	Seafire XV		8/46–2/47		
	Seafire XVII	M	1/47–4/49	SX112	
	Seafire F.47	179/P	4/49–11/50	VP459	
801	Spitfire VA		9/42–10/42	P7664	
	Spitfire VB	W	9/42–10/42	AD513	Hooked
	Seafire IB	R	9/42–6/44	MB348	
	Seafire IIC		10/42–5/43	MB151	
	Seafire IIC		4/44–6/44	NF582	
	Seafire III	P8Q	5/44–11/45	PP994	
	Seafire XV	125/N	9/45–4/46	SR596	

Seafire FR.47 VP458 pictured ashore at Hal Far, Malta, was on the strength of No. 804 Squadron. FAAM Yeovilton

Seafire FR.47 VP441 is pictured at Culdrose where it was preserved. The aircraft has since been restored by Ezell Aviation, Texas, where it made its first flight in April 2004 displaying the markings of its first operator, No. 804 Squadron. FAAM Yeovilton

Squadron	Variant	Code	Dates	Example	Remarks
802	Seafire III		5/45–8/45	RX345	
	Seafire XV	102/Q	8/45–4/48	PR407	
803	Seafire III		6/45–12/45	RX218	
	Seafire XV	F	8/45–7/47	PR470	Royal Canadian Navy
804	Seafire XV	133/T	10/46–3/48	SW853	
	Seafire F.47	139/O	1/48–8/49	VP483	
805	Seafire III		7/45–8/45	RX162	
	Seafire XV	O5G	8/45–8/46	SW846	
	Seafire XVII	117/O	4/47–6/48	SX196	
806	Seafire III		8/45–9/45	NF578	
	Seafire XV	5H	10/45–10/47	PR362	
807	Seafire IB		6/42–8/42	MB357	
	Seafire IIC	HL	6/42–10/44	LR753	
807	Seafire III	D5P	6/44–12/45	PP984	
	Seafire XVII	D	12/45–9/47	SX129	
	Seafire III		9/46–10/46	PX960	
808	Spitfire VB		12/42–4/43	BM453	Hooked
	Seafire IIC	3D	12/42–5/44	MB312	
	Spitfire PR.XIII		3/44–3/44	BM591	
	Spitfire VB		2/44–5/44	BL613	
	Spitfire VB	1H	5/44–7/44	EN964	LF
	Seafire III	3A	6/44–10/44	NN341	
809	Spitfire VA		3/43–6/43	L1096	
	Seafire IB		4/43–8/43	NX919	
	Seafire IIC	SS	3/43–10/44	MB133	
	Seafire III	D6M	7/44–12/45	PP972	
	Seafire XV		11/45–12/45		
	Seafire XVII		11/45–1/46	SX138	
816	Seafire IIC		6/43–8/43		
	Seafire IB		8/43–12/43	NX988	
833	Seafire IIC		6/43–9/43	MB326	
834	Seafire IIC	Q	6/43–8/44	NM972	
842	Seafire IIC		7/43–8/43	NM921	
	Seafire IB	D	7/43–3/44	PA120	
879	Spitfire VA		3/43–3/43	P7694	
	Spitfire VB		3/43–3/43	W3846	Hooked
	Seafire IB		3/43–6/43	NX889	

LA561 was a Seafire F.46 assigned to No. 1832 Squadron at Culham. The aircraft later served with No. 767 Squadron before withdrawal from service in 1951. FAAM Yeovilton

Seafire XVII SR572 of Culham-based No. 1832 Squadron starts its take-off run. FAAM Yeovilton

Squadron	Variant	Code	Dates	Example	Remarks
	Seafire IIC	AE	6/43–11/45	MB317	
	Seafire III	D4Y	3/44–11/45	PR292	
	Seafire XVII		11/45–1/46	SX363	
880	Spitfire VB		8/42–2/43	W3756	
	Seafire IIC	7B	9/42–8/43	MB240	
	Seafire IIC		8/43–3/44	LR691	
	Spitfire I		11/43–1/44	R6716	
	Seafire III		3/44–2/45	LR858	
	Seafire III	115/N	2/45–9/45	NN621	
883	Seafire III	Y	9/45–11/45	RX162	
	Seafire XV		11/45–2/46	SW872	
	Seafire XV	AAY	5/47–9/48	SW815	Royal Canadian Navy
884	Spitfire VA		9/42–10/42	P8246	
	Spitfire VB		9/42–10/42	AA866	
	Spitfire VB		9/42–10/42	BL253	Hooked
	Seafire IIC		9/42–7/43	MB237	
885	Spitfire VA		9/42–10/42	R6722	
	Spitfire VB		9/42–10/42	BL343	Hooked
	Seafire 1B		10/42–8/43	MB346	
	Seafire IIC	O6L	9/42–11/43	MB318	
	Seafire III	2A	2/44–11/44	NF426	
	Seafire III		2/44–11/44	LR853	
	Seafire IIC		8/44–11/44	MB257	
886	Spitfire VB		2/43–3/43	AB190	Hooked
	Seafire IIC	B	3/43–2/44	LR641	
	Spitfire VB		2/44–3/44	AA964	Hooked
	Spitfire PR.XIII		3/44–3/44	P8784	
	Seafire III		3/44–7/44	NF537	
889	Seafire IIC		4/44–7/44	MB179	
	Seafire IIC		4/44–7/44	LR699	
	Seafire III		4/44–7/44	LR807	
894	Spitfire VB		3/43–4/43	X4172	
	Seafire IB		2/43–3/43	MB358	
	Seafire IIC		3/43–11/43	MB257	
	Seafire IIC		3/43–11/43	MB306	
	Seafire III	1G	11/43–11/44	LR859	
	Seafire III	H6Z	11/44–3/46	NN460	

Seafire XVII SX194 was on the strength of No. 1832 Squadron, which was based at Culham when this portrait was taken. CP Russell Smith

Pictured at Bramcote displaying the codes of No. 1833 Squadron, Seafire XVII SX282 was lost in a crash in December 1949. FAAM Yeovilton

Squadron	Variant	Code	Dates	Example	Remarks
895	Seafire IIC		3/43–6/43	MB316	
897	Seafire IIC		8/42–9/42	MA981	
	Spitfire I		3/43–3/43	X4337	
	Seafire IB		3/43–7/43	NX892	
	Spitfire VB		3/43–12/43	EP762	Hooked
	Seafire IIC		8/43–5/44	MA982	
	Spitfire VB		3/44–7/44	BL895	
899	Seafire IIC	6Q	12/42–1/44	MB244	
	Spitfire VB		12/43–3/44	AB867	
	Spitfire VB		12/43–3/44	AD187	Hooked
	Seafire III	KP	2/44–9/45	NN599	
1830	Seafire XVII		8/47–5/48	SX245	
1831	Seafire XV	109/JA	6/47–8/51	SW800	
	Seafire XVII	108/JA	6/47–8/51	SX168	
1832	Seafire III		7/47–11/47	RX158	
	Seafire F.46	105/CH	8/47–1/50	LA555	
	Seafire XVII	101/CH	6/48–5/53	SX198	
	Seafire XV	116/CH	4/49–8/51	SW856	
1833	Seafire XVII	156/BR	8/47–7/52	SX279	
	Seafire XV	164/BR	7/49–8/51	SW786	
	Seafire F.47	156/BR	6/52–5/54	VP474	

Seafires Sold Overseas

Burma

Seafire XV Identity	Date delivered	Date withdrawn
UB-401, was SR451	1952	1957/58
UB-402, was SW799	1952	1957/58
UB-403, was SR642	1952	1957/58
UB-404, was SW863	1952	1957/58
UB-405, was SR471	1952	1957/58
UB-406, was PR355	1952	1957/58
UB-407, was SR534	1952	1957/58
UB-408, was PR455	1952	1957/58
UB-409, was PR376	1952	Preserved
UB-410, was PR400	1952	1957/58
UB-411, was PR423	1952	1957/58
UB-412, was SW818	1952	1957/58
UB-413, was PR453	1952	1957/58
UB-414, was SR462	1952	Sold to USA
UB-415, was PR422	1952	Preserved
UB-416, was PR454	1952	1957/58
UB-417, was SR470	1952	1957/58
UB-418, was PR407	1952	1957/58
UB-419, was PR462	1952	1957/58
UB-420, was SW899	1952	1957/58

Canada

Seafire XV Identity	Operator	Date delivered	Date withdrawn
PR375	803, 1 TAG	June 1946	January 1950
PR410	803, 1TAG	June 1946	April 1954
PR425	883, 1 TAG	November 1946	June 1949
PR428	803	November 1946	July 1947
PR434	803	January 1946	February 1949
PR451	803, 883	February 1946	May 1949
PR458	803	February 1946	January 1950
PR460	803, 1TAG	February 1946	June 1949
PR461	803, 883	February 1946	crashed August 1949
PR470	803, 1TAG	February 1946	January 1950
PR471	803	June 1946	July 1949
PR479	803, 883	March 1946	June 1949
PR494	803	February 1946	June 1952
PR496	803	June 1946	January 1950
PR498	803	February 1946	February 1950
PR499	Winter test aircraft	February 1946	March 1952
PR500	802, 803	February 1946	crashed December 1948
PR501	803, 1TAG	February 1946	February 1950
PR502	803, 1TAG	February 1946	crashed August 1949
PR503	803, 1TAG	February 1946	June 1952

Seafire XV

Identity	Operator	Date delivered	Date withdrawn
PR504	803,	February 1946	February 1950
PR505	803,	February 1946	crashed September 1948
PR506	1TAG	February 1946	November 1950
SR464	802, 803	February 1946	June 1949
SR491	803	February 1946	March 1952
SR530	803, 883	March 1946	January 1949
SR545	803	March 1946	April1947
SW793	803, 883	February 1946	January1950
SW802	803, 883	March 1946	May 1951
SW809	803, 1TAG	February 1946	June 1949
SW815	803, 883	February 1946	July 1947
SW860	803, 1TAG	March 1946	June 1949
SW869	803, 1TAG	March 1946	January 1950
SW870	803, 1TAG	March 1946	January 1950
SW909	883, 1TAG	March 1946	January 1950

France

Seafire III

Identity	Operator	Date delivered
LR793		June 1946
LR815		June 1946
NF454		January 1947
NF482		June 1946
NF507		September 1949
NF561	54S.9	April 1948
NN136		April 1948
NN149		June 1946
NN157		June 1946
NN188	54S.28	June 1946
NN235		June 1947
NN267		June 1946
NN303		September 1946
NN391		June 1946
NN396		June 1946
NN456	54S.24	June 1946
NN467		June 1946
NN546		June 1946
NN604		June 1947
NN620		June 1946
NN623	spares use	June 1948
NN641		June 1946
PP972	IF.9 then 12F.2	1947
PP990		June 1946
PR132		April 1948
PR146	54S.14	June 1946
PR170		June 1946
PR249	1F.11	June 1946
PR257		1946
PR265		June 1946
PR266		June 1946
PR293	54S.6	June 1946
PR304		June 1946
PR322		June 1946
PR329	1F.3	June 1946

Seafire III Identity	Operator	Date delivered
PR333		1948
PX932	1F.22	June 1946
SP136	1F.16	June 1948
SP137		May 1948
SP143	1F.19	June 1946
SP144		June 1946
SP147		June 1946
SP148	1F.1	March 1946
SP150	1F.10	March 1946
SP156		March 1946
SP163		1948
SP166	1F.5	1948
SP167	1F.6	1948
SP182		February 1947
SP183		January 1948
SP190	1F.12	1948
SP192		1948
SR519	1F	June 1949
SR520	1F.23	June 1949

Seafire XV Identity	Operator	Date delivered
PR347	12F.15	June 1949
PR360	1F.22	June 1949
PR397	54S.22	June 1949
PR405	1F.27	June 1949
PR414	1F.27	June 1949
PR429		June 1949
PX916		June 1949
PX919		1949
PX931		June 1949
PX932	1F.22	June 1948
PX933	1F.23	June 1949
PX951		June 1949
PX954		1949
PX962		June 1949
RX165	54S.12	June 1949
RX166	1F.3	June 1949
RX183		June 1949
RX192	1F.2	March 1946
RX216		March 1946
RX223	1F.25	March 1946
RX224		1946
RX226	1F.6	1946
RX229		February 1946
RX231		June 1948
RX240	1F.24	1946
RX242	1F.23	1946
RX244		1948
RX247		1948
RX253		June 1948
RX254		1946
RX255		March 1946
RX271		1948
RX278		1948

Seafire XV

Identity	Operator	Date delivered
RX279		April 1948
RX281	12F.3	1948
RX283	54S.3	1948
RX286	3S.10	1948
RX290	1F.9	1946
RX293	1F.5	1946
RX296		1948
RX298		1946
RX301	1F.27	1946
RX305	1F.3	1946
RX309		1946
RX327		1948
RX333		1948
RX338	1F.10	1946
RX342		1948
SR452		June 1949
SR455		June 1949
SR460	1F.24	June 1949
SR474	1F.21	June 1949
SR520	54S.26 then 1F.23	June 1949
SR522		June 1949
SR526		June 1949
SR529	54S.26	June 1949

Ireland

Variant	Identity	Date delivered	Date withdrawn
LF.III	IAC 146 was PR302	17 Feb 1947	June 1954
LF.III	IAC 147 was PR315	17 Feb 1947	written off 5 Sept 1947
LF.III	IAC 148 was PP950	17 Feb 1947	written off 22 May 1953
LF.III	IAC 149 was PP948	17 Feb 1947	June 1954
LF.III	IAC 150 was RX210	11 July 1947	1950
LF.III	IAC 151 was PP941	11 July 1947	written off 29 June 1951
LF.III	IAC 152 was PP929	11 July 1947	written off 1 Sept 1949
LF.III	IAC 153 was PP924	11 July 1947	June 1954
LF.III	IAC 154 was PP915	27 Sept1947	written off 28 May 1951
LF.III	IAC 155 was PR236	27 Sept1947	Aug 1954
LF.III	IAC 156 was PP936	27 Sept1947	June 1954
LF.III	IAC 157 was RX168	27 Sept1947	Oct 1953

Seafire Technical Details

Merlin-powered aircraft

Wingspan: 36ft 10in (11.3m) full span, 32ft 7in (10m) clipped

Length: 30ft 2.5in (9.3m)

Height: 8ft (2.5m) over cowling, 13ft (4m) over propeller

Wing area: 242sq ft (32sq m) full span, 234sq ft (31sq m) clipped

Powerplant: Rolls Royce Merlin   45 (Mks IB and IIC)
     46 (IIC)
     50A (IIC)
     32 (Mks L.IIC LR.IIC)
     55 (Mk III)
     55M (Mks L.III and FR.III)

Armament: Two 20mm Hispano cannon and four 0.303in Browning machine-guns

Internal fuel capacity: 48gal (218ltr, fuselage top tank), 37gal (168ltr, fuselage lower)

External fuel capacity: 30 or 45gal (136 or 205ltr); 90gal (409ltr, Mk III/FR.III)

Engine oil capacity: 5.8gal (26ltr), 8.5gal (39ltr, late production variants)

Weights: lb (kg)

	Empty	Loaded	With 45gal tank	With 90gal tank	With 500lb bomb
Mk 1B	5,910 (2,686)	6,718 (3,054)	7,122 (3,237)	–	–
Mk IIC	6,103 (2,774)	7,004 (3,184)	7,414 (3,370)	–	7,543 (3,429)
Mk L.IIC	6,106 (2,775)	7,006 (3,185)	7,420 (3,373)	–	7,546 (3,430)
Mk LR.IIC	6,245 (2,839)	7,146 (3,248)	7,550 (3,412)	–	–
Mk III	6,204 (2,820)	7,104 (3,230)	7,508 (3,413)	7,950 (3,477)	–
Mk L.III	6,204 (2,820)	7,104 (3,230)	7,508 (3,413)	7,950 (3,477)	7,640 (3,472)
Mk FR.III	6,286 (2,857)	7,186 (3,266)	7,590 (3,450)	8,130 (3,695)	–

Level Speed: mph (km/h)

Height	Mk 1B	Mk IIC	Mk LIIC	Mk III	Mk L.III
sea level	295 (472)	280 (448)	316 (506)	304 486)	331 (530)
6,000ft (1,850m)	–	–	335 (536)	–	358 (593)
11,500ft (3,500m)	–	–	–	352 (563)	–
13,000ft (4,000m)	355 (568)	335 (536)	–	–	–
15,000ft (4,600m)	–	–	350 (560)	–	–
19,000ft (5,800m)	341 (547)	345 (552)	328 (525)	345 (552)	331 (530)

Griffon-powered aircraft

	Mk XV	Mk XVII	F.45, F.46 and F.47
Wingspan	36ft 10in (11m)	36ft 10in (11.3m)	36ft 11in (11.4m)
Length	32ft 3in (9.9m)	32ft 3in (9.9m)	34ft 4in (10.7m)
Height	11ft (3.4m)	11ft (3.4m)	12ft 9in (3.9m)
Wing Area	242sq ft (32.2sq m)	242sq ft (32.2sq m)	243.6sq ft (32.4sq m)

Powerplant: Rolls Royce Griffon VI (Mk XV and Mk XVII); Griffon 61 (Mk 45); Griffon 85 (Mk 46); Griffon 87/88 (Mk 47)

Armament: two 20mm Hispano cannon and four 0.303in Browning machine-guns (Mks XV and XVII); four 20mm Hispano cannon (Mks 45, 46 and 47)

Internal fuel capacity (Mks XV and XVII): fuselage tanks – 80.5gal (366ltr); wing root tanks –19.5gal (89ltr)

(Mk 47): fuselage tanks – 84gal (374ltr); rear fuselage tank 32gal (145ltr); wing root tanks – 11gal (50ltr); wing tanks – 25gal (114ltr)

External fuel capacity (Mks XV and XVII): jettisonable 30/45 (136/205ltr) or 50gal (227ltr) or two 22.5 gal 102ltr) under-wing tanks (Mk XVII)

(Mk 47): 50 or 90gal (227 or 409ltr) centre-line tanks; 45gal (205ltr) under-wing tanks

Engine oil capacity (Mks XV and XVII):10.5gal (48ltr)

(Mk 47): 9gal (40ltr)

Weights: lb (kg)

	Empty	Loaded	With max fuel	With one 500lb bomb
Mk XV	6,965 (3,166)	7,960 (3,619)	8,370 (3,805)	8,515 (3,870)
Mk XVII	7,015 (3,189)	8,010 (3,641)	8,781 (3,991)	8,565 (3,893)
F. 45	8,090 (3,677)	9,357 (4,253		
F. 46	8,530 (3,877)	10,078 (4,581)	11,236 (5,107)	10,628 (4,831)
F. 47	8,680 (3,945)	10,700 (4,864)	11,480 (5,218)	10,778

Level speed: mph (km/h)

	Mk XV	Mk XVII	F.47
Sea level	352 (563)	358 (573)	353 (565)
5,000ft (1,500m)	371 (594)	374 (598)	376 (602)
9,500ft (3,000m)	368 (589)	372 (595)	405 (648)
13,500ft (4,000m)	383 (613)	387 (619)	–
23,000ft (7,000m)	378 (605)	383 (613)	–
24,250ft (7,500m)	–	–	434 (694)

Technical Details of Royal Navy Aircraft Carriers

Illustrious Class fleet carrier

R87 Illustrious, R92 Indomitable, R38 Victorious

Builder	Harland and Wolff
Machinery	Three-shaft Parsons geared turbines; six Admiralty boilers 111,000shp, 30.5kt (55km/h)
Displacement	23,207 tons (23,578 tonnes) standard; 28,619 tons (29,077 tonnes) deep load
Dimensions	740ft 9in (228m) long overall; 106ft 9in (32.8m) max beam; 28ft (8.6m) deep draught
Armament	Eight twin 4in; six octuple 2pdr Pom-Pom; twenty twin Oerlikon; fourteen single Oerlikon
Endurance	14,000 miles (22,400km) @ 12kt (22km/h)
Flight deck	740ft (228m) long; 95ft 9in (29.5m) wide, armoured steel
Arrester wires	Seven 11,000lb (5,000kg) @ 55kt (99km/h) plus two 20,000lb (9,000kg) @ 60kt (108km/h)
Hangar	456ft (140m) by 62ft (19m) by 16ft (5m)
Catapults	One hydraulic 14,000lb (6,000kg) rated @ 66kt (119km/h)
Aircraft	Fifty-four operational

Modified Illustrious Class fleet carrier

R86 Implacable, R10 Indefatigable

Builder	Fairchild Shipbuilding and Engineering Co
Machinery	Four-shaft Parsons geared turbines; eight Admiralty boilers, 148,000shp; 32kt (58km/h)
Displacement	23,450 tons (23,825 tonnes) standard; 32,110 tons (32,624 tonnes) deep load
Dimensions	766ft (236m) long overall, 131ft 3in (40.4m) max beam; 29ft (9m) max draught
Armament	Eight 4.5in, five octuple 2pdr Bofors; twenty-one 20mm Oerlikon; nineteen 20mm Oerlikon
Endurance	12,000 miles (19,200km) @ 10kt (18km/h)
Flight deck	760ft (234m) long, 90ft (28m) wide, armoured steel
Arrester wires	Nine 20,000lb (9,000kg) @ 60kt (108km/h), three 20,000lb (9,000kg) @ 60kt (108km/h)
Hangar	Upper: 456ft (140m) by 62ft (19m) by 14ft (4.3m)
	Lower: 208ft (64m) by 62ft (19m) by 14ft (4.3m)
Catapults	One hydraulic 20,000lb (9,000kg) rated @ 56kt (101km/h)
Aircraft	Eighty-one operational

Argus fleet carrier

I49 Argus

Builder	Beardmores
Machinery	Four-shaft Parsons geared turbines, twelve boilers 20,000shp; 20.2kt (40km/h)
Displacement	14,000 tons (14,224 tonnes) standard, 16,500 tons (16,764 tonnes) deep load
Dimensions	560ft (172m) long overall, 79ft 6in (24.5m) beam, 22ft 6in (6.9m) max draught
Armament	Six 4in, four 3pdr, thirteen 20mm Oerlikon
Endurance	5,200 miles (8,320km) @12kt (22km/h)
Flight deck	470ft (145m) long, 85ft (26m) wide, steel; later 548ft (169m) long, 85 ft (26m) wide
Arrester wires	Four 11,000lb (5,000kg) rated @ 53 kt (95km/h)

Hangar	350ft (106m) by 68ft (21m)
Catapults	One hydraulic 12,000lb (5,500kg) rated @ 66kt (119km/h)
Aircraft	Max twenty; normal fifteen

Furious fleet carrier

47 Furious

Builder	Armstrong Whitworth
Machinery	Four-shaft Brown Curtis geared turbines, eighteen Yarrow boilers, 90,820shp; 30kt (54km/h)
Displacement	22,450 tons (22,800 tonnes) standard, 27,165 tons (27,600 tonnes) deep load
Dimensions	786ft 5in (242m) long overall, 90ft (28m) max beam, 29ft 11in (9.2m) deep draught
Armament	Six twin 4in, four octuple 2pdr Pom-Pom, four 20mm Oerlikon, seven 20mm Oerlikon
Endurance	3,700 miles (5,920km) @ 20kt (36km/h)
Flight deck	596ft (182m) x 91ft 6in (28m) steel
Arrester wires	Four 11,000lb (5,000kg) rated @ 60kt (108km/h)
Hangar	Upper: 520ft (160m) by 50ft (15m) by 15ft (4.6m)
	Lower: 550ft (169m) by 50ft (15m) by 15ft (4.6m)
Catapults	None
Aircraft	Thirty-three operational

Majestic Class light fleet carrier

CVL-21 Magnificent

Builder	Harland and Wolff
Machinery	Two-shaft Parsons geared turbines, four Admiralty boilers, 40,000shp; 24.5kt (44km/h)
Displacement	15,700 tons (15,950 tonnes) standard, 19,550 tons (19,860 tonnes) deep load
Dimensions	698ft (215m) long overall, 112ft 6in (35m) max beam, 25ft (7.7m) max draught
Armament	Eight twin 40mm Bofors, fourteen 40mm Bofors
Endurance	8,300 miles (13,280km) @ 20kt (36km/h)
Flight deck	690ft (212m) long,106ft (32.6m) wide, steel
Arrester wires	Nine 20,000lb (9,000kg) rated @ 87kt (157km/h)
Hangar	275ft (84.6m) by 75ft (23m) by 52ft (16m) by 17ft 6in (5.4m)
Catapults	One hydraulic 20,000lb (9,000kg) rated @ 56kt (101km/h)
Aircraft	Thirty-seven operational

Colossus Class light fleet carrier

15 Colossus (later *Arromanches*), R68 Ocean, R51 Perseus, R76 Pioneer, R64 Theseus, R16 Triumph, R31 Warrior

Builder	Vickers Armstrong
Machinery	Two-shaft Parsons geared turbines, four Admiralty boilers, 40,000shp; 25kt (45km/h)
Displacement	13,190 tons (13,400 tonnes) standard displacement, 18,400 tons (18,700 tonnes) deep load
Dimensions	695ft (214m) long overall, 112ft 6in (34.6m) max beam, 23ft 5in (7.2m) max draught
Armament	Six quad 2pdr Pom-Pom, eleven twin Oerlikon, ten Oerlikon
Endurance	8,300 miles (13,280km) @ 20kt (36km/h)
Flight deck	690ft (212m) long, 80ft (25m) wide, steel
Arrester wires	Eight 15,000lb (6,800kg) rated @ 60kt (108km/h)
Hangar	275ft (85m) by 75ft (23m) by 52ft (16m) by 17ft 6in (5.4m)
Catapults	One hydraulic 16,000lb (7,300kg) rated @ 66kt (119km/h)
Aircraft	Forty-two operational

Ruler Class assault escort carrier

D31 Arbiter, D51 Atheling, D98 Emperor, D42 Empress, D62 Khedive, D21 Shah, D26 Slinger

Builder	Seattle-Tacoma Shipbuilding Corp, USA
Machinery	One-shaft General Electric Geared turbine, two Foster Wheeler boilers, 8,500shp; 18.5kt (33km/h)
Displacement	11,200 tons (11,400 tonnes) standard, 15,400 tons (15,650 tonnes) deep load
Dimensions	492ft (151m) long overall, 108ft 6in (33m) beam, 25ft 5in (7.8m) draught
Armament	Two 5in US Mk 12, eight twin 40mm Bofors, four twin Oerlikon, twenty-five single Oerlikon
Endurance	27,500 miles (44,00km) @ 11kt (20km/h)
Flight deck	450ft (138m) long, 80ft (25m) wide, wood covered by steel
Arrester wires	Nine 19,800lb (9,000kg) rated @ 55kt (99km/h)
Hangar	260ft (80m) by 62ft (19m) by 18ft (5.5m)
Catapults	One H4C 16,000lb (7,200kg) rated @ 74kt (133km/h)
Aircraft	Thirty operational, ninety ferry

Attacker Class assault carrier

D02 Attacker, D18 Battler, D32 Chaser, D64 Fencer, D80 Hunter, D91 Stalker, D12 Striker, D24 Tracker

Builder	Western Pipe and Steel Corp, USA
Machinery	Single-shaft General Electric geared turbine, two Foster Wheeler boilers, 8,500shp; 18kt (32km/h)
Displacement	10,200 tons (10,400 tonnes) standard, 14,400 tons (14,600 tonnes) deep load
Dimensions	491ft (151m) long overall, 105ft (32m) max beam, 21ft (6.5m) max draught
Armament	Two 4in, four twin Bofors, eight twin Oerlikon, four single Oerlikon
Endurance	27,000 miles (43,200km) @ 11kt (20km/h)
Flight deck	442ft (136m) long, 88ft (27m) wide, steel covered wood
Arrester wires	Nine 19,800lb (9,000kg) rated @ 55kt (99km/h)
Hangar	262ft (80m) by 62ft (19m) by 18ft (5.5m)
Catapults	One hydraulic 7,000lb (3,180kg) rated @ 61kt (110km/h)
Aircraft	Twenty operational, ninety ferry

Pretoria Castle trials and training carrier

F61 Pretoria Castle

Builder	Harland and Wolff, conversion carried out by Swan Hunter
Machinery	Two-shaft diesels, 16,000shp; 18kt (32km/h)
Displacement	19,650 tons (19,960 tonnes) standard, 23,450 tons (23,800 tonnes) deep load
Dimensions	592ft (182m) long overall, 76ft 4in (23.4m) max beam, 29ft 10in (9.2m) max draught
Armament	Two 4in, ten twin 20mm Oerlikon, two quad Pom-Pom
Endurance	16,000 miles (25,00km) @ 16kt (29km/h)
Flight deck	550ft (169m) long, 76ft (23.4m) wide, steel
Arrester wires	Six 15,000lb (6,800kg) rated @ 60kt (119km/h)
Hangar	354ft (109m) by 46ft (14m) by 17ft (5.2m)
Catapults	One hydraulic 14,000lb (6,400kg) rated @ 66kt (119km/h)
Aircraft	Twenty-one operational

Unicorn aircraft repair ship

R72 Unicorn

Builder	Harland and Wolff
Machinery	Two-shaft Parsons geared turbines, four Admiralty boilers, 40,000shp; 24kt (43km/h)
Displacement	14,750 tons (15,000 tonnes) standard, 20,300 tons (20,625 tonnes) deep load
Dimensions	640ft (197m) long overall, 90ft (27.7m) max beam, 24ft 10in (7.6m) max draught
Armament	Four twin 4in, four quad 2pdr Pom-Pom, five twin 20mm Oerlikon, six single Oerlikon
Endurance	7,500 miles (4,700km) @ 20kt (36km/h)
Flight deck	640ft (197m) long, 90ft (27.7m) wide, armoured steel
Arrester wires	Six 20,000lb (9,000kg) rated @ 60kt (108km/h)
Hangar	Upper: 324ft (99.7m) by 65ft (20m) by 16ft 6in (5m)
	Lower: 360ft (111m) by 62ft (19m) by 16ft 6in (5m)
Catapults	One hydraulic 12,500lb (5,700kg) rated @ 66kt (119km/h)
Aircraft	Thirty-five operational, twenty under repair

Bibliography

Andrews, CF and Morgan, EB, *Supermarine Aircraft since 1914* (Putnam, 1981)

Brown, Capt Eric CBE DSC AFC RN, *Wings of the Navy* (Airlife, 1987)

Crossley, Cdr R DSC RN, *They gave me a Seafire* (Airlife, 1986)

Frelaut, Jean and Pierquet, Claude-A, *Les Seafire dans l'Aeronatique Navale Francais* (Oest France, 1983)

Hobbs, Cdr David MBE RN, *Aircraft Carriers of the Royal Navy and Commonwealth Navies* (Greenhill Books, 1996)

Morgan, Eric and Shacklady, Edward, *Spitfire, The History* (Key Publishing, 1987)

Sturtivant, Ray and Burrow Lee Howard, Mick, *Fleet Air Arm Fixed Wing Aircraft since 1945* (Air Britain, 2004)

Index